DAYTRIPS
—IN—
ISRAEL

——— 25 ———

**One Day Adventures
by Bus or Car**

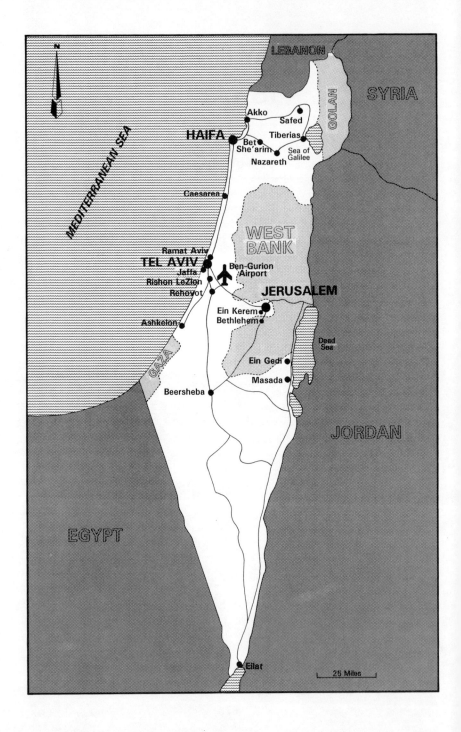

DAYTRIPS
— IN —
ISRAEL

— 25 —

One Day Adventures
by Bus or Car

by
Earl Steinbicker

HASTINGS HOUSE
MAMARONECK, NEW YORK

We are always grateful for comments from readers, which are extremely useful in preparing future editions of this or other books in the series. Please write directly to the author, Earl Steinbicker, c/o Hastings House, 141 Halstead Avenue, Mamaroneck, NY 10543; or FAX (914) 835-1037. Thank you.

The author would like to thank the following people for helping to make this book possible:
Sheryl Stein, of El Al Israel Airlines.
Barbara Bahny, of the Israel Government Tourist Office.

All photos and maps are by the author except as noted.

Distributed to the trade by Publishers Group West, Emeryville, CA.

ISBN: 0-8038-9342-6

Library of Congress Catalog Card Number 91-077902

Printed in the United States of America
10 9 8 7 6 5 4 3 2 1

Contents

6   CONTENTS

Introduction

For such a small nation—hardly a dot on the world map—Israel certainly gets a lot of attention. Seldom does a week go by without major news bulletins originating from Jerusalem, Tel Aviv, or the West Bank. But then, earth-shattering events are nothing new to Israel—for all of the world's Jews, Christians, and Moslems too, this is where it happened first.

Ten thousand years of history and a passing parade of Canaanites, Israelites, Greeks, Romans, Byzantines, Arabs, Christian Crusaders, Egyptian Mamluks, Turks, and returning Jews have all added to the wealth of fascinating remains and lingering cultural traditions that make this crossroads of civilization one of the most intriguing places on Earth to visit.

Although Israel has excellent beaches, luxurious resorts, great hotels, restaurants, shopping, world-class museums, and even ski slopes and a golf course, these amenities are not what lure the tourists. Its chief draws are the numerous holy sites sacred to Jews, Christians, and Moslems alike; the artifacts of history; and the sheer adventure of discovering an emerging democracy still in its infancy.

Within its compact boundaries lies an amazing variety of experiences, cultures, and even climates. Here you can encounter the Arab way of life without journeying to Amman or Cairo, and get a good introduction to the entire Middle East while you're at it. Even when the streets of Jerusalem are dusted with snow, you can travel only a few miles to Ein Gedi on the Dead Sea and enjoy a sub-tropical paradise, or to nearby Masada to work on your tan while exploring King Herod's palace. From the stark Negev Desert to the lush, forested mountains above the Galilee, most of Israel's attractions can be seen by taking easy daytrips from a base in Jerusalem, Tel Aviv, or Haifa.

Daytrips in Israel takes a fresh—*and very thorough*—look at 25 of the most intriguing destinations, including several within the cities themselves, and describes in step-by-step detail a pleasurable way of exploring them on self-guided walking tours.

Walking is by far the best way to probe most places. Not only is it undeniably healthy, but it also allows you to see the sights from a natural, human perspective; and to spend just as much or as little time on each as you please. The carefully tested walking tours were designed to take you past all of the attractions worth seeing, without wasting time, effort, or money. Which of these you actually stop at is up to you, but you won't have any trouble finding them with the large, clear maps provided.

Dining well is a vital element in any travel experience. For this reason, a selection of particularly enjoyable restaurants along the walking routes has been included for each of the daytrips. These are price-keyed, with an emphasis on the medium-to-low range, and have concise location descriptions that make them easy to find.

All of the daytrips can be made by bus or by private car, and a few even by train. Specific transportation information is given in the "Getting There" section of each trip, and general information in the "Daytrip Strategies" chapter.

Time and weather considerations are important, and they've been included in the "Practicalities" section of each trip. These let you know, among other things, on which dates the sights are closed, when the colorful outdoor markets are held, and which places should be avoided under certain conditions. The location and telephone number of the local Tourist Information Office is also given in case you have questions.

Many of the attractions have a nominal entrance fee—those that are free will come as a pleasant surprise. Places of worship depend on small donations to help pay their maintenance costs, so it is only fair to leave some change when making a visit.

Please remember that places have a way of changing without warning, especially in this restless part of the world, and that errors do creep into print. If your heart is absolutely set on a particular sight, you should check first to make sure that it isn't closed for renovations, or that the opening times are still valid. The local tourist offices are always the best source of such up-to-the-minute information.

One last thought: It isn't really necessary to see everything at any given destination. Be selective. Your one-day adventures in Israel should be fun, not an endurance test. If they start becoming that, just saunter over to the nearest café and enjoy yourself while watching the world stroll past. There will always be another day.

Happy Daytripping!

Section I

The charms of Old Jaffa are only minutes away from modern Tel Aviv

DAYTRIP
STRATEGIES

The word "Daytrip" may not have made it into dictionaries yet, but for experienced independent travelers it represents the easiest, most natural, and often the least expensive approach to exploring many of the world's more interesting countries. This strategy, in which you base yourself in a central city and probe the surrounding region on a series of one-day excursions, is especially effective in the case of such a compact, but varied, nation as Israel.

ADVANTAGES:
   While not the answer to every travel situation, daytrips have significant advantages over point-to-point touring following a set itinerary. Here are ten good reasons for considering the daytrip approach to seeing Israel:

1. Freedom from the constraints of a fixed itinerary. You can go wherever you feel like going whenever the mood strikes you.
2. Freedom from the burden of luggage. Your bags remain in your hotel while you run around with only a guidebook and camera.
3. Freedom from the anxiety of reservation foul-ups. You don't have to worry each day about whether that night's lodging will actually materialize.
4. The flexibility of making last-minute changes to allow for unexpected weather, serendipitous discoveries, changing interests, new-found passions, and so on.
5. The flexibility to take breaks from sightseeing whenever you feel tired or bored, without upsetting a planned itinerary. Why not sleep late in your base city for a change, or go to the beach?
6. The opportunity to sample different travel experiences without committing more than a day to them.
7. The opportunity to become a "temporary resident" of your base city. By staying there for a while you can get to know it in depth, becoming familiar with the local restaurants, shops, theaters, night life, and other attractions—enjoying them as a native would.
8. The convenience of not having to pack and unpack your bags each day. Your clothes can hang in a closet where they belong, or even be sent out for cleaning.
9. The convenience (and security!) of having a fixed address in your base city, where friends, relatives, and business associates can reach you in an emergency. It is exceedingly difficult to reach anyone who changes hotels frequently.
10. The economy of staying at one hotel on a discounted longer-term basis, especially in conjunction with airline package plans. You can make advance reservations for your base city without sacrificing any flexibility at all.

   Above all, daytrips ease the transition from tourist to accomplished traveler. Even if this is your first trip abroad, you should be able to handle uncomplicated one-day excursions such as those to Masada or Akko on your own. The confidence gained will help immensely when you tackle more complex destinations, freeing you from the limitations of guided tours and putting you in complete control of your own trip.

DISADVANTAGES:

For all of its attractions, the daytrip concept does have certain restrictions. There are always a few areas where geography and the available transportation have conspired to make one-day excursions impractical, or at least awkward. In Israel, neither the resort town of Eilat, most of the Negev Desert, nor the Golan Heights lend themselves to comfortable daytripping. To see these, you'll have to temporarily resort to more conventional travel.

Another disadvantage is that you'll have to forego the adventure of staying at a *kibbutz* in the country instead of a city hotel, bed-and-breakfast, hospice, or hostel. You could, however, enjoy the best of both worlds by using daytrips most of the time, and the "touring" approach the rest.

Perhaps the greatest drawback to daytripping is that all of the to-ing and fro-ing involved can increase your total travel mileage. This will surely result in higher costs if you're using a rental car. Bus and train fares, however, are so inexpensive that the additional cost is insignificant. The extra time spent on public transportation is not wasted as you will continue meeting people, seeing, and learning even as you travel.

ESCORTED DAY TOURS:

Commercially operated one-day bus tours to historical sites and other attractions are offered from Jerusalem, Tel Aviv, Haifa, and Eilat. Described in colorful brochures, these are heavily promoted by hotels (who get a commission) and by local tourist offices. On the surface, they may seem like an effortless way to take in the sights. While certainly better than no tour at all, they are no substitute for exploring on your own. Among their shortcomings is the fact that the tours go where their operators want to go, not where you want to. All too often, this is where it's easiest to park the bus. Some of the "attractions" visited are just souvenir shops from which they get extra income, while others reflect someone's idea of the "average" person's interests. Worse, people who take these tours are often treated as part of a crowd to be efficiently catered to for profit rather than as real guests. You'll get no genuine adventure on these trips, and feel no sense of accomplishment on completing them. On top of that, they tend to be a bit expensive. You might, however, want to consider commercial tours to destinations in the Occupied Territories of the West Bank, where you may feel uncomfortable traveling on your own; or to the Negev Desert, where solo travel by the inexperienced can be dangerous.

WALKING TOURS:

Each daytrip in this book includes a highly-detailed do-it-yourself walking tour. No one has yet invented a better way to experience the towns and sites of Israel than to stroll through them on foot. Not only do you get to see the attractions from a human, eye-level perspective, but all along the way you'll be mixing with local residents, meeting with and absorbing their cultures as if by osmosis.

Walking is good for you as well. Besides being an excellent aerobic exercise, it also stimulates the brain while it burns off all of those nasty calories from last night's feast.

The suggested walking routes described in the text and shown on the maps are designed so as not to waste time or effort. They often include more sights than you'll care to see in a day, but this allows you to pick and choose.

BASE CITIES

Israel is such a small country that you can make daytrips to nearly all of its varied attractions from a base in either Jerusalem, Tel Aviv, or Haifa. Only in the case of Eilat, the Negev Desert, or the Golan Heights will this prove difficult. Those traveling by bus or train will find, however, that it is considerably easier to take certain excursions from Jerusalem, others from Tel Aviv, and all of the northern trips from a base in Haifa. The book is arranged with this in mind.

FINDING ACCOMMODATIONS:

For the best choice of hotels, you should make advance reservations through your travel agent, possibly choosing one of the **package plans** that combine air fares to and from Israel, hotel rooms, and a rental car into one discounted price. **El Al Israel Airlines** offers a nice selection of these budget plans, with many options concerning length of stay, hotel selection, and car category. Similar arrangements are available from some other carriers.

Failing that, you can always find a room of some sort upon arrival by going straight to the **Government Tourist Information Office** counter at Ben-Gurion International Airport. This is located in the arrivals area, close to the baggage claim, and the phone number is (03) 971-1485.

Government tourist offices throughout Israel and around the world can supply you with an up-to-date copy of the **Israel Tourist Hotels** booklet, which gives highly detailed listings of hundreds of hotels in all price ranges. Most Israeli hotels are **graded** from one to five stars, according to the level of comfort and amenities they provide. In general, the average tourist will probably be content with any hotel rating three or more stars. Prices are nearly always quoted in U.S. dollars, and you'll save yourself a hefty tax by **paying in dollars** (or other "hard" currency) instead of shekels. This can be done with cash, traveler's checks, or credit cards.

When selecting a hotel in **Jerusalem**, note that some of those listed are in the Old City or East Jerusalem, where local transportation can be a problem. These hotels usually have considerably lower rates to compensate for the inconvenience. Before booking, check the address against a map to determine if the savings are worth the bother.

If you come to Israel during the off-season or a slack period, you might be able to bargain the price down, especially if you're staying for a week or more. The slowest season is from mid-fall through winter; with the exception of the Channukah, Christmas, and New Year's holidays. Hotels tend to be heavily booked in mid-summer and on Jewish and Christian holidays. Eilat is an exception to the rule; there the winters are pleasantly warm and the summers fiercely hot.

Among the low-cost alternatives to hotels are some 30 **youth hostels**, including several in the heart of the major cities. You don't have to be young or belong to the I.Y.H.A. to stay at them, but you'll get a discount if you do. Other inexpensive places to sleep include **Christian hospices, bed & breakfast** rooms, and—way out in the countryside—the delightful **kibbutz guest houses**. Ask the Government Tourist Information Office, in Israel or abroad (see page 24), for current information about these bargains.

GETTING THERE

Unless you're one of the few who come by boat, you'll almost certainly arrive in Israel at **Ben-Gurion International Airport**, located about 12 miles southeast of Tel Aviv near the town of Lod, along the main highway to Jerusalem. Although many international carriers fly there, none can compare with **El Al Israel Airlines** at providing a genuine Israeli experience all the way. Few, if any, airlines manage to capture the spirit of their native land quite so well. Perhaps this is because it is the choice of the high-spirited Israelis themselves, whose personalities fill the plane with an engaging ambiance.

El Al is also noted for its extraordinary security measures, which rely on psychological profiles as well as baggage checks. Expect to be asked some strange questions when you check in; these are designed to reveal potential troublemakers before they can act. As a result, the airline has a safety record that is envied throughout the industry.

Since El Al is the national airline of Israel, it has a stake in seeing to it that both your flight and your total visit are so enjoyable that you'll come back again. To this end they offer a variety of flexible **package plans** that independent travelers will find especially attractive, as they combine airfares, hotel stays, and a car rental into one discounted price. Short extensions to Eilat, Cairo, or even London can be added at relatively little additional cost. Seniors over 60 receive a special discount, and both youth and family fares are available. Passengers making **connecting flights** through New York's La Guardia Airport can check in right there and receive free transportation to their El Al flight at JFK Airport. **Advance check-ins** may be made at El Al's satellite terminate in Boro Park, Brooklyn. When **departing Israel**, you can conveniently check in earlier in the day at satellite facilities in Tel Aviv, Jerusalem, and Haifa; sparing yourself the trouble of hauling luggage to Ben-Gurion Airport and allowing you to arrive there much closer to departure time.

El Al offers more non-stop service and flies more passengers to and from Israel than any other carrier, serving 39 cities worldwide including seven U.S. gateways in New York, Baltimore/Washington, Boston, Chicago, Dallas/Fort Worth, Los Angeles, and Miami. For up-to-date detailed information contact your travel agent or phone 1-800-El-AL-SUN.

Upon arrival, your options for getting to your first destination in Israel are:

AIRPORT BUSES:

Buses operated by **Egged** depart Ben-Gurion Airport fairly frequently for Jerusalem, Tel Aviv, and Haifa. These go directly to the central bus station in their respective cities, from which you can take a taxi or local bus to your hotel. This is the cheapest way in from the airport. Passengers heading for Tel Aviv may prefer the **United Tours** bus number 222, which makes stops along the waterfront at most of the city's hotels. Ask for current information at the tourist office counter in the Arrivals Hall of the airport.

SHERUTS:

Common throughout the Middle East, *sheruts* are shared vehicles going to a more-or-less common destination—sort of a compromise between a taxi and a bus. Although these are usually seven-passenger stretch Mercedes cars, you shouldn't expect limousine comfort. Fares are a bit higher than buses but much lower than taxis, and are fixed and payable in shekels. Usually, you buy a ticket from the dispatch stand to your right as you leave the terminal building. Assuming that your hotel is not out in the boondocks, the driver should take you directly to it. Service is available to Jerusalem, Tel Aviv, and Haifa.

TAXIS:

If you're going to Tel Aviv and have bulky luggage, you might want to splurge for a regular taxi, usually called a "Special." The fares for these are fixed; ask at the tourist office in the terminal building for current information. Israelis rarely tip the drivers, but foreigners are more or less expected to. If you want to take a regular taxi to Jerusalem, you'll have to negotiate a price with the driver first.

GETTING AROUND

All of the daytrips in this book can be taken by either bus or by private car, and a very few even by train. In general, your options for all transportation within Israel are:

BY BUS:

Buses go nearly everywhere in Israel, and for the most part run quite frequently. With the exception of local services around Tel Aviv, East Jerusalem, and the West Bank, they are almost invariably operated by the **Egged Cooperative.** Schedules are printed in Hebrew and occasionally in English, while the departure boards in the stations are in both languages and there is almost invariably an English-speaking agent at the information counter. You can also phone toll-free (177) 022-55-55 for current **route and schedule** information anywhere in the country. A variety of discount **fares** and passes are available, but the regular fares are so inexpensive to begin with that it's easier to just pay each time you board a bus. You can buy a ticket either at the ticket window or from the driver, who is usually able to make change. Departure platforms are numbered and marked in both Hebrew and English. **Advance reservations** are not necessary except for the long haul to Eilat during peak periods.

Riding an Israeli bus is an experience in itself. Providing convenient, fast, and cheap transportation in a struggling country, they are very popular and often crowded, especially with gun-toting soldiers in uniform. Don't be surprised to find yourself sitting next to the butt of an Uzi, and be thankful that you're so well defended in this turbulent part of the world. Most of the buses are air-conditioned, and generally quite modern. A few even border on the luxurious, but now and then you'll encounter an ancient rattletrap.

Every town of any size has a **Central Bus Station**, and most of these have an **Egged Cafeteria** where you can get decent kosher food at bargain prices. Buses can also be boarded (or left) at numerous **bus stops** along the route, which are well-marked in Hebrew and English with the route numbers that will stop there on request. They usually have a shelter and posted schedules. To make sure that a passing bus stops to pick you up, stand in full view of the driver and point to the spot where you want the bus to halt.

Most buses throughout Israel operate on Sundays through Thursdays from early morning until mid- or late evening; on Fridays and Jewish holiday eves until a few hours before sunset; and on Saturdays (the Sabbath) and holidays not at all until the sun has safely set in the evening. There are a few exceptions to this rule, mostly in Arab areas.

Local bus services are described in the "Getting Around" section of each chapter where their use is relevant.

BY *SHERUT:*

For a real Middle Eastern experience, try to make at least one trip on a *sherut,* also called a service taxi. These are shared vehicles, usually stretch Mercedes-Benz cars, that carry up to seven passengers along a common route. Charging slightly more than buses, they do not follow a schedule, but depart when there are enough passengers—which is usually fairly frequently. The fares are fixed and should always be confirmed with the driver first. Since so many different small companies operate *sheruts* and the services keep changing to meet the competition, you'll have to ask locally for current information. *Sheruts* can take you all over Israel, and also run locally in the larger cities. Advance reservations may be made so you'll be sure of a seat. Unlike most buses, these shared cars often run on the Sabbath, albeit at higher prices. Be sure not to confuse *sheruts* with the much more expensive regular taxis.

BY TRAIN:

Israel Railways offers good passenger service between Tel Aviv (Central/North Station) and Haifa, and from there north to Akko and Nahariya. They also have an infrequent service between Tel Aviv (South Station) and Jerusalem, which makes up in scenic splendor what it decidedly lacks in speed. The passenger cars are old, but quite comfortable, and there is usually a kosher buffet car. **Fares** are even lower than on the buses! Buy tickets at the station or from the conductor. Naturally, trains do not run from mid-afternoons on Fridays until Sunday mornings, nor or religious holidays or the eve preceding them. For **schedules**, phone (03) 542-15-15 in Tel Aviv or (04) 564564 in Haifa. Dedicated railfans will want to check this out, and perhaps visit the small train museum in Haifa.

BY CAR:

Driving your own rental car is, of course, the most convenient way to get around Israel. Unfortunately, it is not cheap. By the time you've added the kilometer charge, fuel costs, and collision damage waiver to the basic rental, you'll find that it's often less expensive to hire a private taxi. You can cut these costs substantially by using one of the **package plans** offered by **El Al** and some other airlines, especially if the plan selected allows unlimited mileage. These plans must be arranged for when you first book your trip.

Most of the major car rental chains including Hertz, Avis, National, and Budget have outlets in Israel. In addition, there are several Israeli firms, most notably Eldan, that offer somewhat lower rates. Be wary about dealing with small, unknown operators without first checking them out—their prices may seem small but the fine print on the contract often contains imaginative charges that you never dreamed existed.

Although it varies from firm to firm, in general you must be at least 21 years old and not older than 70 to drive a rental car in Israel. **Drivers' licenses** from countries with diplomatic relations with Israel are accepted, as long as they are in English, but the International Driving Permit is preferred. This can be obtained in America from the A.A.A., and from similar motor clubs in other countries.

Major highways in Israel are excellent and well marked in English. Secondary roads, while nicely surfaced and maintained, are usually narrow and often wind their way through twisting, hilly terrain. The real downside to driving in Israel is not the roads, however, but the careless drivers who make this an such exceptionally accident-prone country. Fast, aggressive driving is a national trait that has to be dealt with.

Try to avoid driving in the Occupied Territories of the **West Bank**, where your yellow Israeli license plates provide a tempting target. If you must pass through this troubled area, stick to the main roads and stay away from towns like Hebron or Nablus.

Driving in the center of Jerusalem is difficult until you get to know its confusing street layout. **Parking** in any city is always a challenge, and requires a parking card on which you indicate the time the car was parked. These are sold at newsstands and by lottery vendors.

BY AIR:

Israel may be a tiny country, but if you're going to Eilat the distance is still substantial enough that you can save many hours of travel time by flying. **Arkia Israel Airlines** offers service to Eilat from Jerusalem, Tel Aviv (Dov Airport), Ben-Gurion Airport, and Haifa; as well as flights to Rish Pinna (for Tiberias and Safed) and other domestic services.

FOOD AND DRINK

Happily for visitors, Israel's collective taste buds have been maturing for the past decade or so. Where food was once regarded simply as fuel, civilized dining is now well established. Most of the world's cuisines, from French to Chinese—and way beyond—can be readily found in the cities, and sometimes even in the countryside.

Several choice restaurants that make sense for daytrippers are listed for nearly every destination in this book. Most of these are long-time favorites of experienced travelers, are open for lunch, are on or near the walking route, and provide some atmosphere. Their approximate price range is shown as:

> $ —Inexpensive.
> $$ —Reasonable.
> $$$—Luxurious and expensive.
> X: —Days closed.

Menus are generally printed in both Hebrew and English, and are prominently displayed outside the entrance. Prices are nearly always quoted on shekels. If the menu or your bill says something like "service not included," a tip of 10–15% is expected.

KOSHER:

Regardless of which country's cuisine it comes from, most of the food in Israel, and most of the restaurants that serve it, are kosher. This simply means that the establishment and its suppliers follow the dietary laws of kashrut, which prohibits the mixing of meat and dairy products, as well as the eating of certain "unclean" foods such as pork and shellfish. You will never see a ham-and-cheese sandwich in any kosher establishment. Or a cheeseburger. Or get real ice cream after a steak dinner. In practical terms, these restraints are hardly noticeable and should not interfere with your dining pleasures.

SHABBAT:

Shabbat is the **Sabbath**, when most of the restaurants in Israel are closed, and many hotels will serve only food prepared in advance. It begins at sundown on Fridays (restaurants usually close at 2 P.M.) and continues until after dark on Saturday evening. The same rule applies on religious holidays and the eve preceding them. In the cities and urban areas, however, plenty of non-kosher restaurants remain open, so you won't have to starve.

BREAKFAST:

Hotel room rates usually include a "full Israeli breakfast," which can be quite a formidable meal—easily enough to sustain you throughout much of the day. Commonly served as a buffet, it typically consists of fresh fruit and juices, eggs, cereals, salads, cheese, fish, rolls, blintzes, yogurt, and coffee. And quite likely even more, though no one expects you to eat it all.

MIDDLE EASTERN FOOD:

The closest Israel comes to having a native cuisine is in its ubiquitous "Middle Eastern," or "Oriental" specialties, largely borrowed from the Arab and Mediterranean worlds. Among the many dishes to try are: *shishlik* (charcoal-grilled meats), *kebab* (spicy chopped meat on a skewer), *hummus* (a paste of mashed chickpeas with tehina and oil), *pita* (a round, flat bread), *malawah* (pancakes stuffed with meat or vegetables), *couscous* (cooked semolina with meat and vegetables), *fuul* (beans with oil, lemon, and caraway), and *bourekas* (pastry filled with meat, cheese, potatoes, spinach, or other ingredients).

FAST FOOD:

Felafel is the national dish of Israel. Sold by sidewalk vendors everywhere, it has the merits of being delicious, nutritious, cheap, and fast. *Felafel* consists of ground chickpeas fried into balls, usually served in a *pita* bread pocket to which you add salads, vegetables, and sauces to taste. It is a mess to eat, so have plenty of paper napkins handy, and look for a *felafel* stand that offers places to sit. Also be sure to choose one that does a thriving business among the locals and is at least partially enclosed, well away from exhaust fumes. Many of these stands also sell *shwarma*, a similar dish in which the *felafel* balls are replaced with slices of lamb, veal, or turkey from a spit. Either of these delights, along with fruit juice, makes a wonderfully cheap lunch that's actually good for your health.

Should you tire of *felafel*, you can still eat on the run at one of the many **pizza** stands, especially those in Arab areas that feature Egyptian-style pizzas. And if you're homesick for hamburgers, you'll find them at the many Burger Ranch and McDavid's (!) outlets in the larger towns, and at Wendy's in the big cities.

BEVERAGES:

Israelis drink lots of **fruit juices**, which cost less than sodas and are sold everywhere. Their idea of **coffee** usually means the Turkish variety, in which the grounds reside at the bottom of the cup, waiting for the hapless victim to swallow. The uninitiated can often order *espresso* or *cappuccino* instead, or at least the American-style *caffe filter* or instant *nes kafeh.*

Although the per-capita consumption of alcohol is rather low, Israel does make some excellent **beers** that are available just about anywhere. *Maccabee* is a well-balanced, tasty lager; and *Goldstar* a slightly darker, even tastier brew, often served on tap.

Wines have been made in Israel since around 3000 B.C. After a long dry spell under Moslem rule, this industry was revived in the late 19th century and today produces excellent vintages that can compete in the world market. Some superb labels to look for are: *Rothschild*, *Monfort*, *Yarden*, and *Gamla*.

PRACTICALITIES

LANGUAGE:

It's a good thing that so many Israelis speak fluent English; unlike European tongues, Israel's two official languages—modern Hebrew and Arabic—are totally incomprehensible to most travelers. Fortunately, you'll have absolutely no trouble getting around with only a command of English. Nearly all public signs, including road directions, are in both Hebrew and English, and often Arabic as well.

There is a problem, however, in transliterating Hebrew or Arabic words and names into the Latin (English) alphabet, which cannot cope with the unusual sounds of these languages. Thus a town name like Safed can also be spelled as Zefat, Zfat, Tzfat, Safad, and other ways as well. Since there is no correct way of doing this, you'll encounter many different variations on maps and destination signs. Try pronouncing the name—if it sounds right, it probably is right.

While walking around the towns, you'll notice that street-name signs sometimes use English words like boulevard, road, and so on; and other times their transliterated Hebrew equivalent. Some of these are: *rehov* (street), *sderot* (avenue or boulevard), *derech* (road), and *kikar* (square, plaza, or circle).

Other languages that are frequently used in Israel include Russian, French, German, Yiddish, Spanish, Polish, and Hungarian.

MONEY MATTERS:

The New Israeli **Shekel** (NIS) is the basic unit of currency, and is divided into 100 *agorot*. Paper money comes in denominations of 100, 50, 20, and 10 NIS; and coins in 5, 1, and ½ NIS as well as 10 and 5 *agorot*. Although it is generally good advice throughout the world to change your money at banks rather than hotels, in Israel you *might* do better at your hotel. Ask and compare the rates, taking commissions into account.

Hotel rates, car rentals, airfares, and some other major tourist expenses are usually quoted in U.S. dollars rather than shekels. If you pay these in dollars (or other "hard" currency), you can avoid the stiff 18% **Value Added Tax** that is figured into the price of anything paid for in shekels. You can use cash, traveler's checks, or (usually) credit cards. For meals (not charged to your hotel bill), local transportation, museum entrance fees, small purchases, and so on, you'll need shekels, although quite a few restaurants and merchants happily accept dollars.

Automated Teller Machines (ATMs) are now quite common in Israel, with both the Cirrus and Visa networks represented. Check with your issuing bank before leaving home to make sure that your PIN code will work there.

TELEPHONES:

Two types of **public telephones** are used througout Israel, usually paired together so you have a choice. The older kinds use tokens, called *asimonim*, which are sold at post offices, newsstands, and hotels. More convenient are the newer phones that operate on a *Telecard*, a pre-paid magnetic debit card from which the cost of each call is subtracted until its face value is all used up. These cards are available at post offices and bus stations in various denominations.

Israel is divided into **area codes**, which are dialed only when calling from outside that area. All phone numbers in this book indicate the area code in parentheses.

International calls are best made from the newer pay phones, from post offices, or from the Bezek phone centers in larger towns. For collect or credit-card calls from any phone, dial the overseas operator at 188. Holders of AT&T or MCI phone cards can call home directly and inexpensively by dialing, toll-free, 177-100-2727 or 177-150-2727 respectively. These calls are charged to your home account and are placed through live operators in the U.S.A.

MEDIA:

It's important to keep up with the news while in Israel, since so much of it happens there. The widely-respected, English-language *Jerusalem Post* is published every day except Saturdays, and is your best source for in-depth news. On Mondays it carries a reprint of the "News in Review" section from the Sunday *New York Times*. Larger newsstands also carry the *International Herald Tribune*, *USA Today*, and several English-language magazines.

On **AM Radio**, you can listen to the Voice of America at 1260 kHz, the BBC at 1322 kHz, or the Voice of Peace at 1540 kHz. Radio Kol Israel has brief English News bulletins at 7 A.M., and 1, 5, and 8 P.M. at 576 and 1548 kHz. You can also pick up English news from Jordanian, Lebanese, and other stations.

WEATHER:

In general, central and northern Israel has warm, dry weather from about April through October, sometimes becoming uncomfortably hot by July and August except in mountainous areas such as Jerusalem and Safed. Winters are mild and often rainy from November to March, with occasional snow around Jerusalem and in the northern mountains. The southern resort of Eilat is a special case, with warm, dry winters and hot summers. As in most temperate-climate destinations, the best time to visit Israel is in the spring or fall, when it's pleasantly warm and yet dry.

HOLY DAYS & HOLIDAYS:

Most activities in Israel come to a halt on **Shabbat**, the Jewish Sabbath and the nation's only weekly day of rest. This officially begins at sundown each Friday and continues until the sun has completely set on Saturday. Shops, restaurants, and businesses start closing around 2 P.M. or so on Fridays. Nearly all public transportation ceases to operate later in the afternoon, with the exception of some *sheruts* and taxis, and a few buses in and around Haifa. *Shabbat* is not observed in Arab towns, where the Moslem Holy Day is Friday and the Christian Sabbath Sunday. An increasing number of non-kosher restaurants in the cities now remain open, so you won't go hungry.

For most Israelis, *Shabbat* is not quite as holy a day as you might think. They take full advantage of this singular day off from work to drive around and enjoy themselves, and to visit places of entertainment once that sun has set on Saturday. Most of the major tourist attractions, such as museums, are open for at least a few hours on Saturdays, although you might have to purchase admission tickets in advance.

Possibly to make up for having only one weekly day of rest, Israel celebrates a great many **holidays**, both religious and secular. Like *Shabbat,* holidays begin at sundown on the preceding evening and end after dark on the holiday itself. For religious holidays, the same rules apply.

The date on which Jewish holidays fall is determined by the **Jewish calendar**, which is based on a lunar year of 354 days and is therefore always out of step with the secular *Gregorian* calendar of 365 solar days, used universally throughout the world for day-to-day living. To further add to the confusion, Orthodox Christians employ the ancient *Julian* calendar to date their holidays. The lunar *Moslem* calendar is similar to the Jewish, but has no leap years, so holidays such as the month of *Ramadan* can fall at any time of the year.

Confused? The tourist office can furnish you with a current list of holidays and the dates of the regular Western, or *Gregorian*, calendar on which they fall. The major Jewish religious holidays are:

Passover (*Pesach*) (falls in March or April; the first and last days are celebrated)

Pentecost (*Shavu'ot*) (falls in May or June)

Jewish New Year (*Rosh Hashana*) (two days in September or October)

Day of Atonement (*Yom Kippur*) (falls in September or October)

Feast of Tabernacles (*Sukkot*) (falls in September or October)

Rejoicing of the Law (*Simhat Torah*) (falls in September or October)

Feast of Lights (*Channukah*) (falls in November or December; the first day is a holiday)

SUGGESTED TOURS

The do-it-yourself **walking tours** in this book are relatively short and easy to follow. They always begin at the local bus stop or station since most readers will be using public transportation. Those going by car can make a simple adjustment. Suggested **routes** are shown by heavy broken lines on the maps, while the circled numbers refer to major attractions or points of reference along the way, with corresponding numbers in the text.

You can estimate the amount of time that any segment of a walking tour will take by looking at the scaled map and figuring that the average person covers about 100 yards a minute. The walks will be easier if you wear real walking shoes, especially those sneakers that are specifically designed for walking rather than jogging or sports. Layered clothes are a good idea to cope with changing temperatures during the cooler seasons, and you'll need protection from the sun during most of the year. Many of the religious sites require a head covering of some sort—you can usually borrow one at the entrance—and prohibit bare knees or, in some cases, even bare shoulders. These requirements are mentioned in the text.

Trying to see everything in any given town could easily become an exhausting marathon. You will certainly enjoy yourself more by being selective and passing up anything that doesn't catch your fancy in favor of a friendly café. Not all museums will interest you, and forgiveness will be granted if you don't visit *every* religious site.

Practical information, such as the opening times of various attractions, is as accurate as was possible at the time of writing, but everything is subject to change. You should always check with the local tourist information office if seeing a particular sight is crucially important to you.

* OUTSTANDING ATTRACTIONS:

An * asterisk before any attraction, be it an entire daytrip or just one exhibit in a museum, denotes a special treat that in the author's opinion should not be missed.

TOURIST INFORMATION

Nearly every town of any tourist interest in Israel has an information office that can help you with specific questions. Usually identified by a logo of two figures bearing a huge bunch of grapes, they always have someone there who speaks English. These offices are almost always closed on the Sabbath and Jewish holidays. Their locations are shown on the town maps in this book by the word "**info.**," and repeated along with the phone number in the "Practicalities" section for each trip.

ADVANCE PLANNING INFORMATION:

The **Israel Ministry of Tourism** maintains **Government Tourist Information Offices** in various countries to help you plan your trip. Some convenient ones are located at:

350 Fifth Avenue
New York, NY 10118
Phone (212) 560-0600

5 South Wabash Avenue
Chicago, IL 60603
Phone (312) 782-4306

6380 Wilshire Boulevard
Los Angeles, CA 90048
Phone (213) 658-7462

180 Bloor Street West
Toronto, Ontario M5S 2V6, Canada
Phone (416) 964-3784

18 Great Marlborough Street
London, W1V 1AF, England
Phone (071) 434-3651

Section II

DAYTRIPS IN
CENTRAL ISRAEL

- **from Jerusalem**
- **from Tel Aviv**

All of the daytrips in this section can be taken from either Jerusalem or Tel Aviv, as these two base cities are less than an hour apart by either bus or car. Still, you'll find it easier (and cheaper) to use Jerusalem as your headquarters for the first nine excursions, and take the remaining eight from Tel Aviv. A few of the tours are within the cities themselves, visiting the most interesting parts of town.

One of the trips described further on in Section III, that to Caesarea, can be just as easily taken from Tel Aviv as from Haifa.

Jerusalem

(Yerushalayim, El-Quds)

*The Old City I

From the Jaffa Gate to the Western Wall

"Pray for the peace of Jerusalem: they shall prosper that love thee" declares the Book of Psalms (122:6). Getting to know this most complex of cities is difficult; heeding David's call to actually love it could be harder. Still, the rewards that come with even a glimmer of understanding are so immense that a successful visit here can well be one of the highlights of your life.

Sacred to the three great monotheistic religions, Jerusalem is the repository of some 3,000 years of turbulent history—a cultural cauldron still bubbling away. Ironically, this world center of spirituality is also the focus of ancient animosities that remain unresolved to this day, but that's what makes this such a vital, dynamic place. You may love it or hate it, but you can only gain by sampling its infinite experiences. In all the world, there is no other place like Jerusalem.

Settlements have existed on this hilly site, perched about 2,700 feet above sea level, as far back as the Stone Age. The first recorded town was founded by the Canaanites around 3000 B.C. on Mount Ophel, just south of the Temple Mount and close to the only source of water, the Gihon Spring. It was here, to the Temple Mount (Mount Moriah), that according to the Bible Abraham was sent to sacrifice his son Issac (Genesis 22), probably in the 18th century B.C.

The real history of Jerusalem as a significant center begins with King David, who purchased the top of Mount Moriah around 1000 B.C. (2 Samuel 24:18–25) and there built an altar housing the Ark of the Covenant. His son Solomon erected the magnificent First Temple on the same spot, which lasted until the Babylonians under Nebuchadnezzar plundered the city in 586 B.C., sending its people into exile. A second temple was begun after their return; under Roman rule this was greatly enlarged by that master builder and psychopathic despot, Herod the Great, in 18 B.C.

This sign says it all

Jesus practiced his last ministry here, was arrested and then crucified around A.D. 30. Jewish rebellions against Roman injustice in A.D. 66 and 132 led to the expulsion of Jews from the city, an exclusion that lasted until the 13th century. Under the emperor Constantine, Jerusalem became a Christian center, only to be taken by Islamic forces in A.D. 638. The Christian Crusaders of the 12th century held it for nearly a hundred years; after which the Egyptians and later the Turks ruled until modern times.

Increasing European influence in the 19th century restored much of Jerusalem's former greatness. After World War I, the city became the administrative capital of the British Mandate in Palestine, and following the 1948 War of Independence was brutally divided between Israel and Jordan. This situation was finally rectified by the Six Day War of 1967, when all of Jerusalem became part of Israel.

For diplomatic reasons, Jerusalem's status as the capital of Israel is not yet officially recognized by many nations including the United States and the United Kingdom, who maintain their embassies in Tel Aviv and have separate consulates in both East and West Jerusalem.

These first two walking tours explore the very heart of historic Jerusalem—the Old City. The second begins where the first left off; both can be done in the same day if you don't spend much time at museums. However, it is better to take them on separate days at a more leisurely pace. After that, the next few chapters describe do-it-yourself tours in East Jerusalem, The New City, and the suburbs.

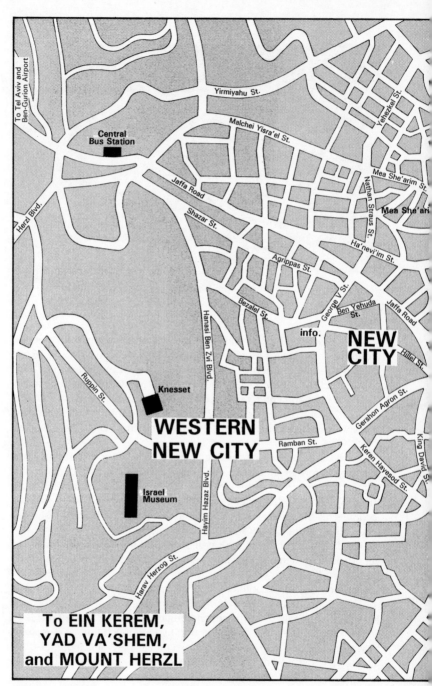

To Tel Aviv and Ben-Gurion Airport

Yirmiyahu St.

Malchei Yisra'el St.

Central Bus Station

Jaffa Road

Shazar St.

Herzl Blvd.

Mea She'arim St.

Yehezkel St.

Nathan Straus St.

Mea She'ari

Ha'nevi'im St.

Agrippas St.

Bezalel St.

George V St.

Ben Yehuda St.

Jaffa Road

Hanasi Ben Zvi Blvd.

info.

NEW CITY

Hillel St.

Ruppin St.

Knesset

WESTERN NEW CITY

Ramban St.

Gershon Agron St.

Keren Hayesod St.

King David St.

Israel Museum

Hayim Hazaz Blvd.

Harav Herzog St.

To EIN KEREM, YAD VA'SHEM, and MOUNT HERZL

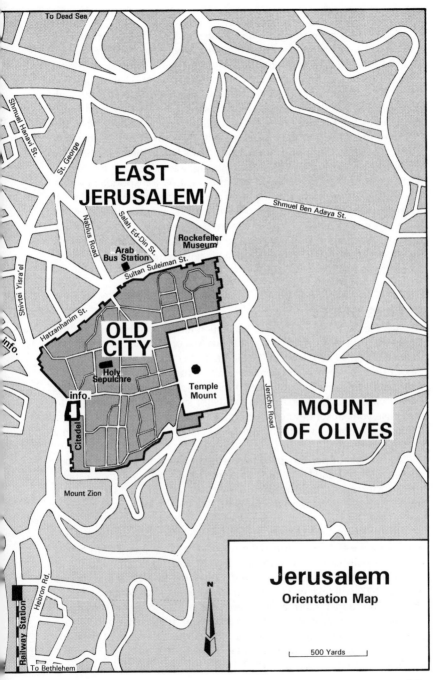

To Dead Sea

Shmuel Hanavi St.

St. George

EAST JERUSALEM

Shmuel Ben Adaya St.

Nablus Road

Salah Ed-Din St.

Rockefeller Museum

Arab Bus Station

Shivtei Yisra'el

Sultan Suleiman St.

Hatzanhanim St.

info.

OLD CITY

Holy Sepulchre

info.

Temple Mount

Citadel

Jericho Road

MOUNT OF OLIVES

Mount Zion

Hebron Rd.

Railway Station

To Bethlehem

N

Jerusalem
Orientation Map

500 Yards

Most of the historic and religious sites of Jerusalem are contained within the 16th-century walls of the Old City, which is conveniently divided into four sectors plus the original Temple Mount, or Mount Moriah. These are, in tour sequence: the Armenian and Jewish quarters (Walk I), and the Moslem and Christian quarters (Walk II). Although considerably less than a square mile in size, the Old City holds such treasures as the Citadel, the Western Wall (a.k.a. the Wailing Wall), the Dome of the Rock, the Via Dolorosa, and the Church of the Holy Sepulchre. Besides these and many other attractions, there are bustling markets along several of the ancient passageways that pass for streets, adding colorful life to the sacred stones of history. Transportation within the walls is entirely by foot as the lanes are much too narrow for vehicles.

You cannot possibly see all of the Old City in a single day, or even in a week. Perhaps later, after you've digested the experiences along these two "get acquainted" walking tours, you can find the time to explore it in greater depth, armed with one of the many fine archaeological or historic guidebooks that are devoted solely to Jerusalem.

GETTING THERE:

Buses leave Tel Aviv's Central Bus Station almost continuously for the 50-minute ride to Jerusalem's Central Bus Station, located at the northwest end of Jaffa (*Yafo*) Road in the New City. Service to and from Haifa, a 2-hour ride, is nearly as frequent. In general, the buses run from about 6 a.m. until late evening, but do not operate at all from mid-afternoon on Fridays until Saturday evenings, nor on major Jewish holidays. It is best to purchase your ticket before boarding, and to wait in line at the posted departure platform—where the signs are in English on one side, Hebrew on the other.

Sherut Taxis operated by different companies depart from various points in Tel Aviv and Haifa for Jerusalem. These shared vehicles, usually stretch Mercedes, have fixed fares that are roughly the same as the buses, with higher rates on the Sabbath. Ask locally for current information.

Airport Buses and Sheruts depart Tel Aviv's Ben-Gurion Airport frequently for the 45-minute ride to Jerusalem. The buses operated by Egged run every half-hour or so from about 6:30 a.m. to 8 p.m. and go to Jerusalem's Central Bus Station. *Sheruts* operated by Nesher Taxi, phone (02) 22-72-27, will take you to or from anywhere in Jerusalem for an extra charge. The Tourist Information Desk in the arrivals lounge at the airport can give you current information about your transport options. Passengers departing Israel on **El Al** should ask the airline about their advance check-in and airport transportation programs.

Trains connect Jerusalem with Tel Aviv, but they run so infrequently and slowly that only the most devoted railfan or scenery watcher would want to ride them.

By car, Jerusalem is 39 miles southeast of Tel Aviv via Route 1; and 99 miles southeast of Haifa via Route 2 to Tel Aviv followed by Route 1 into Jerusalem.

GETTING AROUND:

Local buses operated by Egged serve the New City and most of the surrounding areas, but do not venture inside the walls of the Old City or go deep into Arab East Jerusalem. For the purpose of this daytrip, you'll have to get off outside the Jaffa Gate and hoof it from there. Depending on which part of the city you're coming from, take any of the following bus route numbers: 1, 3, 13, 19, 20, 23, or 30. Ask the driver to make sure you're going in the right direction. He'll sell you the correct ticket, which you keep until leaving the bus. There is no service from mid-afternoon on Fridays until after sunset on Saturday evenings, nor on major Jewish holidays.

Bus Number 99, the **Jerusalem Circular Line,** runs during the tourist season and makes stops at most of the major attractions in the New City, the Mount of Olives, and Mount Scopus. This route begins and ends just outside the Jaffa Gate. You can buy a single-ride ticket, or an unlimited-use ticket valid for one or two days. Ask at the tourist office for current information on this handy service.

Taxis, usually called "Specials," are the easiest way to get around Jerusalem. They can be hailed in the street or summoned by phone, and are not too terribly expensive—especially if several people are traveling together. Be sure that the driver uses the meter! Fares are higher after 9 p.m. and on the Sabbath or holidays. Most Israelis don't leave tips, but foreigners are more or less expected to. Not that it matters on this trip, but many drivers from the New City refuse to drive to addresses in East Jerusalem—people staying in hotels there sometimes have to change cabs at the "border" on Suleiman St., opposite the Arab Bus Station.

Driving a car yourself anywhere in Jerusalem is definitely not recommended. Israeli drivers are extremely aggressive, and the streets are so confusing that you'll surely get lost. Even if you do find your destination, there will most likely be no place to park nearby. Do yourself a favor and leave the driving to locals.

PRACTICALITIES:

These two walking tours visit places that are sacred to Jews, Christians, and Moslems—so there are three different **Sabbaths** to respect. If you are intent on seeing *absolutely everything*, you should avoid making the trips on a Friday, Saturday, Sunday, or religious holiday. That said, however, there are enough places open on any given day to keep you

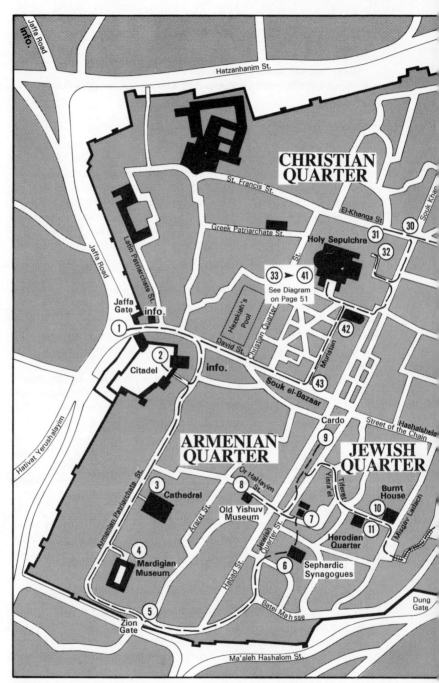

CHRISTIAN QUARTER

Hatzanhanim St.

St. Francis St.

El-Khanga St.

Greek Patriarchate St.

Holy Sepulchre

Jaffa Road

Latin Patriarchate St.

Jaffa Gate

info.

(1)

(2)
Citadel

info.

Hezekiah's Pool

David St.

Christian Quarter

(33) ► (41)
See Diagram
on Page 51

(31)

(30)

(32)

Souk Khan

(42)

Souk el-Bazaar

(43)

Muristan

Cardo

Street of the Chain

Hashalshela

ARMENIAN QUARTER

(9)

JEWISH QUARTER

Hativat Yerushalayim

Armenian Patriarchate St.

(3) Cathedral

Ararat St.

(8)

Or HaHayim St.

Old Yishuv Museum

Yistra'el

Tiferet

Burnt House

(10)

(7)

Herodian Quarter

(11)

Misgav Ladach

(4)
Mardigian Museum

Habad St.

Jewish Quarter St.

(6)

Sephardic Synagogues

(5)
Zion Gate

Batei Mahsse

Dung Gate

Ma'aleh Hashalom St.

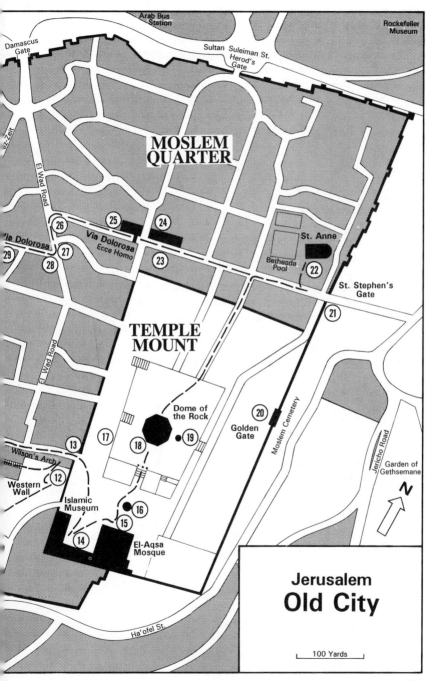

Jerusalem
Old City

100 Yards

33

happily occupied. Many of the sites along the route require that you be **modestly dressed**, meaning no shorts or bare shoulders. Head coverings of some sort are needed at some sites; if you don't have one, they'll loan one to you.

A common complaint among visitors to the Old City are the frequent **annoyances** caused by self-appointed "guides," excessively zealous merchants, and dubious beggars. These pests are especially thick along the Via Dolorosa and around the Jaffa Gate. Do whatever it takes to discourage them, remembering that saying "yes" to one will surely bring on hordes of others. Also remember that all legitimate guides must be licensed by the government; self-styled "guides" offering their services along the street are violating the law. If you do encounter problems, contact the Old City Tourist Police, phone (02) 27-32-22, near the entrance to the Citadel.

As in other large cities around the world, you should be on guard against pickpockets and bag thieves. Either keep your arm around your possessions at all times or use a money belt. Wearing flashy jewelry or expensive accessories only invites trouble. Although the Old City of Jerusalem is actually quite safe, **tensions** do occasionally erupt into violence. In the highly unlikely event that you might actually encounter an incident, you should leave the scene immediately, exiting discreetly and quietly. Do not run or take photos—just vanish.

Visitors coming to Jerusalem in **winter** should not be surprised to find it blanketed with snow, so bring some warm clothes with you. It also rains a lot in that season.

The **Government Tourist Information Office,** phone (02) 75-49-12, is located at 24 King George St. in the New City. They have a handy branch office, phone (02) 28-22-95, just inside the Jaffa Gate in the Old City. The city operates a **Municipal Information Office** at 17 Jaffa Road, a block northwest of the Old City walls, phone (02) 22-88-44. If you need help on a Friday afternoon or Saturday morning, when these offices are closed, try the **Christian Information Center,** phone (02) 28-76-47, near the Citadel entrance in the Old City.

Jerusalem has a **population** of nearly 500,000, of which about 26,000 live in the Old City. Citywide, roughly about 75% are Jews, 20% Moslems, and 5% Christians and others.

FOOD AND DRINK:

For a variety of reasons, there are few decent places to eat in the Old City. You might try the following:

> **Abu Saif** (just inside the Jaffa Gate, beyond the tourist office) Middle Eastern specialties at modest prices. X: Sun. $

> **The Coffee Shop** (near the Citadel entrance and the Anglican Church) Light meals in an attractive setting. X: Sun. $

Quarter Café (upstairs, next to the Burnt House in the Jewish Quarter) An excellent self-service restaurant with a great view. Kosher. X: Fri. eve., Sat. $

SUGGESTED TOUR:

Begin your walk at the **Jaffa Gate** (*Sha'ar Yafo*) (1), one of the eight openings in the 16th-century walls that physically define and enclose the **Old City.** The present walls, about two-and-a-half miles in circumference, were built by the Ottoman ruler, Suleiman the Magnificent, between 1537 and 1542. Until the late 19th century, the area contained by his ramparts was the only inhabited part of Jerusalem. The site of David's original town of 1000 B.C. lies just outside the southeast corner. From that time until the 16th century, the city and the walls surrounding it expanded and contracted several times as Jerusalem's fortunes waxed and waned. The location of the walls was always determined by the city's strategic location atop hills bordered on three sides by deep valleys, a position defensively vulnerable only to the north.

The **Jaffa Gate** is the main aperture to the New City, or West Jerusalem. It opens directly onto Jaffa (*Yafo*) Road, the old route linking Jerusalem with the ancient seaport of Jaffa (see page 115). Originally, the gate was L-shaped to slow down any attacking armies, but in 1898 the moat outside it was filled in and a large breach punched through to enable the visiting Kaiser Wilhelm II of Germany to pass through on his white charger in the manner of a Crusader, complete with white silk burnoose and sun helmet. He came to dedicate the Lutheran Church of the Redeemer. Another official visitor, Britain's General Allenby, passed through in 1917, but he arrived on foot. Cars and trucks enter this way today, although they can't go very far into the Old City. Just inside the gate, behind a wrought-iron fence to the left, are two graves thought to be those of Suleiman's architects, who were reportedly beheaded for not including Mount Zion within the walls they designed. *That* taught them a lesson!

It is possible to **walk** along the top of the **ramparts** for some wonderful views of the Old City and the surrounding hills and valleys. There are access points at the Jaffa Gate, the Citadel, and the Damascus Gate; and extra exit points at most of the other gates. For security reasons, the walls surrounding the Temple Mount are off limits. Women are strongly advised not to make this walk alone as there have been numerous sexual assaults. The walls are open daily from 10 a.m. to 4 p.m., closing at 3 p.m. on Fridays. In season, the section between the Citadel and Zion Gate remains open in the evening. Tickets are not sold on Saturdays or holidays, so purchase in advance.

To your left, once inside the gate, is the helpful **Government Tourist Information Office;** and around the corner the **Christian Information**

Center, which can give more detailed information on Christian sites. The massive ***Citadel** (2), often called the **Tower of David** although it has nothing to do with the Israelite's second king, now houses the fascinating **Museum of the History of Jerusalem.** Even without its splendid new museum, this magnificent fortress would be well worth a visit for the building and its views alone. First built in 24 B.C. as a palace for horrible Herod the Great, it was later used as a residence for the Roman procurators and severely damaged in the Jewish rebellion of A.D. 66. Although tradition says otherwise, it is quite likely that this was the praetorium from which Pontius Pilate sent Jesus to his crucifixion (John 18:28–19:16). The Citadel was altered many times over the centuries, most notably by the Crusaders in 1128, the Mamluks in 1312, and Suleiman the Magnificent in 1538; but parts of Herod's original structure still survive. The minaret near the southwest corner is a relatively modern addition, having been built in 1655.

Cross the bridge spanning the dry moat and enter the Citadel. You will have a choice of taking a guided tour in English or going through on your own, following the clear signs and explanations and perhaps renting a cassette player as your personal guide. Begin your visit with the audiovisual show "Shalom Jerusalem," screened frequently in the **Phasael Tower** above the entrance hall. This is one of the original towers built by Herod, with the upper levels of smaller stones added by the 14th-century Mamluks. Be sure to go all the way to the top for a marvelous ***view** that lets you see just how the disjointed parts of the entire complex fit together into a functional whole. It also provides a great panorama of the Old City.

Color-coded routes lead you through **exhibits of Jerusalem's history** in chronological order, to several observation sites, and to recent excavations. There is also a walk through the dry moat, a special route for people with limited mobility, a museum shop, and a cafeteria. Don't miss the 19th-century **model of Jerusalem,** a 13x15-foot re-creation in zinc of the Old City that was recently discovered in a Swiss basement. During the summer months, a 45-minute **sound-and-light show** is presented every evening at 9:30 except on Fridays and holiday eves. If you come back for this, be sure to bring warm clothes with you. The Citadel, phone (02) 28-32-73, is open on Sundays through Thursdays from 10 a.m. to 4 p.m., and on Fridays and Saturdays from 10 a.m. to 2 p.m. Allow plenty of time for this exceptional attraction.

Leave the Citadel and stroll into the quiet **Armenian Quarter,** one of the four residential sections of the Old City that are still loosely defined by the main north-south and east-west streets of Roman Jerusalem. The Armenians converted to Christianity in the 4th century, the first nation to do so, and have been represented in Jerusalem since Byzantine times. Today, just a few thousand Armenians still live in continued exile in this neighborhood after many centuries of persecution in their native land. Their **Cathedral of St. James** (3) is reached via a doorway on the left marked "Couvent Armenien St. Jacques," immediately after the first vaulted segment of Armenian Patriarchate St. It is open only during services held daily at 2:30 or 3 p.m., but it's a worthwhile sight if you can make it. The present church was built in the 12th century during the Crusader occupation on remnants of earlier Christian churches from the 5th and 11th centuries, and has a strikingly beautiful interior. It commemorates both St. James the Greater, the martyred apostle believed to have been beheaded on this spot in A.D. 44 on the orders of Herod Agrippa I; and St. James the Lesser, a cousin of Jesus and the first bishop of Jerusalem. Both are entombed within. An unusual feature of this church is the set of clappers used to summon the faithful to worship, which neatly circumvented a 9th-century ban on the use of bells.

Continue down the street to the **Mardigian Museum** (4), which is devoted entirely to the history and culture of the Armenian people. Its exhibits, housed in a former theological seminary of 1843, range from 1st century frescoes found buried on Mount Zion to the unspeakable genocide perpetrated on the Armenians by the Turks in 1915. The museum is open on Mondays through Saturdays, from 10 a.m. to 4 p.m.

Just around the corner is the **Zion Gate** (5), an opening in the Old City walls that leads onto Mount Zion. The outer walls of the gate bear extensive scars from the 1948 War of Independence, when the Old City was lost to the Jordanians. You might want to come back at some other time and explore the attractions of Mount Zion, which was once within the town walls but which was left out by Suleiman's builders as an economy measure—the oversight for which they lost their heads. The sights here, all relatively minor, include the **Cenacle** (the supposed site of the Last Supper), **David's Tomb** (which probably isn't), the **Dormition Church** (a lovely Roman Catholic church on the traditional site of the Virgin Mary's death), and the **Chamber of the Holocaust** (a grim collection of artifacts from the Nazi genocide).

In the meantime, back within the city walls, you can continue on into the prosperous **Jewish Quarter.** Almost completely rebuilt since the Six Day War of 1967, this neighborhood is a harmonious blend of the new, the old, and the very ancient. Every opportunity to unearth the archaeological treasures of three millennia was taken before the carefully designed new structures went up, and many of the discoveries can be enjoyed *in situ* by visitors today.

Follow the map to the four **Sephardic Synagogues** (6), a spiritual center of the Mediterranean Jews since the 16th century. The complex was begun by Jews driven out of Spain and Portugal in the late 15th century, who migrated to Palestine after that became part of the Ottoman Empire. Set about ten feet below street level to comply with an old law that forbade synagogues from being taller than the surrounding buildings, they were severely damaged during the 19 years of Jordanian occupation from 1948 until 1967, when they were used to stable donkeys. The synagogues have since been elegantly restored and are again used for regular services. Visitors are welcome on Sundays, Mondays, Wednesdays, and Thursdays from 9:30 a.m. to 4 p.m.; and on Tuesdays and Fridays from 9:30 a.m. to 12:30 p.m.

From here it's just a few steps north to the **Hurva and Ramban Synagogues** (7). Set adjacent to the Jewish Quarter's only minaret, these historic synagogues are both built on the ruins of a 12th-century Crusader church. The **Ramban Synagogue** honors Rabbi Moshe Ben Nahman, a great Spanish scholar who escaped to Jerusalem in 1267 after unwisely debating the merits of Judaism vs. Christianity in his native land. Here he established the first Jewish community since the Crusader period. This structure, set below street level and originally built around 1400, served both Sephardic (Spanish) and Ashkenazi (Eastern European) Jews until 1585, when the ruling Turks turned it into a flour mill, then a warehouse, and later a food factory. By the end of the 19th century the building had completely deteriorated, and was reconstructed from total ruins after the 1967 war. Currently, it is open only for morning and evening prayers.

Behind the Ramban is the famous arch of the ruined **Hurva Synagogue,** which suffered destruction in 1720 at the hands of angry, unpaid Arab creditors, was rebuilt in 1856 after the debts were forgiven, and again destroyed by the Arab Legion in 1948. Its lonely, poignant arch was restored after 1967, but there are presently no plans to rebuild the synagogue.

The **Old Yishuv Court Museum** (8), a block or so to the west at 6 Or HaHayim St., takes you back to a more recent past. Here the focus is on everyday family life in the Jewish Quarter from the mid-19th century until the end of Ottoman rule in 1917. Occupying a typical Old City house built around an interior courtyard, the museum has two floors with rooms completely furnished in period decor, representing both the Sephardic and Ashkenazi traditions. This interesting little diversion, phone (02) 28-46-36, is open on Sundays through Thursdays, from 9 a.m. to 4 p.m.

Whenever the Romans laid out the streets of a town, they always included a *cardo* as the main north-south axis. And so it was in Jerusalem when the emperor Hadrian built his Cardo Maximus in the 2nd century A.D. Running from the Damascus Gate to as far south as David St., this was extended to the southern wall sometime between the 4th and 6th centuries. Parts of the extension were dug up in the early 1980s, revealing an ancient thoroughfare some 75 feet wide, lined with shops and colonnades of the Byzantine and Crusader eras. Sections of this are under-

Pillars at the Cardo
(Photo courtesy Israel Ministry of Tourism)

ground; others well below the present street level but open to the sky. Beautifully restored, the **Cardo** (9) of today is an intriguing combination of an upscale shopping mall and a fascinating archaeological site; a mixture of boutiques and Roman columns, cafés and Crusader arches. Someday it may be possible to excavate northward to the Damascus Gate, uncovering the earliest Roman constructions, but to do this requires the demolition of many houses in the Moslem and Christian quarters.

The route on the map leads past some barely visible traces of 8th-century-B.C. walls and a section of rough paving stones laid in the 1st century A.D. as part of a project to relieve unemployment. Continue down Tiferet Yisra'el St. to the **Burnt House** (10), a.k.a. the Kathros House. When the Romans destroyed the Second Temple in A.D. 70 after a Jewish uprising, they also set this neighborhood ablaze and slaughtered its inhabitants. Firsthand evidence of the wanton brutality can be seen in the excavated basement of an aristocratic Jewish family named Kathros. A wide range of artifacts is on display there, along with one room left just as it was right after the conflagration. The site, phone (02) 28-72-11, is open on Sundays through Thursdays from 9 a.m. to 5 p.m., and on Fridays from 9 a.m. to 1 p.m. A 15-minute slide show in English is given at 9:30, 11:30, 1:30, and 3:30. Those planning to also visit the next attraction should purchase a joint admission ticket.

Another recent discovery of great importance is the nearby **Herodian Quarter—Wohl Archaeological Museum** (11). Here you can descend into excavations of six mansions from the Herodian era (37 B.C. to A.D. 70); opulent priestly homes preserved as they were in the time of Jesus. They are located underneath a present-day religious school, and are furnished with household artifacts uncovered in the digs. This most fascinating site is open on Sundays through Thursdays from 9 a.m. to 5 p.m., and on Fridays from 9 a.m. to 1 p.m. The phone number is (02) 28-81-41, and a joint admission including the Burnt House (above) is offered.

Now follow the route down steps to what for many is the most significant spot in Jerusalem, the ***Western Wall** (*Kotel HaMa'aravi*) (12). For centuries this was known as the "Wailing Wall" because it was as close as Jews could come to the site of their ancient Temple, and where they came to lament its destruction. The Western Wall is actually part of a massive retaining wall erected around 20 B.C. by Herod the Great to support the Second Temple, which he rebuilt and which was later destroyed by the Romans in A.D. 70. The hill on which this stood, now called the Temple Mount, was the Biblical Mount Moriah where Abraham went to sacrifice Issac nearly four millenia ago. Since about A.D. 700 it has been sacred to the Islamic faith, and can be visited on the next walk.

From 1948 until 1967, when the Old City was in Jordanian hands, Jews were denied access to this most holy place. Before the Six Day War it was also hemmed in by narrow alleyways and crowded Arab housing. Then, almost immediately after Israeli forces entered the Old City in June, 1967, the bulldozers arrived to demolish the neighborhood and create the large open plaza of today. The Wall, looming above you, is about 50 feet high—but that's only half of it as the unexcavated lower levels extend another 50 feet or so down into the accumulated rubble of centuries. The large blocks of dressed stone comprising the lower courses are Herodian, the next layer Roman, and the top stones Arab and Turkish.

Although not officially a synagogue, the Western Wall and the plaza immediately in front of it is a holy place subject to the same rules that govern Orthodox synagogues. A fence divides the men's section (at the shady north end) from the women's section (at the sunny south end). To enter the sacred enclosed area, which is always open, you'll need to pass a security checkpoint and be properly dressed. Cardboard *yarmulkas* are provided free for hatless men, and women with bare shoulders may borrow shawls. You are allowed to take photos at any time except on the Sabbath or a Jewish holiday, when it is also forbidden to smoke.

Worshipers visit the Wall at all hours, many of whom are Orthodox Jews dressed in their distinctive black clothes. The practice of stuffing written prayers into the cracks of the Wall is an ancient one still honored by many. Small groups conduct services here according to their beliefs,

The Western Wall and the Dome of the Rock
(Photo courtesy Israel Ministry of Tourism)

and *Bar Mitzvah* celebrations are common. This is also a venue for national events and often a place of joyous communal dancing.

At the northern end of the Wall are 19th-century excavations known as
Wilson's Arch after the English archaeologist who discovered it. The arch
itself, inside a large room, was part of an ancient bridge that connected
the Jewish Quarter with the Temple Mount. You can peer down two deep
shafts that extend to the very base of the Wall itself, and explore other
discoveries that are still being made. Parts of this area are considered
holy, and the usual rules apply. Visits to the "Western Wall Heritage" can
usually be made on Sundays, Tuesdays, and Wednesdays from 8:30 a.m.
to 3 p.m.; on Mondays and Thursdays from 12:30–3 p.m.; and on Fridays
from 8:30 a.m. to noon.

This is the end of the first walk. If you're not tired, you might want to
continue on the second walk, which follows the same map and whose
text begins on page 42.

Jerusalem

(Yerushalayim, El-Quds)

*The Old City II

From the Temple Mount to the Holy Sepulchre

"If I forget thee, O Jerusalem, let my right hand forget her cunning. If I do not remember thee, let my tounge cleave to the roof of my mouth; if I prefer not Jerusalem above my chief joy" cries out the Book of Psalms (137: 5–6). Fear not—you will never, ever, forget the sights along this walking tour, which begins where the previous one left off and follows the same map (pages 32–33). Since this is a continuation, the summary beginning on page 26 still pertains.

GETTING THERE:

GETTING AROUND:

PRACTICALITIES:

FOOD AND DRINK:
See the appropriate entries on pages 30–34.

SUGGESTED TOUR:
Leaving the **Western Wall** (12) (pages 40–41), climb the steps near the northwestern corner of the plaza, and turn right onto the **Street of the Chain** (*Ha Shalshelet* or *Bab el-Silsileh* Road). This is the ancient east-west axis of the Old City, the Roman *decumanus* that leads eastward past some intriguing Mamluk buildings of the medieval period to the Temple Mount. Pious Jews will not enter this area as the precise location of the Temple destroyed in A.D. 70 is not known and they might inadvertently step on sacred ground. The Temple Mount is in Moslem territory that is sometimes closed to non-Moslems. Tourists may be denied entry by the Arab guards for a variety of reasons, including what they might regard as

improper dress or suggestive behavior. It should also be avoided during periods of civil unrest. *If you cannot or would rather not explore the Temple Mount, you should turn left on El Wad Road and follow the map to the Via Dolorosa.*

Enter the **Temple Mount,** known in Arabic as the **Haram esh-Sharif,** through the **Chain Gate** (*Bab el-Silsileh*) (13), one of the few entry points for non-Moslems. Sacred to Moslems, Jews, and Christians alike, the Mount has—with the exception of the 12th-century Crusader period—been in Moslem hands ever since the 7th century A.D. After the stunning Israeli victory in the Six Day War, it was assumed by many that the Jews would regain possession of their most sacred site, but the Israeli flag flew over the Mount for only three hours on June 7, 1967, before Defense Minister Moshe Dayan ordered it removed as a peace gesture—and the Mount returned to the Arabs.

Steeped in a blend of legend, fact, and religious belief, the **history of the Temple Mount**—presumed to be the Biblical Mount Moriah—begins around 1800 B.C. when the patriarch Abraham was sent there to sacrifice his son Issac (Genesis 22:2–19). Through God's intervention the boy was spared; and this steep, rocky, windswept summit became a holy place for all time. Around 1000 B.C., the Israelite king David captured a Jebusite settlement on the adjoining Mount Ophel, purchased a threshing floor atop Mount Moriah, and there placed an altar (2 Samuel 24:18–25). The **First Temple** was erected on the same spot by his son Solomon as a fitting shrine for the Ark of the Covenant (1 Kings 5 & 6). This lasted for nearly 400 years until the Babylonians under Nebuchadnezzar destroyed it and the city in 586 B.C., sending the Israelites into captivity.

Upon their release from Babylon, the Israelites put up a **Second Temple** on the site, finished in 516 B.C. (Ezra 3 & 6), which King Herod the Great began rebuilding around 18 B.C. To support his massive structure, Herod first surrounded the summit with enormous retaining walls on the east, south, and west sides; the void this contained was filled with rubble to create the huge (nearly 40 acres in size) **platform** that you see today. The southeast corner of this rises a dramatic 213 feet above the Kidron Valley, while the southern end of its west side is the Western Wall visited on the previous walk.

Several of the most significant events in the life of Jesus occurred at the Temple, as recounted in Luke 2:22–28, Luke 2:41–47, Luke 4:9–12, Matthew 21:12–16, John 5:14, John 7:14–53, John 8:2–11, John 10:22–39, Mark 12:41–44, Matthew 24:1–25, Matthew 27:2–10, and Matthew 27:51. For Christians, too, this is a holy place.

Herod's Temple was destroyed by the Romans in A.D. 70, and its final remnants obliterated by the emperor Hadrian in A.D. 135. Early Christians generally avoided the area, which remained bleak until Jerusalem was conquered by the armies of Islam in A.D. 638. The Rock of Abraham on Moriah's peak, the center of the previous Temple, was according to the Koran also the spot from which Muhammad made his mystical Night Journey into Heaven. Except for a relatively brief period of Christian rule during the Crusader times of the 12th century, the Temple Mount has remained under Moslem control from the 7th century A.D. right up to the present, and will almost certainly continue to be so in the future. It is the splendid Moslem buildings, some dating from as far back as the 7th century, that draws non-Moslem visitors from all over the Earth to this third-holiest place (after Mecca and Medina) in the Islamic world.

Entry to the Temple Mount is at the discretion of the Arab authorities, and is free except for the holy sites and the Islamic Museum. Visits may be made on Saturdays through Thursdays from 8 a.m. to 3 or 4 p.m., closing at 11 a.m. during Ramadan, but not on Fridays or Moslem holidays. You must be modestly dressed and refrain from any suggestive behavior, such as holding hands. Do not wander away from obvious tourist areas, as some sections are off limits but not marked as such. Any bags that you may be carrying will be searched, and they along with cameras and shoes must be left outside the holy sites. Purchase your **ticket** for the sites at the booth between the gate and the museum. Although the hours vary according to a complex pattern, the museum is usually closed from about noon until 1 p.m.; and both the mosque and the Dome of the Rock close for prayers from roughly 11 a.m. to 12:15 p.m. and again from 2–3 p.m. Since they are all near each other, you can see them in any sequence.

The entrance to the **Islamic Museum** (14) dates only from the 19th century, but most of it is housed in an adjacent former mosque from 1194, and in an earlier Crusader structure. The collections focus on the traditional artistry and craftsmanship of Islam, and especially on original architectural elements removed from the Dome of the Rock and the El-Aqsa Mosque during renovations. Other noteworthy items include huge 18th-century cooking pots used to feed the poor, a 19th-century cannon that announced the beginning and end of fasting during Ramadan, lovely religious ceremonial objects, armaments, and illuminated manuscripts and Korans.

Standing next to the museum is the venerable **El-Aqsa Mosque** (15), first built in A.D. 715 by the Caliph al-Walid. It was twice destroyed by earthquakes within 60 years of its completion, as was its successor of 780. The present structure, greatly modified and rebuilt over the years, dates from 1035 and was used by the Crusaders as a royal residence and later as the headquarters of the Knights Templar. The name of the mosque, *Masjid el-Aqsa*, once applied to the entire Temple Mount platform, and means the "Farther Sanctuary," a reference to Muhammad's famous Night Journey from this hill.

It was here, in 1951, that King Abdullah of Jordan was assassinated by

The Arcade and the Dome of the Rock
(Photo courtesy Israel Ministry of Tourism)

a Palestinian nationalist while in the company of his young grandson, the present King Hussein. A deranged Christian tourist from Australia caused enormous damage, since repaired, in 1969 when he tried to rid the Temple Mount of "abominations" by fire so that the Messiah could come. President Anwar Sadat of Egypt prayed on this spot during his 1977 mission of peace to Jerusalem.

Before entering the mosque, you must heed the Biblical command to ". . . put off thy shoes from off thy feet, for the place whereon thou standest is holy ground." (Exodus 3:5). And leave your bags and camera behind, too.

Accommodating some 5,000 worshipers, the vast **interior** of El-Aqsa is a forest of marble columns donated in 1938 by Italy's Benito Mussolini, with ceiling decorations done at the same time courtesy of Egypt's King Farouk. The *mihrab*, or prayer niche, on the south side indicates the direction of Mecca. Almost above it is the dome, surfaced in silvery lead in contrast to the Dome of the Rock's golden glow.

Now stroll north past the round **El-Kas Fountain** (16), built in 709, in which devout Moslems wash their feet before entering the mosque. The olive tree on the right is said to date from the time of Muhammad. Ascend the steps and walk beneath the graceful 10th-century arcade from whose arches, many believe, the scales of judgment will be suspended on the Last Day. To the left, in the southwest corner of the elevated esplanade, is the often-overlooked but quite remarkable **Fountain of the Sultan Qaytbay** (17), a classic Mamluk structure of 1482.

Straight ahead stands Jerusalem's most visible landmark, the ***Dome of the Rock** (*Qubbat al-Sakhra*) (18), erected on the ancient summit of Mount Moriah—the very spot where Abraham is supposed to have come to sacrifice his son. This was also the site of the Jewish First Temple of Solomon (953 B.C.) and, later, the Second Temple, destroyed by the Romans.

Completed in A.D. 691, the Dome of the Rock was the first major Islamic sanctuary and has remained intact through some 13 centuries of earthquakes and other disasters because it is built on a solid rock foundation, while the surrounding structures rest atop rubble fill. Commemorating Muhammad's mystical Night Journey to Heaven astride his steed Burak (Sura XVII of the Koran), which traditionally began atop this rock, the Dome's astonishing beauty was at least partially created to offset the powerful influence of nearby Christian churches during the Byzantine era, which were busy making converts of Arabs. Thus its splendor helped spread the cause of Islam, and instilled a sense of pride among the Moslem faithful. Its appropriation of Abraham's rock no doubt sent the message to many that Judaism had been superseded by the new religion. The Dome of the Rock is regarded as the third holiest place in Islam, after the Kaaba in Mecca and Muhammad's tomb in Medina.

Much of the Dome's loveliness derives from the near-mathematical perfection of its proportions, relating to and reflecting the inner circle surrounding the rock. The exterior **tiles** were replaced by Suleiman the Magnificent in the 16th century, although a few of noticeably lower quality were added in the 1960s by Jordan's King Hussein. Once made of real gold, the **dome** itself was melted down to pay a caliph's debts, and lead put in its place. The "gold" you see today is actually an aluminum-bronze alloy added after 1958; it is currently planned to gild this with 24 kt. gold.

Remove your shoes, leave your bag and camera behind, and enter the Dome of the Rock. In its center is the ***Holy Rock** (*Kubbet es-Sakhra*) itself, surrounded by a wooden fence through which you can touch it. Pious Moslems believe that they can see the hoofprints of Muhammad's horse, and the fingerprints of the Archangel Gabriel. A nearby reliquary holds hair from Muhammad's beard. Steps near the southeast corner lead down to a cave called the **Well of the Souls**, where according to tradition, voices of the dead mingle with the rivers of paradise as they drop into eternity. Overhead, and all around you, the exquisite ***decorations** of the interior are in geometric and floral designs, as Islamic law forbids the representation of human or animal forms.

Immediately east of the Dome of the Rock is the much smaller **Dome of the Chain** (19), built about the same time. Its function remains a mystery, although it is associated with the legend of a chain hung by Solomon to test the honesty of witnesses—anyone who lied while touching the chain would be struck by lightning. A more likely, but unproven, theory is that this was the caliph's treasury, guarded against theft by that rather electrifying myth. Note that each of the 17 columns can be seen at the same time regardless of which angle you view the dome from.

Of the eight gates piercing the walls of Jerusalem's Old City, only seven are open. The eighth, the **Golden Gate** (20), is reserved for the Messiah's entry into Jerusalem. Probably built in the late 7th century A.D., it was blocked in the 8th century, occasionally opened during the Christian Crusader era, and permanently sealed since then.

Exit the Temple Mount via the Bab Hitta Gate and soon turn right to **St. Stephen's Gate**, also called the **Lions' Gate** (21). You are now in the Moslem Quarter, although from here on the walk takes you to mostly Christian sites. The gate is named after Christianity's first martyr, who was stoned to death nearby for blasphemy in A.D. 36. Its other name refers to the 13th-century heraldic emblems on either side of the opening, which later represented the lions who were supposed to eat Suleiman's father if he carried through his evil plan to level Jerusalem in the early 16th century. Franciscan monks lead a *procession of pilgrims from here, going by way of the Via Dolorosa to the Holy Sepulchre, every Friday at 3 p.m. (4 p.m. in mid-summer), which you are welcome to join.

Just north of the gate is the 12th-century **Church of St. Anne** (22), possibly the finest example of Crusader architecture in Jerusalem. Erected over the presumed birthplace of the Virgin Mary, it honors her parents Anne and Joachim. The first Christian chapel on this site may have been built as early as the 2nd or 3rd century A.D.; certainly there was a basilica here in the 5th century, which was rebuilt into the present structure in 1142. This survived as a Moslem school and in 1856 was given to the French for their help in the Crimean War. Its **Crypt**, the traditional place of the Virgin's birth, may be visited. Next to the church is the ruined **Pool of Bethesda**, a source of water for the Temple from the 8th century B.C. until the time of Herod the Great. After that it fell into disuse, but continued to fill with waters that were considered to be miraculous, attracting the lame and sick. According to the New Testament (John 5: 2–9), this is where Jesus cured a man who had been crippled for 38 years. The church and its grounds are open on Mondays through Saturdays from 8 a.m. to noon and 2:30–6 p.m. (5 p.m. in winter). Look for an entrance along the street marked "Ste.-Anne—Pères Blanc."

Continue down the street a short distance to the beginning of the *Via Dolorosa** (Way of Sorrow), the route taken by Jesus, carrying his cross, from condemnation to crucifixion and burial. Of course, no one knows for certain whether this is the exact route since it was determined more by faith than by historical evidence. In fact, the route followed by pilgrims has changed several times over the centuries; the present itinerary was adopted only in the 18th century. Along the way are 14 **Stations of the Cross** representing the chain of events from trial to burial, which were gradually added beginning in the 8th century and given their present number and location in the 19th century. Whether the footsteps are precise or only supposed, and despite the tatty commercialization of the route, following the Via Dolorosa is an intense spiritual experience for devout Christians.

Station I is the site of the **Antonia Fortress** (23), traditionally the place where Jesus was brought before the Roman governor Pontius Pilate for judgment. History suggests that this event would have more likely occurred at Herod's Palace by the Citadel (2), where the governor usually held court. However, since it happened at the time of Passover, it is *possible* that Pontius Pilate may have temporarily moved to the Antonia Fortress to be next to the Temple, where the action was. In any case, there is precious little to see; the fortress was demolished in A.D. 70 and the site is now occupied by a Moslem school. You can climb the steps and possibly gain admittance for a wonderful view of the Temple Mount.

Directly across the street is **Station II**, the **Franciscan Convent** (24), with its **Chapel of the Flagellation** on the supposed spot where Jesus was flogged and given his crown of thorns. To the left is the **Chapel of the Condemnation,** where Pontius Pilate is said to have pronounced sentence. Both chapels are within the site of the former Antonia Fortress, and both may be visited on Mondays through Saturdays, from 8:30 a.m. to noon and 2–6 p.m., closing at 5 p.m. in winter.

Pass under the **Ecce Homo Arch**, said to be the spot where Pilate exclaimed "Behold the Man." The arch itself, however, dates from A.D. 135 and was part of a triumphal gateway to the pagan Roman city. To its right is the **Convent of the Sisters of Zion** (25), where you can see some excavations of a huge underground chamber called the *Lithostrotos*, another part of the sprawling Anotonia Fortress. Along with this are models and graphic displays that help make sense of the complex. You can visit them on Mondays through Saturdays from 9 a.m. to noon and 2–5 p.m., entering at the doorway marked "Notre-Dame de Sion."

Station III (26), where Jesus fell with the cross, is at the junction with El Wad Road and marked by a small Polish chapel with a relief above the door depicting the event. Turn left to **Station IV** (27), the spot where Jesus met his mother in the crowd of onlookers.

Here the Via Dolorosa turns right. Simon of Cyrene, who had come from Libya to celebrate Passover, was forced by the Romans to help Jesus carry his cross at **Station V** (28). Continue on to **Station VI** (29), where a woman named Veronica wiped the face of Jesus with her cloth. Under the weight of his cross, Jesus fell for a second time at **Station VII** (30), which at that time was on the edge of the city. A gate here led up to the place of

*Jesus on the Cross at Station XII in
the Church of the Holy Sepulchre*

execution, and this is where notices of death sentences were publicly
posted. El Khanqa Street goes up to **Station VIII** (31). Here Jesus spoke to
the women of Jerusalem (Luke 23:27–30), foretelling the destruction of
their city.

From this point the direct route to the site of Calvary is blocked by old
buildings, so return to the market street and turn right. Shortly on the
right, a stone staircase takes you up to a Coptic church, the site of
Station IX (32), where Jesus fell for a third time.

Now carefully follow the map to the ***Church of the Holy Sepulchre**
(33), inside of which are the remaining Stations of the Cross. Although
contested by some, there is excellent historical and archaeological evidence supporting the belief that this is indeed the true site of Calvary, the
Biblical Golgotha, where Jesus was crucified, buried, and resurrected.

Many—indeed most—who visit Christendom's central shrine are dis-
appointed in what they see. By no stretch of the imagination is this a
great edifice; rather it is a jumble of poorly maintained miscellaneous
structures stacked together on a hilltop; dark, cavernous, and confusing
within. Bitter rivalries between different denominations prevent it from
being what its site and history deserve. It takes an act of faith to tran-
scend the chaos all around and derive satisfaction from your visit, but it
can be done and it's worth the effort.

Worship at this site apparently began with the very first Christians, who preserved a living memory of the exact location. In an effort to stamp out the new religion, the Romans erected a pagan temple on the spot in the 2nd century A.D. By the 4th century, however, the Empire had adopted Christianity and the emperor Constantine decided to build a great church. The precise location of the tomb was determined by his mother, the empress Helena, and confirmed by excavations beneath the temple. Work on the new basilica began in A.D. 326 and was completed in 348.

Constantine's Byzantine basilica was destroyed by invading Persians in 614, but rebuilt only 15 years later. This lasted until 1009, when it was reduced to rubble by the Fatamid caliph el-Hakim. A modest replacement soon rose; it was this structure that the Crusaders expanded into approximately the church that you see today, consecrated in 1149. The church has suffered desecrations and inept repairs throughout the centuries. A fire in 1808 and an earthquake in 1927 caused substantial damage, but it was not until 1959 that the warring religious factions got their act together long enough to agree on a long-term program of restoration.

Six different Christian denominations—Greek Orthodox, Roman Catholic, Armenian, Coptic, and Ethiopian—share rights to the Church of the Holy Sepulchre, with major ownership belonging to the first three. Their competing services result in a confusion of overlapping processions, chants, and incense fumes; each constantly getting in the way of the others. Occasionally it breaks out into aggressive behavior, and even fisticuffs, over such silly matters as to who has the right to sweep which floor, and when. The Protestants, meanwhile, have remained above the fray and in the late 19th century established their own symbolic Calvary/Golgotha at the Garden Tomb, just north of the Old City walls in East Jerusalem. It is described in the next chapter.

The Church of the Holy Sepulchre is open daily from 5 a.m. to 8 p.m., closing at 7 p.m. in winter. Admission is free, and modest dress—meaning no shorts or bare shoulders—is required.

Referring to the diagram on page 51, **enter the church** from the courtyard and climb the **steps** to your immediate right. These lead to the summit of **Calvary**, also called Golgotha, the hill on which Jesus was crucified. To the right, at the top, is a Franciscan chapel marking **Station X** (34), where Jesus was stripped of his garments. He was nailed to the cross at another spot in the same chapel, identified as **Station XI** (35). To the left, in the Greek Orthodox chapel, is **Station XII** (36), the actual ***site of the Crucifixion**. It is marked, in no uncertain way, by glittering life-size icons of Jesus on the Cross, Mary, and John the Baptist, surrounded by numerous lamps. The hole in the rock under the altar is purported to be the socket in which the cross was set. Close to this is **Station XIII**, where the body of Jesus was removed and given to Mary.

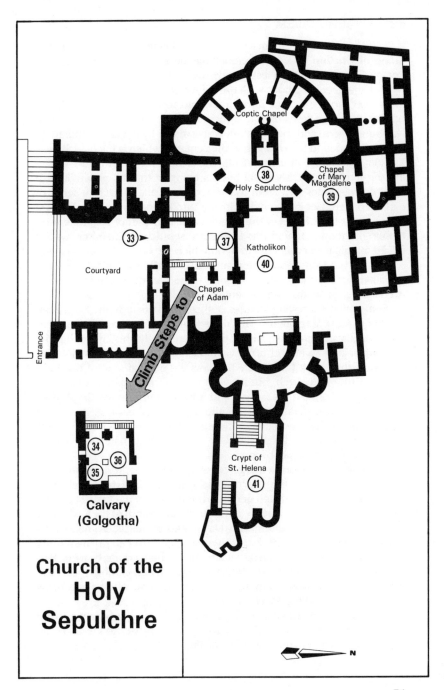

Coptic Chapel

Chapel
of Mary
Magdalene
(39)

(38)

Holy Sepulchre

(33) ▶

(37) Katholikon

(40)

Courtyard

Chapel
of Adam

Climb Steps to

Entrance

Crypt of
St. Helena

(41)

(34)
(36)
(35)

Calvary
(Golgotha)

Church of the
Holy
Sepulchre

N

Descend the steps to the main level. Directly ahead of you is the **Stone of Unction** (37), commemorating the spot where, according to Roman Catholic tradition, Jesus' body was anointed before burial. To the right is the Greek Orthodox **Chapel of Adam**. Here, through a pane of glass, you can see a crack in the rock said to have been caused by an earthquake when Jesus died (Matthew 27:51). Legend has it that Adam was buried here, and that his skull was revealed by the cleft in the rock.

Stroll around to the rotunda, in the center of which is the final **Station XIV** (38), the ***Holy Sepulchre** itself. The present marble structure encasing the tomb, charitably described as being in the full-blown Turkish rococo style, dates only from the 19th century and replaces a series of earlier chapels. Get in line and wait your turn to enter the tomb. The first little room is the **Chapel of the Angel**, containing part of the stone used to seal the tomb; behind this is the tiny **Sepulchral Chamber**, whose raised marble slab covers the rock on which the body of Jesus was laid.

Behind the Holy Sepulchre is a minute **Coptic Chapel** where, for a donation, you can kiss what purports to be part of the original tomb. Archaeologists contest the authenticity of this.

Some other interesting features of the church include the Franciscan **Chapel of Mary Magdalene** (39), where Jesus is said to have appeared to Mary Magdalene after his resurrection. Interestingly, this chapel has the only organ in the whole church. Continue into the **Katholikon** (40), also known as the Greek Cathedral. This was the original nave of the 12th-century Crusader church, but its elegant simplicity has been marred by ornate decorations. At the far east end is the entrance to the **Crypt of St. Helena** (41), incorporating bits of the 4th-century basilica. A suspect tradition holds that the stairs on the right lead down to a cistern where Empress Helena discovered the True Cross, which had been hastily discarded after the Crucifixion.

Leave the church and emerge once again into the fresh air and sunlight. You are now in the heart of the **Christian Quarter**, a relatively prosperous and less crowded neighborhood built on the highest ground in the Old City. Follow the map to the Lutheran **Church of the Redeemer** (42), consecrated on Reformation Day, 1898, by Kaiser Wilhelm II of Germany. The church is built on the ruins of an 11th-century monastery whose cloister survives mostly intact, and is the spiritual heart of Protestantism in the Holy Land. Its **tower,** which you may climb on Mondays through Saturdays from 9 a.m. to 1 p.m. and 2–5 p.m., offers a fine ***view** of the Old City and the Mount of Olives.

Continue down Muristan Road to David Street and turn right into the **Souk el-Bazaar** (43), a colorful old market that leads back to the Jaffa Gate (1), the beginning of your Old City walking tour.

East Jerusalem and the Mount of Olives

Not all of the Christian sites of Jerusalem lie within the walls of the Old City. The Mount of Olives, in particular, is rich in places associated with the life of Jesus. This tour also takes you through a colorful part of Arab East Jerusalem and visits one of the world's foremost archaeological museums. Midway, you'll have the best possible panoramic view of the entire city, and can even have your picture taken riding on a camel overlooking it all!

GETTING THERE:

Local bus numbers 1, 23, 27, and 99 connect most parts of Jerusalem with the Damascus Gate, where the walk begins. For more details see page 30.

Taxis are the easiest way to reach the Damascus Gate. Be sure the driver uses the meter!

PRACTICALITIES:

Avoid making this trip on a Sunday, when most of the sites are closed. If possible, try to get off to an **early morning start**, or allow a long lunch break as many of the attractions close between noon and 2:30 p.m. **Modest dress** (no shorts or bare shoulders) is required for entry to the holy sites. In summer, you'll need a **headcovering** and sunglasses for the fierce sun, and be well supplied with liquids. A flashlight might be helpful in some cases. **Women** should not make this trip alone, and all persons should avoid East Jerusalem during periods of civil unrest. For **tourist information**, see page 34.

FOOD AND DRINK:

There are relatively few restaurants along this route, especially on the Mount of Olives. The best of the lot include:

53

American Colony Hotel (Nablus Rd. at Salah Ed-Din) A long-time favorite for visiting dignitaries and journalists. Continental and Middle Eastern cuisine, great buffet lunch on Saturdays. Restaurant and coffee shop. Non-kosher. $$ and $$$

Philadelphia (9 Ez-Zahara St., just east of Salah Ed-Din) Using the ancient name of Amman, Jordan, this classic restaurant is famous for its Middle Eastern cuisine. Non-kosher. $$

Petra (11 El-Rashid St., a block west of the Rockefeller Museum) Middle Eastern buffet and set dishes. $ and $$

Seven Arches Hotel (at the top of the Mount of Olives) Fabulous view. Restaurant with good Saturday buffet lunches, and a coffee shop. $$

SUGGESTED TOUR:

Begin your walk at the monumental **Damascus Gate** (*Bab el-Amud*) (1), easily reached by public transportation from other parts of Jerusalem. This is surely the most impressive of the Old City's eight gates, and an outstanding example of 16th-century Ottoman architecture. The busiest entrance into the Moslem Quarter, it marks the beginning of the ancient road to Damascus, Syria; which of course no longer extends that far north.

An earlier gate was erected on this site by Herod Agrippa I around A.D. 44 and rebuilt by the Roman emperor Hadrian in A.D. 135. Remnants of this and its medieval additions can be seen below the modern footbridge leading to the arch. If you're really interested, you can visit the small **Roman Square Museum** by the entrance to the ramparts walk, which is set in the excavations and helps explain the layout of Hadrian's *Aelia Capitolina*, as Jerusalem was then called. It is open daily from 9 a.m. to 5 p.m., closing at 3 p.m. on Fridays.

Turning north away from the Old City, cross the broad, busy Sultan Suleiman Street and enter the Arab neighborhood of East Jerusalem. Until 1967 this, like the Old City, was a part of Jordan, and still retains much of that flavor. The old highway to Damascus is now called **Nablus Road** (*Derech Schechem* in Hebrew) after the West Bank city that it now leads to. Follow it a short distance and turn right into an alleyway leading to the ***Garden Tomb** (2). This peaceful, lovely oasis is believed by some Protestants to be the true location of Calvary (Golgotha), the place where Jesus was crucified, buried, and resurrected—although there is virtually no credible evidence to support this view, and a great deal to confirm the Holy Sepulchre (see page 49) as the actual site. Whatever the truth, this is certainly an infinitely more attractive place, a welcome change from the heaviness of so many of Jerusalem's Christian sites.

The Garden Tomb was first discovered in the late 19th century when Britain's General Gordon (of Khartoum fame) noticed the striking resem-

The Damascus Gate

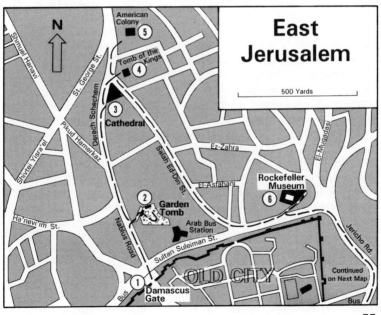

blance of a rock face just north of the Old City walls to the Biblical description of the skull-shaped Golgotha. Excavations nearby unearthed a likely tomb, and the site was then purchased by the London-based group that maintains it today. Interestingly, they do not dogmatically insist on its authenticity. A visit here is a very pleasant, if largely symbolic, experience that can be made on Mondays through Saturdays from 8 a.m. to noon and 3–5 p.m.

Continue on past the U.S. Consulate to **St. George's Cathedral** (3), the seat of the Anglican archbishop of Jerusalem since 1898. It has no set visiting hours, but you're welcome to see its lovely interior whenever the doors are open.

Just beyond this is the so-called **Tomb of the Kings** (*Tombeau des Rois*) (4), once thought to be the final resting place of the ancient Judean kings. It is now known to be the tomb of Queen Helena of Adiabene, a small kingdom north of Baghdad. She had converted to Judaism and moved to Jerusalem around A.D. 46, where she helped relieve a great famine by importing food from Egypt and Cyprus. The tomb complex was built after the death of her son and later used for both herself and her descendants. Archaeology buffs will enjoy exploring these spooky subterranean chambers, which are open daily from 8 a.m. to noon and 2–5 p.m. Bring a flashlight to pierce the gloom.

You are now in the heart of the American Colony, a neighborhood first settled in 1881 by the Spafford family of Chicago after a domestic tragedy. They and their Presbyterian friends spent the rest of their lives here doing charitable works, and acquired an elegant house that became the nucleus of the world-famous **American Colony Hotel** (5). This luxurious outpost of tranquillity in the middle of an often-besieged city is the favorite watering hole of journalists covering the Middle East, and a place where Western diplomats meet discreetly with Palestinian leaders. Neutral all the way, the hotel is under Swiss management. It's a fine place for lunch.

Now follow Salah Ed-Din St., East Jerusalem's busy shopping thoroughfare, back to Sultan Suleiman St. and turn left. After a block or so a ramp on the left leads up to the ***Rockefeller Museum** (6), probably the most important collection of antiquities in the Holy Land. Originally called the Palestine Museum of Archaeology, it was established in 1927 by a grant from John D. Rockefeller II and opened in its present landmark building in 1938. Many of the displays are still in old-fashioned glass cases, but are gradually being upgraded to modern museum standards. Among the treasures are the Galilee Skull from about 200,000 B.C., a skull of the Carmel Man from 100,000 B.C., and a skeleton from 10,000 B.C. Weapons and other artifacts dating from 3500 B.C. to the Middle Ages compete for your attention with Roman jewelry and some of the best Islamic art anywhere. Be sure to visit the beautiful courtyard with its reliefs depicting the history of Palestine. The museum, phone (02)

29-26-27, is open on Sundays through Thursdays from 10 a.m. to 5 p.m.; and on Fridays, Saturdays, and holiday eves from 10 a.m. to 2 p.m.

From here, take a look across the valley to the Mount of Olives, capped by a modern hotel with seven arches. If you think you can walk it, fine, it's good exercise. Those who would rather ride should go to the bus stop at the Damascus Gate (1) and board bus number 42 or 43; or the seasonal number 99 Jerusalem Circular Tourist Bus. A more frequent service is offered by the number 75 Arab bus from the nearby Arab Bus Station on Sultan Suleiman St. east of the Damascus Gate. Better yet, take a taxi. They are usually plentiful in this area.

However you get up the hill, begin your tour of the Mount of Olives at the **Seven Arches Hotel** (7), a modern structure erected during the Jordanian occupation of East Jerusalem. This is another fine place for lunch. From the plaza in front of the hotel you will have a fabulous ***panoramic view** of Jerusalem, enhanced perhaps by the presence of camels that you can sit on while having your picture taken. Be sure to negotiate a price first!

Much of the hillside below you is an ancient Jewish cemetery, the largest in the world and one that remains in use today. This has always been a choice place for burial because of the belief that the Messiah will

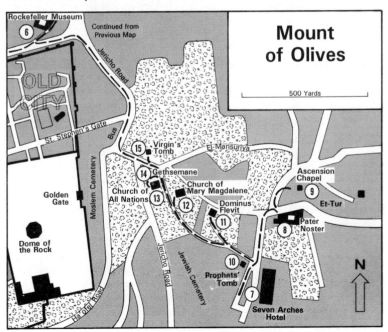

come here on Judgment Day to lead the resurrected into Jerusalem via the Golden Gate (Joel 3 and Zechariah 14).

Follow the road north to the Carmelite Convent, the site of the former **Church of Eleona** and the present **Church of the Pater Noster** (8). Built by the empress Helena in the 4th century A.D. over the grotto where Jesus is thought to have spoken to his disciples about the end of the world, the Eleona Church was destroyed in the 7th century A.D. The site later became known as the place where Jesus taught the Lord's Prayer (*Pater Noster*, Latin for "Our Father"). An oratory was erected over the ruins by the Crusaders in 1106, but the present structure dates only from 1868. It was financed by Princesse de la Tour d'Auvergne, who donated it to the French nation in turn for their perpetual care. Based on an old tradition, The Lord's Prayer has been painted on some 60 tiled panels around the cloister, each in a different language. The complex is open on Mondays through Saturdays from 8:30–11:50 a.m. and 3–4:30 p.m.

Now stroll over to the Arab village of Et-Tur and visit the **Chapel of the Ascension** (9), located on the grounds of a small 17th-century mosque. This is generally agreed to be the spot where Jesus ascended into Heaven (Luke 24:50–51), although the Russian Orthodox Church has its own site a few steps to the east. The earliest chapel here was built in the 4th century and reconstructed in the 12th century by the Crusaders. It has remained in Moslem hands since 1198 and is venerated by them as they also believe in Jesus' ascension, although this is not mentioned in the Koran. Inside, the rock on the floor near the *mihrab* (prayer niche) is allegedly marked with the footprint of Jesus, which some people are able to see. If the compound is not open, just ask around the village for the caretaker; he'll gladly let you in for a small donation.

Return past the Pater Noster Church and turn right, going downhill to the **Tomb of the Prophets** (10). Despite the claim that these are the tombs of Haggai, Zechariah, and Malachi, who wrote the last three books of the Old Testament and lived in the 5th and 4th centuries B.C., all archaeological evidence suggests that the tombs date from between the 1st century B.C. and the 2nd century A.D. At least it's cool inside. The gate is open on Mondays through Fridays from 9 a.m. to 3:30 p.m., and you'll probably need a flashlight. Just below it an orange sign marks the **memorial graves** of those who fell defending the Jewish Quarter during the 1948 War of Independence. Their remains were reinterred here after the 1967 war.

Go down the hill a bit and turn right to the **Church of Dominus Flevit** (11). Built by the Franciscans in 1955 on the foundations of a 7th-century chapel, this tear-shaped church marks the traditional spot where Jesus wept over the coming destruction of Jerusalem (Luke 19:41). Its Latin name means "The Lord Wept," and it's open daily from 7 a.m. to noon and 3–6 p.m., closing at 5 p.m. in winter. Excavations around it have revealed an ancient cemetery dating back to around 1000 B.C., and remnants of a monastery from the 5th century A.D.

Farther down the very steep hill stands the Russian Orthodox **Church of Mary Magdelene** (12), erected in 1888 by Czar Alexander III. Its seven golden onion domes and elaborate 16th-century-Muscovite styling makes it one of the most unusual structures in the Holy Land, and one of the most beautiful. Inside, there is the tomb of the Grand Duchess Elizabeth, assassinated in 1918 by the Bolsheviks, and other members of the Russian royal family. There are also some gorgeous icons and interesting wall paintings. The church is usually open on Tuesdays and Thursdays, from 9 a.m. to noon and 2–4 p.m.

At the bottom of this hill is the **Church of All Nations** (13), also known as the Basilica of the Agony. According to tradition, it was on the rock in front of the altar here that Jesus prayed just before his arrest in the adjacent Garden of Gethsemane, forfeiting his last chance to escape certain death (Mark 14:35). A church was built on this site as early as A.D. 384, which was destroyed by an earthquake around 745. In the 12th century the Crusaders erected a new church that lasted until 1345. The present structure with its extraordinary façade was completed in 1924 with financing from many different countries, which accounts for its name. The deliberately gloomy interior is open daily from 8:30 a.m. to noon and 3–7 p.m. (2–5 p.m. in winter).

Right next to the church, and sharing the same entrance from the street, is the peaceful ***Garden of Gethsemane** (14), where Jesus was betrayed by Judas and taken prisoner. Although they are indeed quite ancient, it is unlikely that the olive trees here date from the time of Christ as the Romans had denuded this hill in A.D. 70. The garden is open at the same time as the church, above.

One last site remains, and that is the **Tomb of the Virgin** (Church of the Assumption) (15), where Mary, and possibly her husband Joseph and her parents, are supposed to be buried. There is no Biblical mention of this; many people believe that she is buried in Ephesus, Turkey, and that the Assumption, her rise into Heaven, took place elsewhere. In any case, this is a holy place for the Eastern Orthodox faiths, and also for Moslems, who believe that Muhammad saw a light here during his mystical Night Journey. Orthodox churches also consider the adjacent **Grotto of Gethsemane** to be the actual spot where Jesus was betrayed. The site is generally open at the same time as the Church of All Nations, above.

From here you can return to central Jerusalem by taking a bus from the stop on the far side of the main road, below St. Stephen's Gate (Lions' Gate). Taxis are usually available near the entrance to the Garden of Gethsemane.

Jerusalem

The New City

Until the mid-19th century, all of Jerusalem was contained within the defensive walls of its Old City. The rocky hills surrounding it were barren, desolate places nearly devoid of life. After four centuries of inept Turkish rule, the Old City itself had become a neglected pesthole where poverty and intolerance reigned.

An edict in 1856 encouraged Jews and Christians to once again settle in the city but, as their numbers grew, so did their distaste for the living conditions. The first tentative moves outside the protective walls occurred around 1860 when Sir Moses Montefiore, a wealthy Jewish philanthropist from England, began his Mishkenot Sha'ananim housing development just west of Mount Zion. The idea slowly caught on and in 1875 a second development began at Mea She'arim. By the turn of the century there were at least a dozen such communities. These now form the nucleus of the New City, an expanding metropolitan area of modern buildings clad in the sandy-gold limestone of the Judean hills.

This self-guided tour explores the oldest parts of the New City, stopping by all of the major attractions that lie within comfortable walking distance. Along the way it visits the ultra-orthodox neighborhood of Mea She'arim, a delightful villa from the turn of the century, the prosperous commercial heart of a modern city, some architectural gems from the British Mandate period, King Herod's family tomb, the original Mishkenot Sha'ananim with its picturesque windmill, and a restored artists' quarter with enticing galleries.

GETTING THERE:

Bus number 1 from the Central Bus Station takes you along Mea She'arim St., the start of the walking tour. There are many other bus options from all over Jerusalem; ask at your hotel for the best route.

Taxis are the easiest way to reach Mea She'arim, and are inexpensive if a few people travel together.

See page 31 for more details on transportation within Jerusalem.

PRACTICALITIES:

Avoid making this trip on a Friday afternoon, Saturday, or Jewish holiday—when everything is closed, buses don't operate, and you're not welcome in certain religious areas.

Modest dress is required for the first segment of this tour, the **Mea She'arim** neighborhood. Posted signs make it perfectly clear just what this means—women must wear long dresses (no pants) and long sleeves, while men can be neither bare-kneed nor bareheaded. Any show of affection is taboo, as is openly taking photos of the residents without permission. These rules stem from the ultra-orthodox religious beliefs of the people who live there; violating them is extremely offensive and can lead to confrontations. *If you would rather not comply, you should begin your tour at the second stop, the Ticho House.*

The **Government Tourist Information Office**, phone (02) 75-49-12, is located at 24 King George V St., a block south of Ben Yehuda St. and right on the walking route.

FOOD AND DRINK:

The paucity of decent restaurants elsewhere in Jerusalem is more than made up for by the marvelous selection along this route. Out of an embarrassment of riches, some choices are:

Mishkenot Sha'ananim (below Montefiore's Windmill) Excellent French cuisine with a Moroccan touch. A beautiful dining experience. For reservations call (02) 22-67-46. X: Fri. $$$

Off the Square (6 Yoel Salomon St. & 17 Yoel Salomon St., south of Kikar Tzion) Two separate restaurants, the first for dairy/fish and the second for meat, keep this traditional Jewish establishment strictly kosher. X: Fri., Sat. $$ and $$$

Europa (42 Jaffa Rd. at Kikar Tzion, upstairs) The local favorite for Jewish home cooking in the Eastern European tradition. Kosher. X: Fri., Sat. $$

The Yemenite Step (12 Yoel Salomon St., south of Kikar Tzion) Set in a charming old house, this Yemenite restaurant features spicy *mellawach* pancakes stuffed with meat, veggies, eggs, and other foods. Kosher. X: Fri. eve., Sat. $$

Fink's Bar (2 Ha' Histadrut St., corner of Ben Yehuda) A hangout for spies, politicians, and journalists since 1933. German cooking with excellent goulash soup. $$

Me Va Me (34 Ben Yehuda St., on the lower shopping level of the Eilon Tower Bldg. at King George V St.) Salads, grilled meats, fish, and other dishes in a friendly, casual, modern place. Nonkosher. $$

The Pie House (26 King David St., in the Y.M.C.A.) Superb meat, fish, and vegetarian dishes with a light touch, in elegant surroundings. Non-kosher. $$

Ticho House Café (at end of alley off 7 HaRav Kook St.) A wonderful vegetarian and dairy restaurant in the garden of the Ticho House, indoor and outdoor dining. Kosher. X: Fri. eve., Sat. $

Atara Café (7 Ben Yehuda St.) Light meals and pastries, caters to the literary set. Try the onion soup. Kosher. $

The best *felafel* stands are along King George V St. between Ben Yehuda St. and Jaffa Road, especially at Agrippas St. For fast food, try Wendy's in the Eilon Tower complex on King George V St. near Ben Yehuda St.

SUGGESTED TOUR:

Begin your walk at the northern end of **Mea She'arim** (1), a neighborhood founded in 1875 as the second Jewish enclave outside the walls of the Old City. Its name means "hundredfold," referring to the passage in Genesis 26:12 that reads: "Then Issac sowed in that land, and received in the same year an hundredfold; and the Lord blessed him." This was part of the reading from the Torah (the first five books of the Bible) for the week that the momentous decision to move here was made.

Mea She'arim is perhaps the world's only remaining example of a true Jewish *shtetl*, the type of ghetto that flourished in Eastern Europe before the Holocaust. Many of its Hassidic residents still dress in the manner of 18th- or 19th-century Poland, with men in long black coats and black hats with broad brims, and women modestly covered from head to toe. They make no secret of the fact that visitors are also expected to be discreet in their attire and behavior, as the many signs in English proclaim.

The community is inhabited by ultra-orthodox Jews of different sects, with a wide range of conservative beliefs, some of which are intensely fundamentalist. Yiddish is the common spoken language, as Hebrew is regarded as a holy tongue reserved for prayer. Some of the residents refuse to even recognize the State of Israel, since it was not founded by the Messiah but by the ungodly Zionists. Accordingly, they don't pay taxes, do military service, or accept legal jurisdiction. A few make their opinions known through the people's medium of spray-can graffiti—in English for the benefit of tourists. Needless to say, these folk are not popular with other Israelis, especially as quite a few also refuse to work, living instead off the taxes of others. Their votes, however, are often crucial to the tightly-balanced political coalitions that have governed Israel since its founding.

There are no particular sights to see in Mea She'arim, but the **entire neighborhood** is of compelling interest. Just discreetly wander around its many little nooks and crannies, being sure to visit the ***Market Place,**

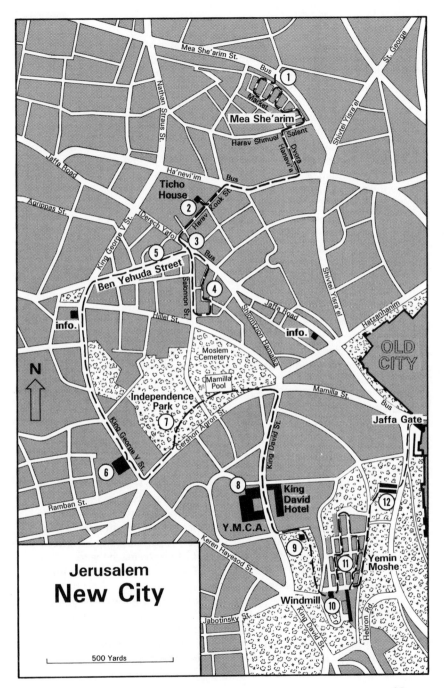

Jerusalem
New City

500 Yards

reached via passageways along the south side of Mea She'arim St. This is a great place to purchase items of Judaica at discount prices, and to discover the most delicious baked goods in Jerusalem.

Leave the neighborhood by way of Harav Shmuel Salant and Dvora Hanevi'a streets, following the map to the *Ticho House (2) at the end of an alleyway off Harav Kook St. One of the most delightful spots in town, this 1860's villa and its gardens serve as a combination small museum, café, library, and reflection of cultured life in Jerusalem earlier in the 20th century. Built by an Arab gentleman and later occupied by a notorious forger of antiquities named Moses Shapira, who had pawned off a fake "world's oldest written text" to the British Museum in 1883, it was eventually acquired by Dr. Abraham Ticho in 1924 for use both as a home and as his ophthalmic hospital. His wife, the artist Anna Ticho, continued to use it as a studio after his death in 1960. When she passed away in 1980, the property was willed to the people of Jerusalem. Some 70 of her works are on display, but the biggest treat is the house itself and its lovely furnishings. The Ticho House, phone (02) 24-50-68, is open on Sundays through Thursdays from 10 a.m. to 5 p.m., on Fridays from 10 a.m. to 2 p.m., and remains open on Tuesdays until 10 p.m. Admission is free. The café here is a marvelous place for lunch.

Continue down the street to **Kikar Tzion** (Zion Square) (3), a major intersection along Jaffa Road (Derech Yafo), the ancient highway from the Old City to the Mediterranean port of Jaffa. Once a rallying point for young Zionists in the 1930s, this is still the busy hub of the New City. Cross the street and stroll south on Yoel Salomon St. into the colorful **Nahalat Shiv'a** (4), a neighborhood named for its seven earliest settlers. It was never a very elegant place, but renewal in the 1980s has preserved much of the original flavor while attracting upscale boutiques, galleries, restaurants, and cafés. Several of Jerusalem's most interesting dining spots are here, and the back alleyways are well worth probing.

Return to Kikar Tzion and turn left into **Ben Yehuda Street** (5), a pedestrians-only mall (midrehov) lined with attractive cafés and shops. This is Jerusalem's unofficial meeting place, where everyone comes to see and be seen. While walking its five-block length, you might want to poke around some of the side streets to the north, or perhaps stop for refreshment. Turn left onto **King George V Street** when you reach the top of the hill, opposite the Eilon Tower complex. The **Government Tourist Information Office** is at Number 24.

Continue down the street to the **Great Synagogue** (6), a modern structure completed in 1983. It is actually two houses of worship, one Ashkenazi and the other Sephardic. Visitors are welcome on Sundays through Thursdays from 9 a.m. to 1 p.m., and on Fridays from 9 a.m. to noon. Immediately south of it is the adjoining **Hechal Schlomo** complex, housing the Chief Rabbinate of Israel and the **Wolfson Museum** with its collection of traditional Jewish ceremonial art and scenes from Jewish history. Located on the fourth floor, the museum is open on Sundays through Thursdays from 9 a.m. to 1 p.m., and on Fridays and holiday eves from 9 a.m. to noon.

Turn left at Gershon Agron St. and follow the map through **Independence Park** (7), a large expanse of green in the center of the New Town. Toward its eastern end, and partially surrounded by an ancient Moslem cemetery, is the **Mamilla Pool.** Probably dating from the time of Herod the Great, this now-waterless reservoir was once part of the Old City's water supply system.

A right turn on **King David Street** (*David Ha'melech*) leads to one of Jerusalem's most visible architectural landmarks, the **Y.M.C.A.** (8) of 1933. No longer the exclusive province of young Christian men, the "Y" caters to both sexes, of all beliefs and ages. It is surely the most beautiful "Imka" in the world, has intriguing public rooms, a superb restaurant, and offers a fabulous panoramic *view of all Jerusalem from its 120-foot **Bell Tower.** Reached by elevator, the tower is open to the public on Mondays through Saturdays, from 9 a.m. to 2 p.m.

Directly across the street is the venerable **King David Hotel,** another magnificent structure from the British Mandate period. Built in 1930 by the Egyptian owners of Shepheard's Hotel in Cairo, it served as British military headquarters from World War II until 1948. As such, it was a tempting target for the Jewish underground, who blew up an entire wing in 1946, killing 91 people. Since reconstructed, the King David is still Jerusalem's most prestigious hotel, if not its most luxurious. You might want to stop for refreshments on the **terrace** overlooking the Old City, an elegant experience that won't cost you too much.

Turn left on the dead-end Abba Sikra St. to **Herod's Family Tomb** (9). This is where horrible Herod the Great (73–4 B.C.) supposedly buried the members of his family that he had executed during various fits of paranoia. Unfortunately, tomb robbers got there before the archaeologists, so little was left inside the underground chambers. Still, you can explore them, but you won't find Herod himself, because he's buried in a yet-to-be-unearthed grave near Bethlehem.

Amble through the Bloomfield Garden to the picturesque **Montefiore Windmill** (10), built in 1867 by Sir Moses Montefiore in a vain attempt to start a new industry. It failed, not for economic reasons, but simply for lack of wind! Today, it's the centerpiece of a delightful residential area and houses a small museum dedicated to his life. The door is open on Sundays through Thursdays from 9 a.m. to 4 p.m., and on Fridays from 9 a.m. to 2 p.m.

Just north of the windmill is the **Yemin Moshe** (11) development of terraced stone cottages dating from 1892. Long considered to be among the best neighborhoods in Jerusalem, it deteriorated rapidly after the

The Montefiore Windmill on the edge of Jerusalem
(Photo courtesy Israel Ministry of Tourism)

Jordanian occupation of the Old City, when this hill was in direct line of sniper fire. After the Six Day War of 1967, its poor inhabitants were evicted and the houses restored, becoming the rather posh "artists'" quarter that it is today. Ironically, few real artists can afford to live here anymore. Follow the route on the map, returning to Montefiore's original **Mishkenot Sha'ananim** of 1860. The first residential area to be built outside the walls, it is located just below his windmill. The now-restored apartments are used to accommodate well-known guests from abroad; mostly artists, musicians, writers, and scholars.

Heading north on Nahon St. takes you past the Mitchell Garden to the **Arts and Crafts Lane** (*Hutzot Hayotzer*) (12). Overlooking the walls of the Old City, these restored stables now house artisans' studios and workshops, where you can admire—and purchase—some of Israel's finest crafts. From here, it's a short walk to the **Jaffa Gate** (see page 35), where you can get a bus or taxi back to your hotel.

The Western New City

One of Israel's greatest treasures—the Dead Sea Scrolls—highlights this walking tour, which visits the world-renowned Israel Museum, the Knesset (Parliament), an exhibition of artifacts that promotes better understanding of the Bible, and a fortress-like monastery that predates the Crusades. Should you have any strength left, you can finish the day off at a huge scale model of Jerusalem as it was around the time of Jesus.

This hilly part of the New City, just west of the central business district, developed only after the 1948 War of Independence. Still sparsely settled, it is occupied mostly by government buildings, cultural institutions, and a university. What brings tourists here is the highly-acclaimed Israel Museum, easily ranking among the finest institutions of its kind on Earth and a "must-see" for all visitors to Jerusalem. The other sights help round off the trip, making for a highly worthwhile day's excursion.

GETTING THERE:

Buses on routes 9 and 24 connect the central part of Jerusalem with both the Knesset and the Israel Museum. Bus number 17 goes directly to the museum, but not to the Knesset. Ask at your hotel for the most appropriate route. During the tourist season the **Jerusalem Circular Line,** route 99, connects all of the sites on this trip.

Taxis are the most convenient way to reach the start of the walking tour, and are not expensive if several people travel together.

See page 31 for more details on transportation within Jerusalem.

PRACTICALITIES:

Avoid making this tour on a Tuesday, when the **Israel Museum** does not open until late afternoon. Also note that the museum closes at 2 p.m. on Fridays, Saturdays, holiday eves, and holidays. Tickets for Saturday or holiday admissions must be purchased in advance.

Those planning to visit the **Knesset** should check the current opening times and ticket availability by phoning (02) 55-41-11. Be sure to bring your passport.

The **Government Tourist Information Office**, phone (02) 75-49-12, is at 24 King George V St. in the center of the New City.

FOOD AND DRINK:

There are precious few places to eat along the route of this tour, but it's only a bit over a mile to the many restaurants described in the previous chapter (page 61). These are easily reached by bus. Otherwise, you might try:

> **Museum Cafeteria** (in the Israel Museum, midway up the central mall) A pleasant self-service cafeteria serving kosher dairy food. $

> **Museum Café** (in the Israel Museum, just inside the main art galleries) Refreshments and snacks in civilized comfort. Bar service. $

SUGGESTED TOUR:

Those planning to tour the Knesset, or watch a debate there, should check the current visiting schedule by phoning (02) 55-41-11. If convenient, begin your walk there; otherwise start at the Israel Museum (2) and come back later or else pass on this attraction.

Israel's massive ***Knesset Building** (Parliament) (1), on a hill overlooking most of the city, was completed in 1966. At that time Jerusalem was still a divided city, with the Jordanian border barely a mile to the east. Originally, the Knesset met in a converted theater in Tel Aviv, but in late 1949 moved to the building in Jerusalem that now houses the tourist office, where it remained until this structure was finished. Interestingly, most major nations, including the United States, still do not recognize Jerusalem as the nation's capital, maintaining their embassies in Tel Aviv instead.

Near the entrance to the Knesset stands an enormous 16-foot-high bronze **Menorah**, the seven-branched candlestick that symbolizes the State of Israel. A 1956 gift from the people of Great Britain, its 29 reliefs depict events and figures from Jewish history.

The Knesset Building itself was financed by the British branch of the Rothschild dynasty, and is decorated with tapestries and mosaics by Marc Chagall. Much of it is underground as a precaution against attack from the air.

Depending on the current schedules, you can either take a free guided tour that includes a discussion of Israeli democracy, or you can watch one of the often-acrimonious debates in Hebrew (or sometimes Arabic). Either way, you'll be subjected to a rigid security check. Bring

Outside the Shrine of the Book

your passport. At the time of writing, the tours are held on Sundays and Thursdays from 8:30 a.m. to 2:30 p.m.; and the visitors' gallery is open (when the Knesset is in session) on Mondays and Tuesdays from 4–7 p.m., and on Wednesdays from 11 a.m. to 7 p.m.

A visit to the *Israel Museum (2), just south of the Knesset, can easily take several hours—so be sure to allow enough time. It occupies several buildings, gardens, and underground galleries arranged around a central mall, covering an area of about 22 acres. Refer to the diagram on page 70 for the location of specific sections, and choose those that interest you. There's really something here for everyone!

Just beyond the entrance pavilion (2) is the museum's greatest single attraction, the *Shrine of the Book (3). This stunning, mostly underground, cave-like structure shelters large segments of one of mankind's most significant discoveries, the fascinating and still-controversial *Dead Sea Scrolls. Aboveground, a long black wall faces a white dome shaped like the lid to one of the clay pots in which the scrolls were hidden for two millenia in the caves at Qumran, high above the Dead Sea. It is this contradiction between black and white that symbolizes the central theme of the scrolls themselves, the eternal struggle between good and evil.

Descend the dark, tunnel-like passageway into a dimly lit subterranean chamber. Inside, you can examine fragments of these 2,000-year-

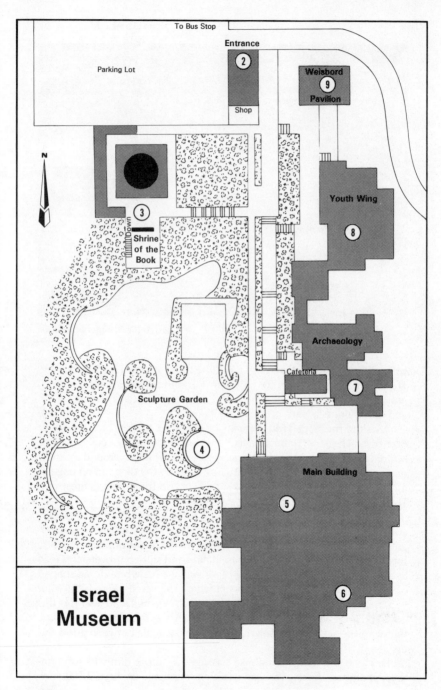

To Bus Stop

Entrance

②

Parking Lot

Weisbord

⑨

Pavilion

Shop

N

③

Shrine
of the
Book

Youth Wing

⑧

Archaeology

Cafeteria

⑦

Sculpture Garden

④

Main Building

⑤

Israel
Museum

⑥

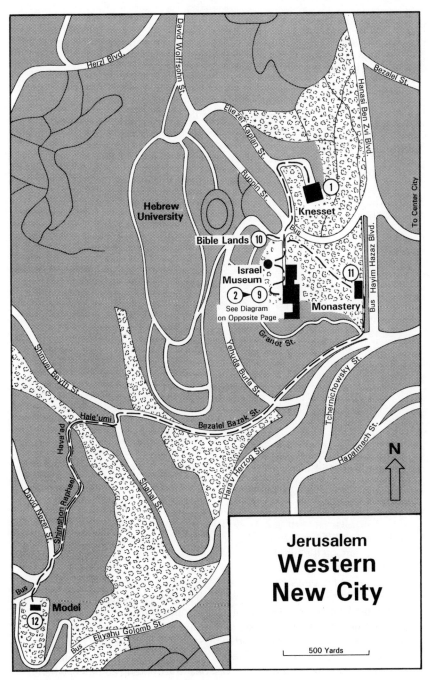

old documents, each lit by timed lights that can only be turned on for a few moments. Among the Biblical manuscripts are all 66 chapters of the Book of Isaiah, inscribed on parchment sometime around the 1st century (B.C. or A.D.) and differing only slightly from later versions. This, and other fragments, confirm the antiquity of the Old Testament and demonstrates how remarkably little it has changed through the ages. Other manuscripts are non-Biblical and refer mostly to forgotten teachings of the breakaway Jewish sect called the Essenes, who lived in a remote monastery at Qumran from the 2nd century B.C. until they were dispersed by the Romans in A.D. 68. It was then that they apparently hid their sacred scrolls in those inaccessible caves.

The first of the Dead Sea Scrolls were discovered quite accidentally in 1947 by a Bedouin shepherd boy looking for his stray goat on a hillside above Qumran. What he found in a cave there was a cache of clay pots filled with bits of old leather. He sold some of these to a shoemaker in Bethlehem, who fortunately passed them on to someone who recognized their true antiquity. A lot of international intrigue followed, with many of the scrolls surfacing in New York, where they were secretly purchased by the famous Israeli general and archaeologist Yigael Yadin and returned to the newly-established State of Israel. Other fragments wound up in the Amman Museum in Jordan. To this day, scholars are still trying to make sense out of these oldest surviving Biblical writings known to man, while here in the Israel Museum you can enjoy seeing some of the best of the fragments with your own eyes.

Continue up the mall to the **Billy Rose Sculpture Garden** (4), named for the New York impresario who donated most of the works. Spread out over lovely gardens designed by the American-born sculptor Isamu Noguchi are some 50 modern pieces by such luminaries as Pablo Picasso, Henry Moore, Auguste Rodin, Jacques Lipchitz, and Jean Tinguely; along with contemporary Israeli sculptors. The sweeping **views** across Jerusalem from here are, as always, spectacular. Enjoy.

Just ahead stands the **Main Building** of the museum, which houses the **Bezalel Art Wing** (5) along with sections devoted to contemporary Israeli art, Jewish ethnography, Judaica, and numismatics. The main art galleries exhibit works from all over the world, from ancient times to the present. Among the highlights are glazed Tang Dynasty pottery from 7th-century China; figures from pre-Columbian Mexico; Impressionist paintings by Renoir, Van Gogh, and Gauguin; Dutch and Flemish Old Masters; 20th-century works by Utrillo, Matisse, Chagall, and Kokoschka; Islamic art; design; and much, much more. The section on **Jewish Communities** (6) displays entire room settings and costumes from Jewish enclaves around the world, while the galleries of **Judaica** have two complete synagogues, ritual objects, and Torah scrolls. If all of this has exhausted you, there's a welcome café near the building entrance, where you can relax before tackling the next sections.

From the lower level of the entrance hall in the Main Building you can stroll directly into the **Bronfman Archaeological Wing** (7), which displays artifacts discovered since 1948. Earlier findings are exhibited in the Rockefeller Museum (see page 56). The collections here are the most comprehensive in Israel, are arranged in chronological sequence, and are refreshingly treated as art objects rather than just as scientific discoveries.

Start in the **Prehistory Hall**, where simple finds from the Old Stone Age blend into the earliest expressions of artistic feelings beginning around the 9th millenium B.C. The next two halls, covering the Canaanite period, have some remarkably beautiful **copper objects** from the 4th millenium, along with fascinating **anthropoid sarcophagi** dating from about 1300 B.C. The **Israelite Halls,** after this, trace the development of the Judean and Israelite monarchies until the 1st century. Among the treasures of the **Roman Gallery** is a magnificent **bronze bust** of the emperor Hadrian from the 2nd century A.D. The Byzantine period is represented by mosaics and architectural elements from both Christian and Jewish sites. Finally, the **Hall of the Neighboring Cultures** presents ancient artifacts from Egypt, Syria, Iraq, Jordan, Iran, Turkey, and Greece.

The lively **Youth Wing** (8) is supposed to be for children, but you'll probably enjoy the ever-changing exhibits and creative activities just as much as the kids. Give it a try! Just opposite the museum entrance is the **Weisbord Pavilion** (9), which features temporary exhibitions that are usually worth seeing.

The Israel Museum, phone (02) 70-88-11, is open on Sundays, Mondays, Wednesdays, and Thursdays from 10 a.m. to 5 p.m.; on Tuesdays from 4–10 p.m. only; and on Fridays, Saturdays, holiday eves, and holidays from 10 a.m. to 2 p.m. Tickets for Saturdays and holidays must be purchased in advance.

Ready for more ancient artifacts from the Holy Land? It's only a short amble from the Israel Museum over to the new **Bible Lands Museum** (10), where over 2,000 objects from Biblical times are arranged in a sequence designed to enhance your understanding of the Bible. The collections are the lifetime work of Dr. Eli Borowski, a survivor of the Holocaust who believes that a return to Biblical values may help prevent future tragedies like that. The opening times for this museum were not yet fixed at the time of writing, so ask locally about them.

Just east of the Israel Museum, down in the valley by a busy highway, stands the 11th-century **Monastery of the Holy Cross** (11). According to tradition, this is the spot where the tree from which the cross that Jesus was crucified on grew. It may be noisy outside, but once within these monastic walls there is a pervasive calm that takes you back to a simpler age. Being located well outside the Old City walls, the monastery was built like a fortress over the ruins of a 5th-century Byzantine church.

Founded by King Bagrat of Georgia around A.D. 1050, the present structure was used by Georgian priests until their numbers became too small, after which it was sold to the Greek Orthodox Church in 1685. An ornate clock tower was added in the 19th century, and the complex remained in use as a seminary until World War I. Don't miss the 17th-century **frescoes** depicting the life of the tree from which the cross was fashioned, which also features a strange combination of Christian saints, Greek philosophers, and pagan gods. The **mosaic floor** to the right of the altar is all that remains of the 5th-century church that was destroyed by the Persians in A.D. 614. You can also see a small museum with an eclectic assortment of sometimes bizarre objects, the communal kitchen, priests' cells, and other monastic chambers. Visits may be made on Mondays through Saturdays from 9 a.m. to 5 p.m., closing at 1:30 p.m. on Fridays. Phone (02) 61-71-21 for further information.

While in the area, you might want to finish off the day at the famous **Model of Ancient Jerusalem** (12) on the grounds of the Holyland Hotel. Be warned, however, that getting there is not half the fun. On foot, it's a bit over two miles following the route on the map. Alternatively, you could take bus number 19 along Harav Herzog St. and walk up the hill, or you could return to the Israel Museum and from there take a taxi the entire distance.

For those who do go, the model is an enormous reproduction of Jerusalem as it was in A.D. 66, the time of the Second Temple, rendered at the generous scale of 1:50. Its construction was supervised by a noted archaeologist and is as accurate in detail as is humanly possible, using original materials wherever practical. Being outside, on a duplication of the actual hilly site, and correctly oriented with regard to the compass, the imposing layout has a startling reality about it, particularly late in the day when the sun is low. The model is open on Sundays through Thursdays from 8 a.m. to 9 p.m., and on Fridays and Saturdays from 8 a.m. to 5 p.m. For further information, phone the Holyland Hotel at (02) 78-81-18. You can return to central Jerusalem by taking bus number 21 from here.

Ein Kerem, Yad Va'shem, and Mount Herzl

It's still within the city limits, but Ein Kerem is really an ancient country village nestled in the scenic Judean hills west of downtown Jerusalem. Tradition has it that John the Baptist was born here, and that this is where the Virgin Mary came to visit her cousin Elizabeth (Luke 1:5–25, 39–80) when the latter was with child. The site has been occupied continuously since around 2000 B.C., although nothing remains from before the 5th century A.D. Now something of an artists' colony, Ein Kerem is an unusually attractive place noted for its two outstanding Franciscan churches. The modern Hadassah Medical Center, within walking distance, attracts visitors with its renowned stained-glass synagogue windows by Marc Chagall.

On the way back to town is Mount Herzl, site of a small museum devoted to the life of Theodor Herzl, and the deeply disturbing Yad Va'shem Holocaust memorial complex—a shattering experience that no visitor to Israel should miss.

GETTING THERE:

Bus number 17 connects central Jerusalem with Ein Kerem (the end of the line) at frequent intervals. From the Hadassah Hospital you can take bus number 27 to Mount Herzl, then return back to central Jerusalem on any of a dozen bus routes.

By car, Ein Kerem is about 5 miles west of central Jerusalem via Herzl Ave. and Ein Kerem Road. This is the most convenient way to make this trip. Parking should present no problem at any of the sites.

PRACTICALITIES:

Avoid making this trip on a Friday or holiday eve, when many of the attractions close early in the afternoon; or on a Saturday or Jewish holiday when they are closed all day. You will probably be visiting one or two synagogues along the way, so males will need a head covering, which can be borrowed at the entrances. In any case, **dress modestly** for both the synagogues and the churches.

The **Government Tourist Information Office,** phone (02) 75-49-12, is at 24 King George V St. in the center of the New City.

FOOD AND DRINK:

Of the very few places to eat along this route, these can be recommended:

> **Goulash Inn** (Ein Kerem village) Fine Hungarian cuisine in a delightful country inn. Phone (02) 41-92-14 for reservations. $$ and $$$
>
> **Yad Va'shem Cafeteria** (at the entrance to the Yad Va'shem complex) A typical self-service museum cafeteria. Kosher. $

SUGGESTED TOUR:

Whether you arrive by bus or car, begin your tour in the charming old village of **Ein Kerem**, once an Arab settlement and now a somewhat artsy suburb of Jerusalem. Stroll north along a narrow alleyway to the **Church of St. John the Baptist** (1), erected over the supposed grotto where St. John was born. The first church on this site was built as early as the 5th century, got restored by the Crusaders in the 12th century, and was later taken over by Moslems. Returned to Christian hands, it was rebuilt by the Franciscans in 1674.

A grotto near the entrance has some fine 5th-century **mosaics** and an inscription in Greek that reads "Hail martyrs of God." Inside the church are steps leading down to a **crypt** with the Latin inscription *Hic precursor Domini natus est,* literally "The Lord's forerunner was born here." Don't miss the **reliefs** depicting events in the life of St. John the Baptist, including the chopping off of his head. The church is open daily from 8 a.m. to noon and 2:30–5 p.m.

Head south through the village and down Hama'ayan St. to **Mary's Well** (2), known as the Spring of the Virgin since Crusader times. The adjacent mosque was abandoned in 1948 when the Arabs fled.

Continue on and go up the steps to the left, climbing to the **Church of the Visitation** (3). According to tradition, this stands on the site of the cottage where the Virgin Mary visited her cousin Elizabeth (or aunt Elizabeth, depending on which translation of the Bible you read), an elderly lady who was soon to give birth to John the Baptist after being barren all her life. The two-level church, partly from the 19th century, sits on the ruins of a 12th-century Crusader basilica whose still-extant apse has pilgrims' crosses scratched into its walls. A few remains from the earlier Byzantine era include the stone behind which the infant St. John is supposed to have hid when the Romans came looking for children to slaughter (Matthew 2:16). Mary's visit is depicted in the mosaic on the

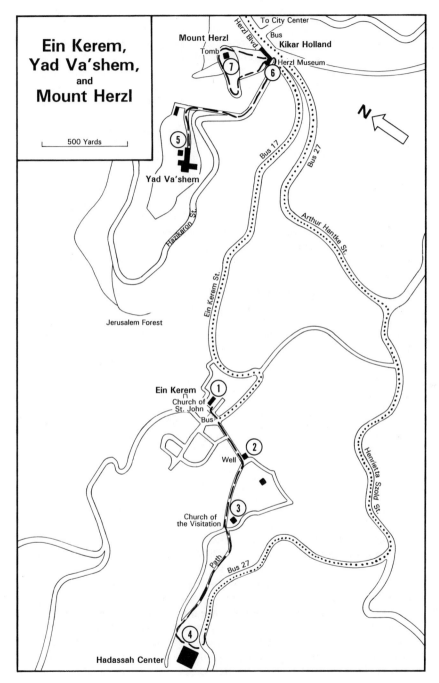

**Ein Kerem,
Yad Va'shem,
and
Mount Herzl**

500 Yards

To City Center

Mount Herzl
Bus
Kikar Holland

Tomb
Herzl Museum

7

6

Herzl Blvd

5

Yad Va'shem

Bus 17

Bus 27

Hazikaron St.

Arthur Hantke St.

Ein Kerem St.

Jerusalem Forest

Ein Kerem
1
Church of
St. John
Bus

Well
2

Henrietta Szold St.

Church of
the Visitation
3

Path

Bus 27

4

Hadassah Center

N

façade of the modern upper church, erected in 1955. The church is open daily from about 8 a.m. to noon and 2:30–5 p.m.

At this point you have three options: you can continue on foot along the road, which soon becomes a difficult-to-follow trail; you can return to the village and take bus number 17 back to Kikar Holland (opposite the Herzl Museum) and there change to bus number 27 to the Hadassah Medical Center; or you can skip that attraction entirely and take bus 17 from the village directly to Kikar Holland and walk over to Yad Va'shem. *If you have a car, of course, you can just follow the map.*

Adventurous souls will probably choose to walk. The road seems to run out after a while, but actually becomes a narrow path following a stone fence to the left. This goes through what appears to be the town dump, then rises directly to the huge hospital complex.

However you get there, the **Hadassah Medical Center** (4) is an impressive sight. Opened in 1962 to replace its namesake on Mount Scopus, which was cut off by the Arabs, it is the largest medical complex in the Middle East. What attracts thousands of tourists is not its therapy but the 12 fabulous ***stained-glass windows** in its synagogue. These are the work of the world-renowned painter Marc Chagall, surely one of the most original figures in 20th-century art. In their brilliant colors, the windows depict the 12 tribes of Israel as described in Genesis 49 and Deuteronomy 33. Four of the windows were destroyed in the fierce Six Day War of 1967 and later replaced by Chagall; another three still bear scars in the form of bullet holes. The synagogue is open to visitors on Sundays through Thursdays from 8 a.m. to 1:30 p.m. and 2–3:30 p.m., and on Fridays from 8 a.m. to 12:45 p.m. Tours in English are conducted a few times in the mornings; phone (02) 44-62-71 for current schedules.

From the front of the hospital you can take bus number 27 to **Kikar Holland**, opposite Mount Herzl and the Herzl Museum (6). Before visiting there, however, follow the map a short distance west to one of the most unforgettable sights in the Middle East. If you haven't had lunch yet, you might want to stop at the cafeteria by the site entrance and eat now because what you're about to witness will surely kill any appetite.

*Yad Va'shem (5) is the most eloquent and moving of all the Holocaust memorials in Israel and elsewhere; and also perhaps the most terrifying. Spread across a peaceful, forested hilltop, it is devoted entirely to the horrors of the Nazi era and to the lessons—and even hope—that can be gleaned from it. A pilgrimage to this place is never pleasant, but is essential for understanding the reality of modern Israel.

Begin your visit at the ***Children's Memorial**, a black cave-like chamber through which you grope your way by feel along a path of darkness. Hundreds of mirrors reflect a single flickering candle, creating the illusion of infinite points of light all around you, each representing the soul of a child killed in the Holocaust. A quiet voice in the background intones a

*The Chagall Windows at the Hadassah Hospital
(Photo courtesy Israel Ministry of Tourism)*

litany of the young victims' names, their ages, and their places of birth.

The **Avenue of the Righteous** honors the Gentiles who risked their lives to save Jews. Follow it to the **Historical Museum**, which documents through artifacts and graphic material the rise of Hitler in 1933, and the subsequent events culminating in the unspeakable Final Solution. A child's empty shoe, whose owner perished, sums up the poignancy of the experience as you exit the building.

In the ***Hall of Remembrance** burns an eternal flame guarding a vault filled with ashes from the ovens. The floor, made of six million stone chips, is shaped into the names of the 22 largest death camps. The only sound is that of birds flying in and out of the open space beneath the roof. Works of art by both victims and survivors of the camps are displayed in the **Art Museum**, while the **Hall of Names** contains biographical material on those who perished.

As you stroll back into the sunlight and around the grounds, you will encounter numerous **sculptures** depicting aspects of the tragedy, and can gaze down into the **Valley of the Destroyed Communities**, where the names of some 5,000 lost communities in 22 countries are memorialized in stone.

Yad Va'shem is open on Sundays through Thursdays from 9 a.m. to 4:45 p.m., and on Fridays from 9 a.m. to 1:45 p.m. Entrance is free, and the phone number is (02) 75-16-11.

Follow the path through the woods back to Mount Herzl and the Kikar Holland square. On the corner is the small **Herzl Museum** (6) document-

Valley of the Destroyed Communities at Yad Va'shem
(Photo courtesy Israel Ministry of Tourism)

ing the life of Theodor Herzl, the visionary who first articulated the concept of Zionism and the creation of a Jewish state. Born in Budapest in 1860, he became the Paris correspondent of a Vienna newspaper and later its literary editor. Among his writings were *Der Judenstaat* (1896), which advocated a separate nation for Jews; and the novel *Altneuland* (1903), which popularized the idea. He was the founder and first president of the World Zionist Organization in Basel. The highlight of the museum is a reconstruction of his **Vienna study** with its original furnishings. Visits to the museum, phone (02) 51-11-08, may be made on Sundays through Thursdays from 9 a.m. to 5 p.m., and on Fridays from 9 a.m. to 1 p.m. Entry is free.

Before leaving the site, take a short walk around **Mount Herzl** (7) to his tomb, from which you can look out over so much of the land that he helped to found. On a clear day, the **view** extends from the Mediterranean to the Dead Sea. Theodor Herzl died near Vienna in 1904; his body was moved here in 1949.

From the far side of Kikar Holland square you can board a bus to just about anywhere in Jerusalem.

Bethlehem

(Bet Lehem, Beit Lahm, Beit Lahem)

Bethlehem—the birthplace of Jesus Christ—is almost an obligatory stop for Christian visitors to the Holy Land. For Jews, too, it is a sacred place, as it is for Moslems. Quietly nestled in the Judean hills a few miles south of Jerusalem, Bethlehem was first mentioned in the 14th century B.C. It entered Biblical history when Rachel, the wife of Jacob, died there while giving birth to Benjamin. Ruth and Boaz had their idyllic romance at this lovely spot during the time of the Judges, and their descendant David was born in Bethlehem and later called away around 1000 B.C. to become king of the Israelites and build Jerusalem.

About a thousand years later, a descendant of King David was also born in Bethlehem. His name was Jesus, and his life profoundly changed the history of mankind. Within two centuries of his birth, the town had become a place of pilgrimage. The Roman emperor Constantine had a basilica erected on the supposed spot of the Nativity in A.D. 325, to which St. Jerome came in A.D. 386 to prepare his Latin version of the Bible, the "Vulgate" that remained in use by Roman Catholics into the 20th century. Destroyed in A.D. 529 by the Samaritans, the church was quickly replaced by Emperor Justinian with the present Church of the Nativity, the oldest Christian church in the world to remain in continuous use.

Visits to Bethlehem are somewhat complicated by the fact that, although only six miles south of Jerusalem, the little town is not in Israel proper but across the "Green Line" in the Occupied Territory of the West Bank. While a trip here should be perfectly safe, it must be remembered that this is in captured Palestinian territory and remains under Israeli military law. As far as the local population is concerned, Bethlehem is in Palestine, not Israel. If this makes you nervous, consider taking a guided bus tour instead of traveling on your own. The folks at your hotel will be only too happy to make arrangements for you, as they get a nice commission on the sale. Also bear in mind that today's Bethlehem is not a particularly attractive place, and that it takes a bit of faith to see beyond the surface and reap any spiritual reward.

GETTING THERE:

Arab bus number 22 provides frequent service between Jerusalem and the bus station in Bethlehem, a ride of roughly a half-hour. Board the bus at the Arab Bus Station on Suleiman St. in East Jerusalem, or at the bus stop across the street from the Jaffa Gate, just west of the Old City.

Guided bus tours operated by Egged Tours and United Tours provide the least problematic—and least adventurous—way to visit Bethlehem. You will get a detailed visit to the Church of the Nativity, and probably make a stop at Rachel's Tomb, but most likely will see nothing else. Ask at your hotel, any Egged Tours office, or at the Government Tourist Information Office in Jerusalem about current schedules, prices, and reservations.

Sherut taxis depart from across the street opposite the Damascus and Jaffa gates in Jerusalem for the roughly 20-minute ride to Bethlehem. The fare on these shared-ride vehicles should be slightly higher than the bus, but confirm this with the driver first.

Driving to Bethlehem is not considered wise at the present time, as your yellow Israeli license plates may attract flying rocks like a magnet in this hostile territory. If you insist on driving, first check with the tourist office or your consulate in Jerusalem about the current political climate. Bethlehem lies 6 miles south of Jerusalem via Hebron Road (*Derech Hevron*, Route 60).

PRACTICALITIES:

All of the sites except the Tomb of Rachel are open daily; that one exception is closed on Saturdays and Jewish holidays. Advance tickets are needed for Christmas celebrations at the Church of the Nativity, held on December 24–25 (Catholic and Protestant), January 6 (Greek Orthodox), and January 17–18 (Armenian Orthodox). **Modest dress**, meaning no shorts or bare shoulders, is required at all of the main sites. *Yarmulkas* (head coverings) may be borrowed at the Tomb of Rachel.

Remember that Bethlehem is in occupied Arab territory, not Israel proper. Expect tensions. For your own safety, be sure to **look like a tourist**, lest you be mistaken for an Israeli or Arab. **Tourists are welcome**, potential Israeli settlers are not. Above all, avoid speaking Hebrew or Arabic. In the highly unlikely event that you should actually encounter an incident, leave the scene immediately, but as discreetly and quietly as possible. Do not run or take photos of it.

Bethlehem can be quite cold, even snowy, in winter. Dress accordingly.

The local **Government Tourist Information Office**, phone (02) 74-15-81, is on Manger Square. Bethlehem has a **population** of roughly 20,000; about half of these are Christian Arabs, the other half Moslems.

FOOD AND DRINK:

Bethlehem has several restaurants that cater to tourists, mostly grouped around Manger Square. There are also a few *felafel* stands in the same area, where you can fill up quickly and cheaply.

St. George's Restaurant (Manger Sq., next to the tourist office) Middle Eastern cuisine, served indoors and out. Open daily. $$

El Andalus (Manger Sq.) Both fixed-price meals and à-la-carte specialties are served here, Middle Eastern and Western style. Open daily. $ and $$

Palace Hotel (Manger Sq.) A coffee shop with self-serve buffet, Middle Eastern and Western dishes. Open daily. $

SUGGESTED TOUR:

It's only a short walk from the **Bethlehem Bus Station** (1) to **Manger Square**, the center of nearly everything in town, including the tourist information office. Always buzzing with the comings and goings of pilgrims, the square practically explodes with excitement during the three annual Christmas celebrations for the three major branches of Christianity: Roman Catholic/Protestant, Greek Orthodox, and Armenian Orthodox.

Facing the east side of the square is the fortress-like ***Church of the Nativity** (2), one of the holiest places in Christendom. The exact site of Jesus' birth was located around A.D. 325 by the Roman empress Helena, mother of Constantine the Great, and a basilica quickly built over it. Actually, this spot had already been venerated by pilgrims for well over a century. Destroyed in the Samaritan revolt of A.D. 529, the small 4th-century basilica was replaced by Emperor Justinian in A.D. 531 with the present church which, although modified several times, remains largely intact today. A mosaic of the Three Kings on its façade spared it from demolition by the conquering Persians in 614. During the 12th century the building was renovated by the Crusaders but later fell into decrepitude under Moslem rule. A thorough restoration was begun in 1670 by the Greek Orthodox Church, which shares the property with the Roman Catholic and Armenian churches in an uneasy truce that still occasionally breaks out in fights.

You'll have to bend over to enter through the tiny four-foot-high **Door of Humility**, but before you do, take a careful look at the outer wall it pierces. Justinian's large 6th-century portal is still visible, filled in by a stone wall with a pointed archway that was added by the Crusaders. This in turn got blocked up and the entrance reduced almost to a crawl space sometime during the Mamluk or Turkish eras to keep the Moslems from riding through on horseback.

Stoop low and enter the church. In the nave are sections of the original **mosaic floor** (3) from Constantine's 4th-century basilica, covered

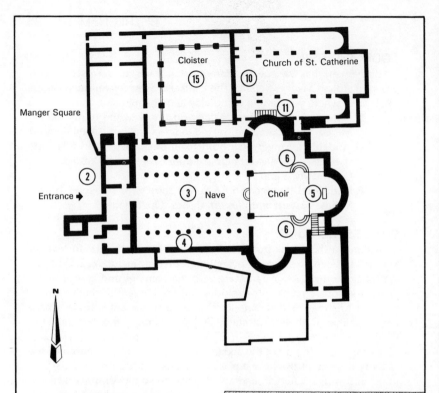

Manger Square

Entrance ➡

Bethlehem

Church of the Nativity

Go down steps to the

Grotto of the Nativity

(right)

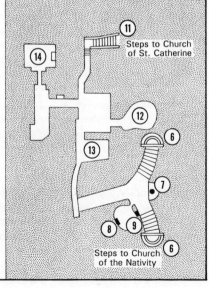

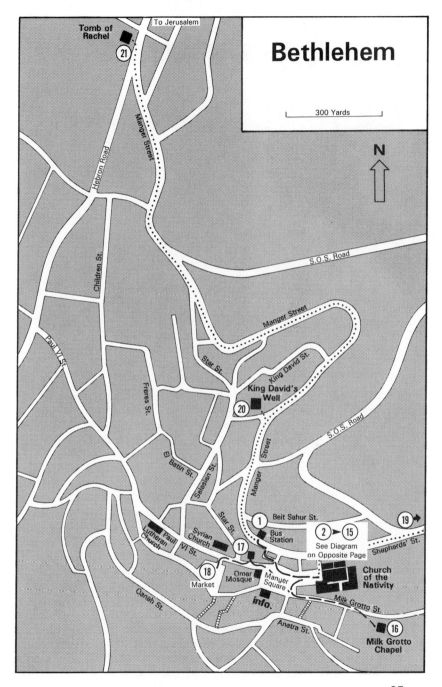

Bethlehem

300 Yards

N

To Jerusalem

Tomb of
Rachel 21

Manger Street

Hebron Road

Children St.

Paul VI St.

S.O.S. Road

Manger Street

Star St.

King David St.

King David's
Well 20

Frères St.

El Batin St.

Salesian St.

Manger Street

S.O.S. Road

Star St.

Beit Sahur St.

1

Bus
Station

2 → 15
See Diagram
on Opposite Page

19 →

Shepherds' St.

Lutheran
Church

Paul
VI St.

Syrian
Church

17

Omar
Mosque

Manger
Square

Church
of the
Nativity

18

Market

info.

Milk Grotto St.

Qanah St.

Anatra St.

Milk Grotto
Chapel 16

The Altar of the Manger in the Grotto of the Nativity

by 12th-century marble and made visible through large trapdoors. The red limestone **columns** topped with marble Corinthian capitals were once thought to be from the 4th century, but are now considered part of Justinian's reconstruction. Some are decorated with **frescoes** of saints, and there is a curious rendering of a swan helmet belonging to Baldwin I, the 12th-century Crusader king of Jerusalem, who was considered to be a descendant of Lohengrin, the Knight of the Swan. Above the columns are the remains of **12th-century mosaics** depicting the ancestors of Jesus as enumerated in Luke 3:23–38, and of the early ecumenical councils. Near the center of the south aisle is a **baptismal font** (4) from the time of Justinian. The raised **choir**, directly above the Grotto of the Nativity, leads to the heavily-decorated Greek Orthodox **High Altar** (5).

You are now ready to visit what is thought to be the actual birthplace of Jesus. Steps along the north and south sides of the choir lead down to the ***Grotto of the Nativity** (6), an ancient cave beneath the church. Forget your typical Christmas-card manger scene—in those days domestic animals were sheltered in hillside caves against which the peasants' houses were built. The "inn" in which there was "no room" was most likely the home of Joseph's parents, and the birth probably took place in a cave adjoining it. The translation of the original Biblical text is tricky and can be taken several different ways, of which this is seemingly the most logical scenario. It can be further argued that Mary and Joseph were natives of Bethlehem, not Nazareth, and that they might have moved to the Galilee area for reasons of security. The "census" described in Luke 2:1–7 took place in A.D. 6, a few years *after* the birth, so Luke may have been mistaken about other details as well. In any case, most scholars believe that this cave is *the* place.

At the bottom, midway between the two sets of stairs, an **altar** (7) stands in a niche beneath a depiction of the Nativity. Under it is a silver star bearing the Latin inscription *Hic de Virgine Maria Jesus Christus natus est*, meaning "Here Jesus Christ was born of the Virgin Mary." The many-pointed star was installed by the Catholics in 1717, but removed by the Greeks in 1847. Shortly afterwards, the ruling Turkish authorities ordered the Greeks to put the star back, an offensive action that helped precipitate the Crimean War of 1853.

On another side of the cave is the Roman Catholic **Altar of the Manger** (8), on the spot where Empress Helena supposedly discovered the original clay manger. A manger is, of course, a trough or box from which livestock feed, and in this instance was used as a crib. Opposite this is the **Altar of the Three Kings** (9), marking the place where the Magi worshipped the Christ Child. The complex of grottoes continues on from here, but is normally only accessible from the next site. Leave the cave the way you came in. The Church of the Nativity is open daily from 6 a.m. to 6 p.m. (8 a.m. to 5 p.m. in winter).

The adjoining **Church of St. Catherine** (10), reached through a door in the north transept, is a refreshing change after the gloomy atmosphere of the Orthodox church. Built by the Roman Catholic Franciscans in 1881 on the site of an earlier church, it possesses some marvelous wood carvings of the Stations of the Cross. **Steps** (11) along the south aisle lead down to the same complex of grottoes that you just left, only this section is under Catholic control.

Here the chambers appear more as they did in Biblical times. The **Chapel of the Innocents** (12) commemorates the massacre of Bethlehem's children by Herod, while the **Chapel of St. Joseph** (13) marks the traditional spot where Joseph had his dream that sent the Holy Family fleeing to Egypt. The **Chapel of St. Jerome** (14) is supposed to be the tiny chamber in which Jerome translated the Biblical texts into the Latin Vulgate during the 4th century A.D. Go back up the steps and stroll through the quiet **medieval cloister** (15), exiting into Manger Square. The Church of St. Catherine is open daily from 6 a.m. to noon and 2–6 p.m.

Milk Grotto St. leads east to the nearby **Chapel of the Milk Grotto** (16), where the Holy Family is said to have hid on their way to Egypt. Tradition has it that a drop of Mary's milk fell to the ground here, changing the walls of the cave into a chalky white stone, now darkened

*Christmas procession in Manger Square
(Photo courtesy Israel Ministry of Tourism)*

with age. Women come to pray for better lactation, assisted perhaps by the powdered stone sold on the spot. The chapel, run by the Franciscans, is open daily from 8–11:30 a.m. and 2–5 p.m. Ring the bell for entrance. Return to Manger Square and stroll west on Paul VI St. to the small **Bethlehem Museum** (17). Traditional Palestinian crafts, costumes, and home interiors may be seen here every day from 8:30 a.m. to noon and 2–5 p.m. Continue into the **Market Place** (*Souk*) (18), where the locals do their shopping. Prices in this colorful bazaar are much lower than in the tourist shops, although most of the merchandise is of little interest to visitors.

From Manger Square it is possible to make a **side trip** to the outlying **Shepherds' Field** (19), where according to Christian tradition the shepherds tending their flock by night were told of Jesus' birth by an angel (Luke 2:9–11). This is also the Field of Ruth, associated with the Old Testament *Book of Ruth*. It lies just east of the Arab village of **Beit Sahur**, which can be reached by bus number 47 from Manger Square, or by taxi. The actual field is a 20-minute walk from the village to a fork in the road; a total distance of about two miles east of Bethlehem. The left fork leads to an interesting Roman Catholic church (open daily from 8–11 a.m. and 2–5 p.m.) and the remains of a Byzantine monastery, while the road to the right goes to the Greek Orthodox field and church (theoretically open about the same times).

Heading back toward Jerusalem from Manger Square, you might want to stop at **King David's Well** (20), which is of historical interest although physically it doesn't amount to much. The story of David's longing for, and then declining to drink, the water of this cistern is told in 2 Samuel 23:13–17. You'll find the well in the parking lot of the King David Cinema.

Of greater interest is the **Tomb of Rachel** (21) at the far northern end of Bethlehem. Sacred to Jews, Christians, and Moslems alike, this is the burial place of the matriarch Rachel, wife of Jacob, who died in Bethlehem while giving birth to Benjamin (Genesis 35:19–20). The simple structure, built by Sir Moses Montefiore in 1841 over earlier remains, is a synagogue visited primarily by women praying for fertility. It is open to visitors on Sundays through Thursdays from 8 a.m. to 6 p.m., and on Fridays from 8 a.m. to 1 p.m. *Yarmulkas* may be borrowed at the entrance.

You can get a ride back to Jerusalem by boarding almost any northbound bus at the bus stop near the intersection.

Ein Gedi
(En Gedi)

During the twilight of the prehistoric era, some five thousand years ago, tribes just emerging from the Stone Age worshipped the moon at a crude temple above the waterfalls of Ein Gedi. This unexpectedly lush oasis in the middle of a hot, arid region next to the lowest spot on Earth must have seemed a garden paradise to its early settlers, as it is for the Israelis of today.

The site belonged to the tribe of Judah during the 13th century B.C. (Joshua 15:62) and was the refuge for David as he fled the wrath of Saul (1 Samuel 24:1) a few centuries later. King Solomon sang "My beloved is unto me as a cluster of camphire (henna blossoms) in the vineyards of En-Gedi" in his *Song of Songs* of the 10th century B.C. (Song of Solomon 1:14). Wiped out by the Babylonians around 582 B.C., by Herod in the 1st century B.C., and by the Romans in A.D. 68, Ein Gedi flourished in Byzantine times before being abandoned sometime after the 5th century.

The oasis remained unoccupied for well over a millenium until 1949, when an Israeli military camp was established on the spot. At the time, this was only two miles south of the Jordanian border. A *kibbutz* followed, and it's still going strong today. The sub-tropical paradise of Ein Gedi is now a protected nature preserve, so you can't pick the flowers or hunt animals, but you can certainly enjoy seeing the wild ibex and hyrax, and just possibly even a leopard. Bird watchers will spot interesting species flying about, naturalists will revel in the luxurious vegetation, and amateur archaeologists can explore some of the oldest remains in Israel.

Used since Old Testament days, the name Ein Gedi means "Spring of the Kid," but you don't have to be a young goat to climb its trails. This is a very popular outing, and attracts numerous visitors, especially on weekends and holidays. It is also an ideal destination in winter, when the temperature is perfectly comfortable.

GETTING THERE:

Buses leave Jerusalem's Central Bus Station just about hourly for the approximately 80-minute ride to Ein Gedi. You can take bus numbers 421, 486, 487, or 966. If there's space, you might be able to get a seat on the faster bus number 444, the express to Eilat. All buses leave from platform 1. Be sure to get off at the **Nahal David** stop, not at the stop marked "Ein-Gedi," which refers to the *kibbutz* over a mile to the south. Note the posted times of return buses. There is virtually no service from Friday

By the waterfalls at Ein Gedi
(Photo courtesy Israel Ministry of Tourism)

afternoons until Saturday evenings, nor or Jewish holidays or the afternoon/evening preceding them.

By car, Ein Gedi is about 50 miles southeast of Jerusalem. Take Route 1 east to the Dead Sea, then Route 90 south to the Nahal David turnoff. Most of the drive goes through the Occupied Territories of the West Bank, but it's a major highway avoiding populated areas, so don't worry.

PRACTICALITIES:

The nature reserve at Ein Gedi is open on Saturdays through Thursdays from 8 a.m. to 4 p.m., remaining open longer in summer; and on Fridays and holiday eves from 8 a.m. to 3 p.m. Phone (057) 842-88 or 843-50 for current information. If you go in the hot season you'll need **protection from the heat and sun**, especially a hat. Be sure to carry enough **liquids** such as water or juice along with you on the trek, and don't drink from the streams. Although the distances look short, the going is slow—so get off to an **early start** and allow enough time if you plan to visit all or most of the sites.

FOOD AND DRINK:

There's a **snack bar** ($) at the Nahal David Reserve entrance, and a self-service **restaurant** ($) at the Holiday Village camping site on the Dead Sea just south of the nature reserve. Both are closed for the day by 5 p.m.

SUGGESTED TOUR:

The **Bus stop** (1) for the Nahal David Nature Reserve is next to the salty **Dead Sea** (*Yam HaMelah*), the lowest spot on Earth. This is the southern end of the Jordan River, where whatever water is left just evaporates, leaving behind a briny solution of about 25% salt. It's so dense that bathers simply can't sink in it. There are also extremely high concentrations of sulfur, magnesium, iodine, bromine, and other chemicals. Some of these are allegedly good for your health, hence the numerous spa resorts. Fish cannot live in this liquid, but some tiny micro-organisms have been discovered lately. The size of the sea is steadily shrinking as more and more water is diverted upstream by Israel and Jordan, a situation that may someday be corrected by a canal from the Red Sea or Mediterranean.

Walk away from the sea to the **Nahal David Nature Reserve entrance** (2), where there's a parking lot and snack bar, and where you pay a small fee to use the park. Ask them for a map, then follow the well-marked trail along the **Nahal David** stream to *David's Waterfall** (3), an area rich in hidden shallow pools. From here, another trail leads uphill to the **Shulamit Spring** (4) where water bubbles out of the earth.

Ambitious climbers may want to make a **side trip** up the cliff to the lovely **Dodim Cave** (*Me'arat Dodim*) (5), a beautiful spot well worth the extra 45 minutes it takes to get there and back.

Continue on from the spring to the ruins of a prehistoric *Chalcolithic Temple** (6), used by primitive man around 3000 B.C. It is speculated that the 416 copper cult objects discovered nearby belonged to this temple, and were removed for safety prior to a raid. A round moon stone found in the remains suggests worship of the moon, and possibly of the springs as each of the two entrances faces a water source farther downhill.

A steep descent brings you in about 30 minutes to the *Ein Gedi Spring** (7), the "Spring of the Kid" mentioned several times in the Old Testament. Not far from it are the remains of an Ottoman **watermill** that once ground flour. If time is running short, you can return from the spring to Nahal David via a different path.

Assuming that you have enough time left, you might want to head south to the modest excavations at **Tel Goren** (8), the original Israelite settlement of Ein Gedi. Northeast of it is a ruined *Byzantine Synagogue** (9) from the 4th century A.D., which has an interesting mosaic floor depicting peacocks eating grapes. The site seems to have been abandoned after the rise of Islam in the 7th century.

Follow the map east to the highway, where you can turn right to the **Holiday Village Camping Site** (10). There's a good cafeteria restaurant here that's open until 5 p.m., and a bus stop from which you can get a ride back to Jerusalem.

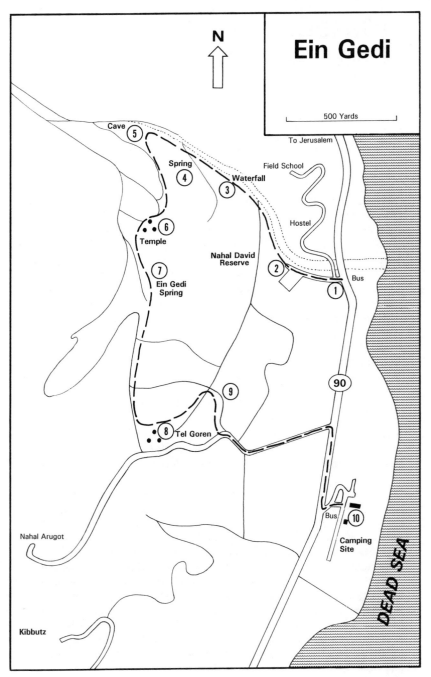

Ein Gedi

N

500 Yards

Cave
(5)

Spring
(4)

Waterfall
(3)

To Jerusalem

Field School

Hostel

(6)
Temple

Nahal David
Reserve

(2)

Bus
(1)

(7)
Ein Gedi
Spring

90

(9)

(8) Tel Goren

Nahal Arugot

Bus
(10)

Camping
Site

Kibbutz

DEAD SEA

*Masada

(Massada, Mezada, Metzadah, Metzuda)

Masada—both the mountain stronghold and the tragic struggle that took place on its summit—is an essential part of the Israeli national experience, a cornerstone of its collective identity. "Masada shall never fall again!" swear young army recruits as they take their oath of allegiance atop this rocky height. That singular catastrophic event, the final defeat of Jewish resistance to Roman rule in the 1st century A.D., has burned itself so deeply into the soul of the Israeli people that you can scarcely understand what makes them tick until you go there yourself.

Towering more than 1,400 feet above the Dead Sea, the small plateau of Masada is cut off from the rest of the world by sheer cliffs and deep gorges. If ever there was a natural citadel, this is it. First fortified by the Judean king Alexander Jannceus early in the 1st century B.C., Masada caught the eye of Herod the Great (74–4 B.C.), who saw it as a personal refuge in the event of an uprising that might threaten his own life. Never one to live in discomfort, he had two luxurious palaces built along with massive fortifications to render the mountain top virtually impregnable. Twice this hideout came in handy for the despised Herod; first in 40 B.C. when his reign was overthrown and he sent his family to Masada while he escaped to Rome, and again in 31 B.C. following the defeat of Antony and Cleopatra at Actium.

The event that forever seared Masada into Jewish consciousness took place nearly a century later. After years of oppressive Roman rule, the Jews of Palestine revolted in A.D. 66, and a group of them called the Zealots captured the lightly-defended Roman outpost of Masada. Isolated from the rest of the land, the mountain fortress played little role in what came to be known as the First Revolt, but it did become a refuge for those fleeing the fighting. After Jerusalem fell to the Roman commander (and later emperor) Titus in A.D. 70, a mopping-up operation began throughout Palestine that finally reached the last Jewish stronghold, Masada, in the year 72. The terrible story that follows is based on the writings of Flavius Josephus, a 1st-century Jewish/Roman historian who, unfortunately, had a tendency to exaggerate, so the tale must be taken with a few grains of salt.

Having decided at last to take Masada, the Romans sent their commander, Flavius Silva, who encircled the mountain with eight fortified camps linked together by a wall. Up to 15,000 Roman soldiers and auxiliaries were massed against the 967 Jewish men, women, and children living in makeshift accommodations atop Masada. One thing that the Zealots had going for them was an abundant supply of food, water, and other necessities; enough, in fact, to hold out for years. Any direct attack straight up the cliffs would have been impossible, so the Romans devised another strategy.

Slowly, using captured Jews as slave labor and as human shields, they built an enormous earthen ramp across a gorge and up the mountain side. Atop this they mounted siege engines that ultimately breached the western wall, bringing inevitable doom to the defenders. At this point, according to Josephus, the Zealot leader Eleazar gave an impassioned speech to his comrades, urging them to choose collective suicide rather than slavery. They then burned their possessions to deny the Romans any loot, leaving only their food stores as proof that they had not been starved into submission. When that was done, each father killed his immediate family and was in turn killed by a group of ten men selected by lot. One, again chosen by lot, executed the remaining nine, and finally himself.

The next morning, as the Romans entered the site, they were greeted by an awful silence. The only living beings they encountered were two women and five children, survivors who hid in a cistern and lived to tell the tragic story. How much of it is true? The sole written record is that of Flavius Josephus, which has several significant errors, including his descriptions of buildings and fortifications. He was nowhere near the scene, yet he recounts Eleazar's lengthy speech word for word. Undoubtedly some of the defenders, realizing that their cause was lost, did commit suicide, but it is equally likely that the rest perished while fighting the Romans. In a way this is more noble, even if less dramatic. In any case, the destruction of Masada put an end to Jewish resistance and established the absolute rule of Rome over Palestine.

The site of Masada was later occupied by Byzantine monks, who built a church and living quarters there in the 4th and 5th centuries. After that it lay deserted and nearly forgotten about until it was rediscovered and correctly identified by two American scholars in 1838. The first ascent of the mountain since Biblical times was made in 1842. Although occasionally explored and mapped, the site was not thoroughly excavated until 1963, when the famed Israeli archaeologist Yigael Yadin began two years of digging, assisted by thousands of largely volunteer workers from all over the globe.

Once so difficult to reach, Masada is now an easy daytrip thanks to its modern cable car and good bus service from Jerusalem. You'll enjoy excellent views of the adjacent Dead Sea both along the way and from the summit. At 1,300 feet below sea level, the sea is the lowest point on Earth. Winters are very mild here, while summers can be uncomfortably hot.

GETTING THERE:

Buses depart Jerusalem's Central Bus Station fairly frequently for the approximately 90-minute ride to Masada. Bus number 444, the express to Eilat, offers the fastest service, but preference is given to passengers going all the way to Eilat. They board first; if seats remain you can get on. Otherwise, take one of the slightly slower number 421, 486, or 966 buses. All leave from platform 1. Buy your ticket first. There is almost no service between late Friday afternoons and Saturday evenings, or on Jewish holidays. A schedule of return buses is posted in the bus stop shelter at Masada.

By car, Masada lies some 60 miles southeast of Jerusalem. Take Route 1 east to the Dead Sea, then Route 90 south to Masada. Most of the drive goes through the Occupied Territories of the West Bank, but it's a major highway avoiding populated areas, and is considered quite safe.

PRACTICALITIES:

Any day is a good day to visit Masada, which is open daily. The cable car operates from 8 a.m. to 4 p.m., closing at 2 p.m. on Fridays and holiday eves. Be sure to check the time of the last ride down, lest you be stranded.

You'll need **protection from the sun**, including a hat, sunblock lotion, and preferably sunglasses. Be sure to bring enough **liquids**, such as water or juice, along with you to avoid dehydration. These are sold at the café near the bus stop. **Water** is available free at the top, but it's warm and you'll need a cup. Only persons in excellent physical condition should attempt climbing on foot, and then only in the early morning before the heat sets in. Everyone else should use the cable car.

For current information, contact the **Government Tourist Information Office**, phone (02) 75-49-12, at 24 King George St. in Jerusalem.

FOOD AND DRINK:

Both a **cafeteria** ($) and a **snack bar** ($) with outdoor tables are located between the bus stop and the lower cable car station, by the parking lot. The food is okay, if somewhat overpriced. There is absolutely nothing available at the summit. For greater comfort, try:

> **Massada Restaurant** (by the parking lot) Adequate "International" cuisine with full service. $$ and $$$

Site of Herod's Northern Palace atop Masada

SUGGESTED TOUR:

Begin at the **Masada Bus Stop** (1) by checking the schedule of return buses posted in the shelter. From here, it's only a short stroll to the **Lower Terminal Complex** (2) and parking lot, where you'll find a restaurant, cafeteria, café, and youth hostel. Just beyond the parking lot is the **Cable Car Station** and the beginning of the serpentine **Snake Path**, the ancient trail to the top that has hardly changed since Biblical times. Take your choice. On foot, it's an arduous one-hour climb of some 1,300 feet. During the warm season you can expect brutal heat from about mid-morning until late afternoon, but in winter it's not uncomfortably hot. The descent on foot is considered to be just as difficult as the ascent, if not worse. For a few shekels more you can ride the **Cable Car**, which deposits you about 50 feet from the top. As a compromise, serious hikers might buy a one-way cable-car ticket and walk the other way.

From the **Upper Terminal** (3), it's a climb of about five stories or so to the site entrance, mostly on steps. At the top, turn right and amble past some partially-restored ruins and the ancient quarry from whence came the stones, to the impressive ***Storehouses** (4). At every site you will find a blue explanatory sign in English. Black horizontal lines on building walls delineate what was found standing by the archaeologists from recent restorations. The authorities have struck an interesting compromise here, rebuilding only a few sites so that untrained spectators would be able to make visual sense of the ruins without losing the atmosphere of an ongoing archaeological dig. Built to supply Herod's stronghold over extended periods of siege, each of the long, rectangular storehouses held a particular type of food, weapons, or other necessities. Some of the containers have been restored and may be seen in one of the structures.

Adjacent to the warehouses stands the partially restored *Bathhouse (5), from whose roof you can get a superb view of the entire Herodian complex. Inside this luxurious Roman structure is a dressing room with traces of its original frescoes and a *mikwe*, or Jewish ritual bath, that was added by the Zealots. The *tepidarium* (warm room) has an interesting tile floor, while the *calidarium* (hot room) reveals the remains of a hypocaust, or heating space beneath the mosaic tiles.

Walk out onto the *Upper Terrace (6) and enjoy the *view that was meant for King Herod the Great. Straight ahead, to the north, you can see Ein Gedi (page 90) and possibly the Plain of Jericho; and to the east the Dead Sea and the hills across the border in Jordan. Surrounding the Masada mountain are the clearly visible outlines of Silva's Roman camps, the connecting wall between them, and to the southwest the ramp that doomed the Zealots. Herod's *Northern Palace was built on three levels, each cut one below the other into the living rock side of the mountain. It was probably intended for his private use, as opposed to the more ceremonial Western Palace. You are now standing on its upper level, where the living quarters were. Modern steps lead down over 60 feet to the **Middle Terrace** (7), thought to have been the king's summer retreat. Nearly 50 feet below that is the spectacular *Lower Terrace (8), a court-yard surrounded by two rows of columns. The rock face wall has interest-ing frescoes and half-columns with Corinthian capitals. Below it, to the east, is the inaccessible private bathhouse of the king, where a few skeletons of the last defending Zealots were found. Before descending to the middle and lower terraces, however, take a good look down and decide whether you can comfortably climb back up.

Continue around the western edge to the **Synagogue** (9), the oldest in Israel and possibly in the world. It is the only known synagogue any-where that is contemporary with the Temple in Jerusalem. Parchment scrolls found buried beneath its floor contained fragments of the books of Deuteronomy and Ezekiel, and can be seen today at the Shrine of the Book in Jerusalem (see page 69). Just beyond is the **Scroll Casemate** (10) of the Western Wall, where a scroll from the Book of Psalms was found along with Essene texts and silver shekels of the Zealot period.

Follow along the path heading away from the cliff to the 5th-century **Byzantine Chapel** (11). Built by Christian monks some four hundred years after the fall of Masada, it has some nicely preserved mosaic floors. Close to this is the **Western Palace** (12), the official residence of King Herod. This is linked to the Western Gate at the top of the **Roman Ramp**,

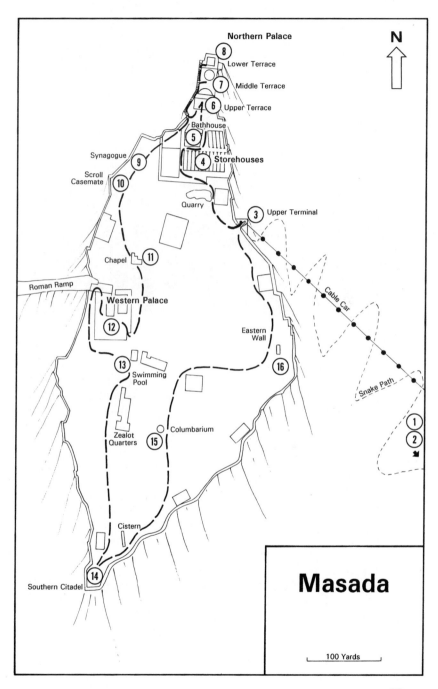

Masada

100 Yards

Ruins of the Northern Palace

still a means of access to the Masada mountaintop for those who come by car and park along the road to Arad. The palace was substantially altered by the Zealots to provide themselves with accommodations, but some interesting Herodian mosaics remain more or less intact.

By now you have left the last of the tour groups behind and can explore the remaining ruins in peaceful solitude. The **Swimming Pool** (13) seems an almost insane luxury in so dry a place, but Herod spared no taxpayer expense in his endless quest for the good life. South of it are some of the **Zealot living quarters** with one room restored to the way it was. Overlooking the south point of the mountain stands the **Southern Citadel** (14), a defensive bastion close to an enormous **water cistern.**

The trail now leads to the **Columbarium** (15), a strange Herodian structure that may have once held the ashes of non-Jews cremated on Masada. Hike over to the **Eastern Wall** (16), part of the Roman defenses that were converted into dwellings by the Zealots. This returns you to the Snake Path Gate and the Upper Cable Car Terminal, from which you can descend back down to the bus stop.

Old Tel Aviv

Thirty-nine miles and a few thousand years separate Tel Aviv and Jerusalem; less than an hour away by land but millennia in attitudes. This is Israel's worldly face, its largest city, its center of commerce, culture, style, social life, and just plain good living.

First-time visitors often get the wrong impression of Tel Aviv, seeing it only as a chaotic urban sprawl with few really attractive sights and little of historic interest. Immerse yourself in the rhythms of its daily life, however, and you'll soon discover an exciting blend of the Mediterranean and the Middle East—a bit of the Riviera, a trace of Cairo, and perhaps even a touch of New York (or at least Miami!).

Strictly a creation of the 20th Century, modern Tel Aviv was little more than sand dunes before 1909. In that year the town was founded as a garden suburb of the teeming ancient port of Jaffa, a place where Jewish residents of the then-Arab town might live peacefully in a European-style community. Its name derives from Theodor Herzl's utopian vision of a Jewish state, described in his 1902 novel *Altneuland*, and poetically connotes the springing to life of an ancient mound of civilization.

Tel Aviv flourished until the outbreak of World War I, when the ruling Turks dispersed the Jews throughout Palestine, suspecting them of pro-British sympathies. These refugees returned to an abandoned town after the conflict; real development did not resume until the establishment of the British Mandate in 1920. Waves of immigration following Hitler's rise to power in Nazi Germany further swelled the population and contributed to the chaotic layout of today's city as well as to the characteristic Bauhaus look of its 1930's architecture. Fortunately, World War II brought only minor damage. After the British pulled out in 1948, the State of Israel was officially proclaimed here by the Zionist leader David Ben-Gurion, who later became the fledgling nation's first prime minister. Tel Aviv served as the capital until the seat of government was moved to Jerusalem in late 1949. In 1950, the old port of Jaffa was annexed by Tel Aviv, now correctly known as Tel Aviv-Yafo.

Besides being a great destination in itself, centrally-located Tel Aviv makes an ideal base for daytrips to most of Israel. Even excursions that are more conveniently taken from Jerusalem or Haifa (see Section III) can usually be accomplished from Tel Aviv, especially if you are driving. The city has a wonderful selection of hotels and hostels in all price ranges, and offers a truly cosmopolitan array of restaurants and night spots to come back to after a hard day's sightseeing. This chapter as well as the next three describe four walking tours that probe different aspects of the city's life. The first takes you through the older, southern part of Tel Aviv and ends at bustling Dizengoff Circle (Kikar Zina), a fabulous square lined with attractive cafés and restaurants, the perfect place to relax. The second tour continues from there through the newer and more prosperous neighborhoods to the north, until it ends at a café-lined square overlooking the Mediterranean. Jaffa, one of the world's oldest ports, is thoroughly explored on the third tour, while the fourth covers Ramat Aviv, an area north of the Yarkon River known for its rich historical treasures.

GETTING THERE:

Buses leave Jerusalem's Central Bus Station almost continuously for the 50-minute ride to Tel Aviv. Service from Haifa's Central Bus Station, a 75-minute ride, is nearly as frequent. In general, the buses run from about 5:30 a.m. until late evening, but do not operate at all from mid-afternoon on Fridays until Saturday evenings, nor on major Jewish holidays. It is best to purchase your ticket before boarding, and to wait in line at the posted departure platform (signs are in English on one side, Hebrew on the other).

Sherut Taxis operated by several different firms depart from various points in Jerusalem and Haifa for Tel Aviv. These shared vehicles have fixed fares that are roughly the same as buses, with a small surcharge on the Sabbath.

Trains also connect Tel Aviv with Jerusalem and Haifa, but do so at such a leisurely pace that they can only be recommended to dedicated railfans or as a scenic trip in itself.

By car, Tel Aviv is 39 miles northwest of Jerusalem via Route 1, and 59 miles south of Haifa via Route 2. Both highways are excellent.

GETTING AROUND:

Local buses in the Tel Aviv area are operated by the DAN Cooperative and run from early morning until about midnight, but not from late afternoon on Fridays until Saturday evenings, nor on major Jewish holidays. Tell the driver your destination and he'll sell you the correct ticket, which you keep until leaving the bus. The #4 route goes from the Central Bus Station into the city center via Allenby Road and Ben Yehuda St.; and the #5 from the bus station via Allenby Road, Rothschild Blvd., and Dizengoff St.

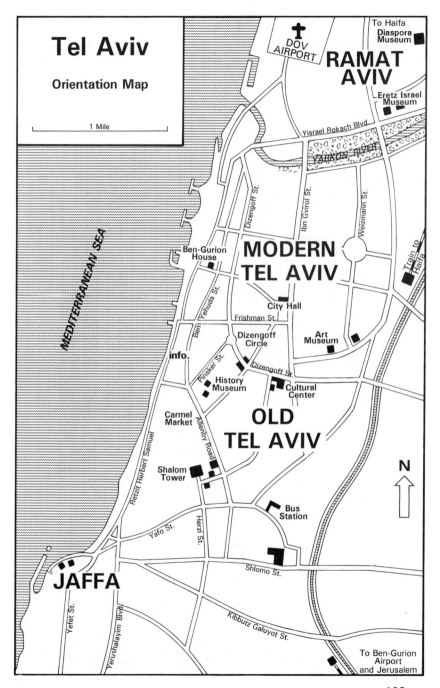

Tel Aviv

Orientation Map

1 Mile

MEDITERRANEAN SEA

DOV AIRPORT

To Haifa
Diaspora Museum

RAMAT AVIV

Eretz Israel Museum

Yisrael Rokach Blvd.

YARKON RIVER

Dizengoff St.

Ibn Gvirol St.

Weizmann St.

Train to Haifa

Ben-Gurion House

MODERN TEL AVIV

City Hall

Frishman St.

Ben Yehuda St.

Dizengoff Circle

Art Museum

info.

Pinsker St.

Dizengoff St.

History Museum

Cultural Center

Carmel Market

Allenby Road

OLD TEL AVIV

Retzif Herbert Samuel

Shalom Tower

N

Bus Station

Yafo St.

Herzl St.

Shlomo St.

JAFFA

Yefet St.

Yerushalayim Blvd.

Kibbutz Galuyot St.

To Ben-Gurion Airport and Jerusalem

103

Sherut **Minibuses** follow the same route as the #4 bus, but leave from the opposite end of the bus station. Their fares are about the same as the regular bus except on the Sabbath, when a premium is charged.

Taxis, usually called "Specials," can be hailed in the street or summoned by phone. Be sure the driver uses the meter. There is a surcharge for service on the Sabbath, holidays, and at night.

PRACTICALITIES:

Most of the sights along this first walking tour of Tel Aviv are closed on Saturdays and major Jewish holidays, and some on Fridays as well. The local **Tourist Information Office** (GTIO), phone (03) 66-02-59, is at 5 Shalom Aleichem St., between the beach and Ben Yehuda St., near the American Embassy. It is closed on Friday afternoons and Saturdays. Tel Aviv has a **population** of some 350,000 within the city limits, and about 1½ million in the metropolitan area.

FOOD AND DRINK:

Some good restaurants along or near the route of this walking tour are:

> **White Hall** (6 Mendele St., 5 blocks west of Dizengoff Circle) A really good steak house with excellent wines. Special lunch menus Sun.–Fri. Non-kosher. $$ and $$$
>
> **Yin Yang** (64 Rothschild Blvd., a few blocks east of Allenby) Great Chinese cuisine. X: Sat. lunch. $$ and $$$
>
> **Maganda** (26 Rabbi Meir St., at the west end of the Carmel Market) Middle Eastern specialties in a lovely setting. Kosher. X: Fri. eve. to Sat. eve. $$
>
> **Zion** (28 Peduyim St., in the southwest corner of the Carmel Market) A favorite Yemenite restaurant in the Yemenite quarter. $$
>
> **Acapulco** (Dizengoff St., a block north of Dizengoff Circle) Light meals at a popular café. Kosher. $

In addition, some of the restaurants listed in the next walking tour are within striking distance of this tour. For good *felafel* and *shwarma*, try the stands near the southwestern end of the Carmel Market, or a block or so east of Kikar Magen David. On the Sabbath, you'll find the best selection on and around Dizengoff Circle, which also has a Wendy's and other fast-food outlets.

SUGGESTED TOUR:

Travelers coming from out of town will probably want to begin their walk at the **Central Bus Station** (1), about as colorfully decrepit and confusing a place as you'll find in Israel. It will eventually be replaced by a

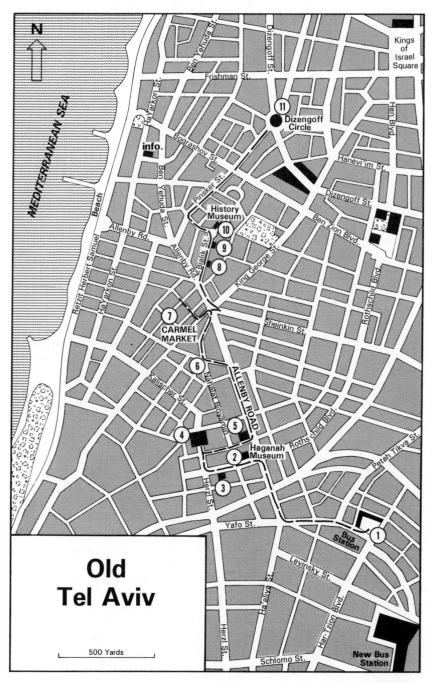

Old Tel Aviv

500 Yards

105

new bus terminal a few blocks to the southeast, but until then you can enjoy this Oriental bazaar with its bustling flea-market atmosphere spread over several square blocks. From here follow the map up HaShomron St., Derech Petah Tikva, and Allenby Road to Rothschild Blvd., where you turn left.

If you are staying in Tel Aviv, you might prefer to begin this tour at its first major attraction, below.

The **Haganah Museum** (2) at 23 Rothschild Blvd. is located in the former home of Eliahu Golomb, one of the co-founders in 1920 of the clandestine Jewish army that later became the Israel Defense Force of today. The exploits of this secretive underground organization, the Haganah, against both the Arabs and the British are chronicled through a series of fascinating displays, including a miniature sound-and-light show of the daring "Night of the Bridges" attack in 1946. The house itself is one of the oldest in Tel Aviv and is authentically furnished in the 1930s style. Operated by the Ministry of Defense, the museum is open on Sundays through Thursdays from 8:30 a.m. to 3 p.m.; and on Fridays and holiday eves from 8:30 a.m. to noon. It is closed on Saturdays. Phone (03) 62-36-24.

Continue along Rothschild Blvd., which until the money moved uptown was once the most prestigious address in Tel Aviv. It still retains much of its original beauty. On the other side, at number 16, is **Independence Hall** (3), where David Ben-Gurion proclaimed the establishment of the State of Israel on May 14th, 1948. Now restored to its appearance on that fateful day, the house was originally the residence of Tel Aviv's first mayor, Meir Dizengoff, and later housed the Tel Aviv Museum of Art until the latter moved uptown in 1959. Exhibits here touch on the history of the *menorah* and Star of David motifs, and examine the first critical months of the nation's existence. Visits may be made from Sundays through Thursdays, from 9 a.m. until 2 p.m. Phone (03) 517-3942. The upper floors of the building house the **Bible Museum** with its exhibits relating to the Bible, and especially to rare translations.

Turn right on Herzl St., Tel Aviv's earliest main thoroughfare. This originally led to the Gymnasia Herzlia, a secular Hebrew high school built in 1910 that soon became the new town's cultural center. After the school moved to larger quarters in the late 1950s, a 35-story office building—reputedly the tallest in the Middle East—rose in its place. Although architecturally undistinguished, the **Shalom Tower** (4) offers a stunning panoramic ***view** that extends (on a clear day) as far as Jerusalem and the Golan Heights. Ride the escalator up to the shopping level, then purchase a ticket for the observatory. There is also a **Wax Museum** here, and a joint ticket is available should you be interested. Continue through the indoor playland to the special Observatory elevator and ride it up to the outdoor terrace level, which also features a café with a view. The

View from Shalom Tower

tower, phone (03) 64-29-45, is open on Sundays through Thursdays from 9:30 a.m. to 7 p.m., on Fridays from 9:30 a.m. to 2 p.m., but never on Saturdays.

Return to Earth and follow the map to the **Great Synagogue** (5), built in 1926 and thoroughly renovated in 1970. Perhaps surprisingly, this is one of the very few obviously religious structures in all of Tel Aviv.

You are now on **Allenby Road** (*Rehov Allenby*), a slightly seedy but pleasant old street that dates from 1917 and was once Tel Aviv's most important commercial and social thoroughfare. It was named after the British general who freed Palestine from the Turks during World War I. Take a close look at the upper stories of the buildings, many of which reveal interesting elements of the architectural styles popular in the Tel Aviv of the 1920s and '30s; especially those combining Bauhaus, Art Nouveau, the International style, and just plain kitsch.

Make a left turn into Rambam St., a traffic-free lane leading to the **Nahalat Binyamin** (6) pedestrian mall (*midrehov*) in the heart of the fashion district. Here, amid the bustling shops and outdoor cafés, can be found some of old Tel Aviv's best domestic architecture. There are often arts-and-crafts activities, music, and even dancing in the street to entertain the clientele. The show gets more exciting as you head north towards **Kikar Magen David** (Star of David Square), then left into the famous ***Carmel Market** (*Shuk HaKarmel*) (7), a noisy and chaotic Oriental bazaar that reminds you that this is indeed the Middle East. Sidewalk merchants sing out the virtues of their goods, often in unison with their competitors, while crowds push and shove as they compare the bargains. You can buy just about anything here, from plucked chickens to cheap polyester underwear, from 9 a.m. to 5 p.m. on any day except Saturdays and major holidays. The already-low prices drop dramatically late on Friday afternoons as the beginning of *Shabbat* draws near. Some of the best deals can be found towards the southwestern end of the market, near the parking lot.

Return to Kikar Magen David, a congested intersection that is more-or-less shaped like its namesake Star of David. On its far side, between HaMelech George St. (King George St.) and Allenby Road, is the **Bezalel Market**, a discount shopping area noted for its good *felafel* stands. **Sheinkin Street**, radiating off to the southeast, is another lively thoroughfare worth exploring.

Continue north on Allenby and turn right into quiet, narrow Bialik St. At number 14 you'll find the **Rubin House** (8), once the residence of the modern Israeli artist Reuvin Rubin and now a small museum largely devoted to his works. Born in Romania in 1893, Rubin moved to Tel Aviv in 1922 and there developed a style that is at once naive and yet mystical. This is where he lived and painted until his death in 1974. The museum, phone (03) 510-3230, is open on Sundays, Mondays, Wednesdays, and Thursdays from 10 a.m. to 2 p.m.; on Tuesdays from 10 a.m. to 1 p.m. and 4–8 p.m.; and on Saturdays from 11 a.m. to 2 p.m. It is closed on Fridays.

Just up the street, at number 22, is the **Beit Bialik Museum** (9), once the home of Israel's most renowned poet, Haim Nahman Bialik. The house itself, dating from the 1920s, is quite charming with its dome, pink balcony, and arched columns. Inside, it remains as it was in his time, and contains manuscripts, archives, and memorabilia of his life and work. Visits may be made on Sundays through Thursdays, from 9 a.m. to 5 p.m.; and on Saturdays from 10 a.m. to 2 p.m. Phone (03) 517-1530, closed on Fridays.

From here it's only a few steps to Kikar Bialik, a small square with a circular fountain, and the **Museum of the History of Tel Aviv-Yafo** (10) located in the former City Hall of 1925. The development of the first all-Jewish city of modern times is brought to life through the use of dioramas, models, photos, artifacts, and an audio-visual presentation in English and Hebrew. The museum, phone (03) 517-3052, is open on Sundays through Thursdays from 9 a.m. until 2 p.m. It is closed on Fridays and Saturdays.

By now, you may feel in need of both rest and refreshment. Fortunately, it's not very far to ***Dizengoff Circle** (11), a.k.a. *Kikar Zina*, which has a wonderful selection of outdoor cafés, the liveliest street scene in Tel Aviv, and one of the weirdest pieces of performing sculpture

The Fire and Water Fountain at rest

in the world. Just follow the map along Idelson and Pinsker streets. A huge, raised circular platform hovers above the traffic intersection, ramps lead down to the cafés and restaurants, and in the center of it all is Ya'acov Agam's monstrous **Fire and Water Fountain**. Most of the time, its brilliantly-colored multi-tiered circles just spew forth water, but at 11 a.m., 5 p.m., 7 p.m., and 9 p.m. the whole contraption comes to life, shooting out flames as its body twists and spins to the beat of banal recorded music. You have to see this to believe it—then you can go to one of the cafés and have a beer. The walk is over.

Tel Aviv-Yafo
Modern Tel Aviv

This second walking tour of Tel Aviv begins where the previous one left off, at Dizengoff Circle in the very heart of town. As the city grew it continued to move north from its origins closer to Jaffa. An increasingly high level of prosperity is evident here, both in the more interesting architecture and in the broader streets with considerably more elbow room between structures. Lovers of modern art will especially appreciate this stroll as it includes two world-class museums, and everyone will enjoy the stunning view across the marina and the Mediterranean as the walk ends in a beachfront square lined with outdoor cafés.

GETTING THERE:

GETTING AROUND:
See the appropriate entries for the first Tel Aviv walking tour on page 102.

PRACTICALITIES:
Some of the major attractions along this walk are closed on Fridays, and one on Saturdays. Apart from the lack of public transportation, this is a fairly good excursion to make on the Sabbath. The other practical information is the same as for the first Tel Aviv walking tour, outlined on page 104.

FOOD AND DRINK:
Some outstanding restaurants and cafés along or near the route of this tour are listed below. In addition, a few of the establishments mentioned for the first walking tour (see page 104) are within reasonable distance of this route as well.

  Kassit Café (117 Dizengoff St., 2 blocks north of Dizengoff Circle)
   Classic Ashkenazi dishes in a genuinely bohemian atmosphere.
   $

Outside the Museum of Art

Nargila (10 Frischmann St., 6 blocks west of Dizengoff Circle, near the beach) Tasty Yemenite specialties along with a convivial ambiance. $

Eternity (6 Kikar Malchel Yisra'el, opposite City Hall) Strictly vegetarian and non-dairy dishes, with interesting meat substitutes. Kosher. X: Fri. eve., Sat. until sundown. $

Cherry (Dizengoff St., corner of Ben-Gurion, 3 blocks east of the Ben-Gurion House) A café with outdoor tables, light meals, and exceptional salads. $

In addition, the art museum has its own cafeteria. Fast-food outlets such as Wendy's and Pizza Hut can be found at Dizengoff Circle and Dizengoff Centre. There are several outdoor cafés and *felafel* stands at Kikar Atarim, the end of the walk.

SUGGESTED TOUR:

On this tour, you'll probably be leaving ***Dizengoff Circle** (1) too early to witness the **Fire and Water Fountain** doing its ridiculous thing (see page 109), but have a look around Tel Aviv's most popular public space anyway. It was named for Zina Dizengoff, the wife of the city's first mayor, and is often known as *Kikar Zina* (the word *kikar* referring to an open plaza). You might want to stop for a morning cup of coffee at one of the many sidewalk cafés and watch the passing parade of humanity before moving on.

Amble down Dizengoff Street, a major shopping thoroughfare, to the stunning **Dizengoff Centre** (2). By now you must realize just how popular Mayor Dizengoff was with the Tel Avivians, as so many places in town are named for him or his wife. A huge shopping complex straddles the street here, with an impressive indoor multi-storied mall on the south side. Stroll through it to get a glimpse of the prosperous side of today's Israel, or perhaps for a snack at an attractive café.

Dizengoff Street now becomes residential for a short distance. Follow it uphill to Tel Aviv's **Cultural Center** on the right. The corner building is the **Helena Rubinstein Pavilion** (3), a branch of the Tel Aviv Museum of Art that displays temporary exhibitions of contemporary art. From 1959 until 1971 it housed the entire museum, which had moved here from the first mayor's residence on Rothschild Boulevard (see page 106). As the collections grew, the space became too confining and a new structure was built a few blocks away, visited later on this tour. Apart from the changing shows, a permanent treat of this pavilion is its exquisite display of miniature room sets from around the world, personally collected by the cosmetics legend, Helena Rubinstein, herself. The pavilion, phone (03) 528-7196, is open on Sundays through Thursdays from 10 a.m. to 8 p.m., and on Saturdays from 10 a.m. to 3 p.m. It is closed on Fridays. The entrance ticket is also valid for the Tel Aviv Museum of Art.

Next to the pavilion is the lovely **Jacob's Garden** (*Gan Yaacov*), a shady, multi-level oasis of cool beauty that links together the various elements of the cultural center. Take a stroll through it, then look at the adjacent **Habima Theater** (4) of 1935. Israel's national theater company, which performs here in Hebrew with English translations, was founded by the Jewish community of Moscow in 1918 and moved to Tel Aviv in 1928. The third major structure here is the **Mann Auditorium** (5), the 3,000-seat home of the world-renowned Israel Philharmonic Orchestra.

Now follow the map north on Ibn Gvirol Street and east on King Saul Boulevard (*Sderot Sha'ul Hamelech*) to the ***Tel Aviv Museum of Art** (6), one of the finest institutions of its type in the world. Its vast holdings include treasures of European art from the 16th through the 19th centuries; Impressionist works by Renoir, Monet, Van Gogh, Pissarro, and others; and major 20th-century creations by Picasso, Chagall, Rouault, Klee, Kokoschka, Pollock, Lichtenstein, and many other luminaries including, of course, quite a few Israeli artists. There are also temporary exhibitions, film shows, dance, music, and theater, along with a well-stocked museum shop and a cafeteria. The museum is open on Sundays through Thursdays from 10 a.m. to 9:30 p.m., and on Saturdays from 10 a.m. to 2 p.m. and 7–10 p.m. It is closed on Fridays. For further information phone (03) 26-12-97. Admission tickets are also valid for the Helena Rubinstein Pavilion, described above.

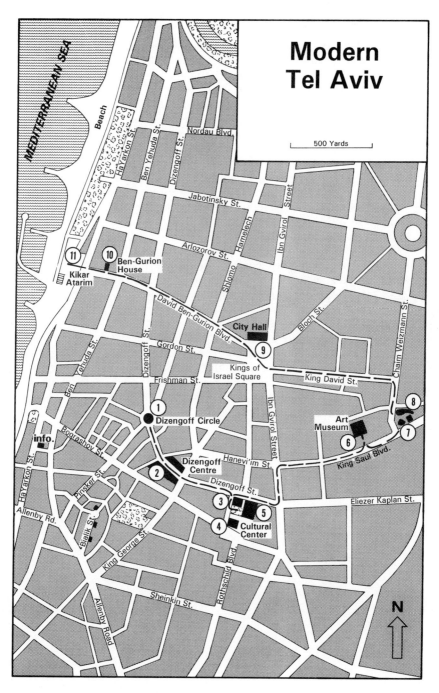

Modern
Tel Aviv

500 Yards

MEDITERRANEAN SEA

Beach

HaYarkon St.

Ben Yehuda St.

Dizengoff St.

Nordau Blvd.

Jabotinsky St.

Street

Arlozorov St.

Hamelech

Ibn Gvirol

Shlomo

⑪

⑩ Ben-Gurion
House

Kikar
Atarim

David Ben-Gurion Blvd.

City Hall

Bloch St.

Chaim Weizmann St.

Ben Yehuda St.

Dizengoff St.

Gordon St.

⑨

Kings of
Israel Square

King David St.

Frishman St.

① Dizengoff Circle

Ibn Gvirol Street

Art
Museum

⑧

info.

Pograshov St.

HaYarkon St.

Pinsker St.

Dizengoff
Centre

②

Hanevi'im St.

⑥

King Saul Blvd.

⑦

Allenby Rd.

Bialik St.

Dizengoff St.

③

④

⑤

Cultural
Center

Eliezer Kaplan St.

King George St.

Rothschild Blvd.

Sheinkin St.

N
⬆

Allenby Road

Just down the street stand several magnificent examples of contemporary architecture, a dramatic break from the boring concrete boxes that dominate the town. The curved, three-sided **IBM Building** (7) rises some 24 stories above its inverted base, while the sensuous lines of the low-slung, white **Asia House** (8) may remind you of a beached whale. Head north on Chaim Weizmann St. and turn left on King David St. (*Sderot David Ha'melech*), following it to **Kings of Israel Square** (*Kikar Malkhei Yisra'el*) (9). This immense open plaza is a favorite gathering place for Tel Avivians, whether for holding celebrations or political demonstrations. At its north end stands the 12-story **City Hall**.

David Ben-Gurion Boulevard (*Sderot Ben-Gurion*) leads west to the rather modest home of Israel's first prime minister, located at number 17 and preserved almost exactly as he left it. Although the interior of the **David Ben-Gurion House** (10) is simply furnished, the memorabilia of his life is absorbing and presents a good insight into the formation of the country. Compare this dwelling with the splendid mansion of Israel's first president, visited on the Rehovot trip (page 129). The house, phone (03) 22-10-10, is open on Sundays, Tuesdays, Wednesdays, and Thursdays from 8 a.m. to 2 p.m.; on Mondays from 8 a.m. to 5 p.m.; and on Fridays from 8 a.m. to noon. Admission is free.

From here it's only a few steps to **Kikar Namir** (11), a.k.a. **Kikar Atarim**, a huge public square on the edge of the sea, overlooking the marina and the Mediterranean. Although heavily criticized for alleged crass commercialism, it's still a fun place and does offer a nice selection of outdoor cafés. Many of Tel Aviv's major hotels are nearby, and can be reached by strolling along the beach.

Jaffa

(Yafo, Yafa, Joppa)

Thousands of years before there was a Tel Aviv, there was a Jaffa. In fact, this is one of the oldest ports on Earth, if not *the* oldest. According to legend, it was established right after the Flood by Noah's son Japheth. Another story links it to Jonah and the whale. In any case, archaeological digs here have definitely established the town as dating from at least the 18th century B.C. To the ancient Greeks, this is where Andromeda, the daughter of Joppa, herself a daughter of Aeolus, the god of the winds, was chained to the rocks until her rescue by Perseus on his winged white horse. In more recent times, the New Testament places the raising of Tabitha by the apostle Peter here in Jaffa.

Throughout history, and under various names such as Yafo, Yafa, Japho, and Joppa, Jaffa has been overrun by a colorful parade of conquerors including Egyptians, Philistines, Israelites, Persians, Greeks, Syrians, Romans, Muslims, Christian Crusaders, Mamluks, Napoleon's armies, Turks of the Ottoman Empire, and finally the British. In 1948, it became part of the new State of Israel after the Arab population fled. Tel Aviv itself began as a mere 20th-century suburb of Jaffa; in 1950 the adjacent towns were reunited into the municipality of Tel Aviv-Yafo.

Today, Jaffa is one of the few really integrated communities in Israel; a place where Jews and Arabs live together in relative harmony. Its oldest quarter, on a hill overlooking the ancient harbor, was thoroughly renovated in the 1960s and made into a quaint "artists' colony" where craft shops, boutiques, artisans, restaurants, and discos vie for the tourist dollars, marks, or yen. The experience is not altogether authentic, but it's a lot of fun, the scenery is great, and there are genuine old neighborhoods rubbing elbows with it. This walking tour takes you through contrasting sights and environs, and ends at the famous Flea Market where you can bargain away to your heart's content or just enjoy the show.

GETTING THERE:

Local buses on routes number 10, 41, 46, 90, and 99 connect Tel Aviv proper with Clock Tower Square in Jaffa. They do not operate between late Friday afternoons and Saturday evenings, nor on Jewish holidays.

115

Regular taxis are a reasonable way to reach Jaffa. Be sure that the meter is used and that you get a phone number to call for the return trip. **On foot**, it's a pleasant 2-mile walk along the seashore from Tel Aviv's main hotels to Jaffa.

PRACTICALITIES:

A visit to Jaffa can be enjoyed at any time, but bear in mind that the colorful flea market is closed on Saturdays and major holidays, and the museum on Fridays. For other tourist information see page 104.

FOOD AND DRINK:

Jaffa is famous for its fine dining. A few choice establishments in all price ranges are:

Alhambra (30 Jerusalem St., 3 blocks east of the Clock Tower) Considered to be Israel's best French restaurant. For reservations call (03) 83-44-53. Not Kosher. X: Fri. $$$

Toutonne (1 Simtat Mazal Dagim, in the artists' quarter) Classic French cuisine, with terrace dining in summer. $$$

Babai (On the Old Jaffa harbor) A popular seafood restaurant. $$

Ifrah (Mifratz Shlomo, next to the Great Mosque) An unpretentious sidewalk café with kebabs, *hummus*, and other Middle Eastern fare. $

Said Abu-Lafiah (7 Yefet St., a block south of the Clock Tower) An old classic bakery selling Arab pizzas and *borekas* along the sidewalk; extremely popular. X: Sun. $

SUGGESTED TOUR:

Begin your walk at the **Clock Tower** (1) on Kikar HaHagana, an open square at the north end of Jaffa. Built in 1906 by the Ottoman sultan Abdul Hamid II to celebrate the 30th anniversary of his rule, the tower has stained-glass windows depicting events in Jaffa's history. Across from it stands the **Great Mosque** (*Mahmudiyeh Mosque*) (2), readily identifiable by its tall minaret, from whose loudspeakers recorded calls to prayer are made. The mosque was built in 1810 by the Turkish governor Pasha Mahmud Abu Nabur, and utilizes columns from antiquity that were removed from Ashkelon and Caesarea but installed upside down.

Turn right on Mifratz Shelomo Promenade, passing several inexpensive restaurants with outdoor tables. On your left, as the road starts going uphill, is the **Antiquities Museum of Tel Aviv-Yafo** (3); a "must-see" if you have an interest in local archaeology, a sight that can be skipped if you don't. The building itself dates from the 18th century and was part of a Turkish administrative complex. It now houses artifacts from prehistoric and Biblical times, mostly found in local digs, and is open on Sundays through Wednesdays from 9 a.m. to 2 p.m., on Tuesdays also

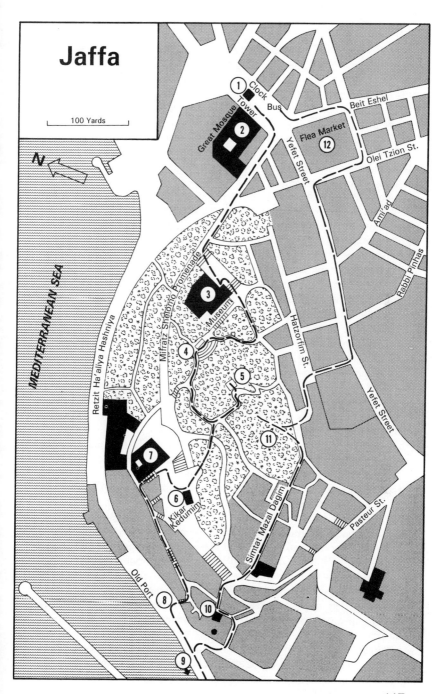

Jaffa

100 Yards

N

MEDITERRANEAN SEA

① Clock Tower
Bus

Beit Eshel

② Great Mosque

Flea Market
⑫

Yefet Street

Olei Tzion St.

Ami'ad

Rabbi Pinhas

Mifratz Shelomo Promenade

③

Museum

④

⑤

⑪

Hatzofim St.

Yefet Street

Retzit Ha'aliya Hashniya

⑦

⑥

Kikar
Kedumim

Simtat Mazal Dagim

Pasteur St.

Old Port

⑧

⑩

⑨

from 4–7 p.m., and is closed on Fridays and Saturdays. For further information phone (03) 82-53-75.

Leave the museum and walk uphill through a park, bearing right to the **HaPisga Amphitheater** (4), a place for alfresco performances with the Mediterranean and modern Tel Aviv as a backdrop. Continue climbing along a path to the highest point, where you will have a spectacular *view of the city. The strange **Statue of Faith** (5) here, a large white sculpture in a vaguely Mayan style, allegedly depicts the fall of Jericho, Issac's sacrifice, and Jacob's dream; although you might have trouble making that connection.

Now go back down the hill and cross a little footbridge to **Kikar Kedumin** (6), the main square of the Old Jaffa restoration. Near its center is an interesting archaeological site where you can look down into exposed ruins from the Hellenistic, Roman, and Byzantine periods. The **Monastery of St. Peter** (7), a Franciscan church first built in 1654 on the foundations of a medieval fortress, is directly opposite. If it's open, take a look at the statue of France's King Louis IX (Saint Louis), who as a leader of the Crusades was one of the many conquerors of Jaffa. Later serving as a hostel for Christian pilgrims, the monastery was visited by Napoleon.

The route now leads through narrow alleyways lined with restored stone walls from antiquity. Were it not for the modern light fixtures and air conditioners hanging from windows, you could very well think that you're back in ancient times. Bear to the right and follow down steps to the **Old Port** (8), whose harbor is still used by fishing boats. This was once the main port of the Holy Land, but commerce has long since moved to larger harbors such as Haifa and Ashdod. Offshore, you can still make out remnants of **Andromeda's Rock**, to which legend has it that the Greek mythological figure was chained as a sacrifice to a sea monster, but was saved by Perseus on his winged white horse.

Stroll along the waterfront to the **Marina** (9), where you'll find several of the seafood restaurants for which Jaffa is famous. Behind it, on the hill, stands the red-and-white **Lighthouse** of 1936.

Returning to the Old Town via the route on the map, you'll soon come to the **House of Simon the Tanner** (10) at number 8 Rehov Shimon HaBurski. According to tradition, this is where the apostle Peter stayed after restoring Tabitha to life (Acts 9, 36–43). Its courtyard contains a well believed to date from the time of Christ, and a stone coffin of the same age that was later used by Moslems for washing themselves before prayers at what was then a mosque. Today it's a private house, but parts of it are usually open to tourists, daily from 8 a.m. to 7 p.m., for a small fee. Just ring the bell.

You are now close to the **Artists' Quarter**, whose narrow stone alleys are named after signs of the zodiac. Follow along **Simtat Mazal Dagim** (Pisces Lane), passing a small synagogue on the right as well as numerous

View of Tel Aviv from the Park

galleries and craft shops. The tiny passageways on either side are also worth exploring.

The end of the lane opens into the **Ramses II Archaeological Garden** (11) where excavations dating from as early as the 18th century B.C. as well as an Egyptian settlement of the 13th century B.C. are on view.

For a complete change of pace, follow the map to Yefet Street, the main thoroughfare of today's Jaffa. Turn left and go downhill, then right on Olei Tzion St. into the noisy, bustling ***Flea Market** (*Shuk HaPishpeshim*) (12). You can find all kinds of things here, from the most awful junk to what might actually be valuable antiques, or at least bargains in decorative crafts, Oriental rugs, clothes, and so on. If you do see something you want, be prepared to haggle and never offer more than half the asking price. This is a great place to witness real *chutzpah* in action. The market is closed on Saturdays and major Jewish holidays. From here you can easily drag your new treasures to the nearby bus stop.

Tel Aviv-Yafo
Ramat Aviv

Two of Israel's greatest cultural treasures lie just north of the Yarkon River, the ancient boundary between the tribes of Ephraim (to the north) and Dan (to the south). Known today as Ramat Aviv, this suburb is home to both the Tel Aviv University and the fabulous Eretz Israel complex of indoor and outdoor museums, incorporating the active Tel Qasile archaeological digs where you can explore some 12 layers of civilization dating as far back as a 12th-century-B.C. Philistine settlement.

Between the Eretz Israel museums and the magnificent, world-renowned Museum of the Jewish Diaspora on the university campus, the tour provides a deeper understanding of the entire Israeli nation and the millennia of history that shaped it. At the end, you can relax in Yarkon Park along the river before returning to the center city.

GETTING THERE:

Local buses on routes 25 and 27 connect central Tel Aviv with the trip sites, and run at frequent intervals from early morning until late evening, but not from late Friday afternoons until Saturday evenings or on major Jewish holidays.

Regular taxis are entirely practical for this trip. Be sure that the meter is used, and that you have a phone number to call for the return ride.

By car, it's a quick trip north on Haifa Road, turning right on University Street. Parking is available near both sites.

PRACTICALITIES:

Avoid making this trip on a Friday, when both attractions are closed. The Diaspora Museum is also closed on Saturdays and major Jewish holidays. Allow at least three hours for the Eretz Israel complex and two hours for the Diaspora Museum. For other tourist information see page 104.

FOOD AND DRINK:

Among the very few places to eat along the tour route are:
> **Museum Restaurant** (in the Eretz Israel Museum complex) An above-average museum restaurant with luncheon specials and a good view. X: Sun. $$

Artisans' stalls at the Man and his Work Pavilion

Eretz Israel Snack Bar (next to the restaurant at the Eretz Israel Museum) *Felafel* and other light meals in a pleasant setting with outdoor tables. X: Fri., Sat. $

There is also a **cafeteria** in the Museum of the Jewish Diaspora.

SUGGESTED TOUR:

Begin your tour at the entrance to the ***Eretz Israel Museum** (1), easily reached by bus, taxi, or car. Formerly known as the Ha'aretz Museum, this enormous complex spreads across some 30 acres of a hillside in the northern part of Tel Aviv known as Ramat Aviv. A wide range of subjects, all relating to the Land (*Eretz*) of Israel, is covered; separate pavilions and open-air exhibits embrace such diverse matters as archaeology, folklore, crafts, and even modern railroading. You can't possibly see it all in a day, but the following tour hits most of the highlights.

Close to the entrance is a major exhibition called ***Man and his Work** (2), which includes a reconstructed outdoor marketplace (*shuk* or *souk*) where artisans demonstrate the ancient trades in their stalls. Indoors, the development of traditional methods of farming, hunting, fishing, transportation, construction, and other forms of work from Biblical times until the 19th century are explained in a series of displays.

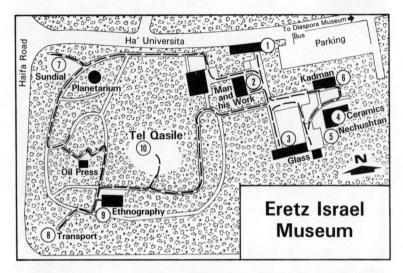

Eretz Israel
Museum

Now stroll over to the **Glass Pavilion** (3), where exquisite glass objects, mostly from the Mediterranean world and covering a time span of well over 3,000 years from ancient Egypt to the present, are on display. Don't miss the ornate 14th-century mosque lamp, a triumph of Islamic glassmaking.

The **Ceramics Pavilion** (4) is next, and of course deals with one of the most vital crafts of the ancient world, pottery. Long before the plastic era, clay vessels were essential for food storage and preparation. There are plenty of them to look at here, dating from as far back as the Neolithic era of the 6th millennium B.C. A full-size reconstruction of an **Israelite House** of the 10th century B.C. demonstrates the many uses of pottery in the ancient world.

Just behind this is the **Nechushtan Pavilion** (5), which tells the story of mining and metallurgy in ancient Israel. Excavated artifacts from the legendary King Solomon's Mines in the Timna Valley, just north of Eilat, are featured along with a model of a copper mine from early times.

Copper also finds its way into the **Kadman Numismatic Pavilion** (6). The long history of coinage and monetary systems from ancient times to the modern era is the subject here, with thousands of glittering coins on display.

Follow the map past **Mosaic Square** and around to **Sundial Square** (7), behind which is the **Lasky Planetarium**. Continue on to the **Garden of Jotham's Parable** and the reconstructed traditional **Oil Pressing Plant**.

From here the trail heads downhill to the **Roads and Railways Site** (8), where the development of land transportation in modern Israel is dem-

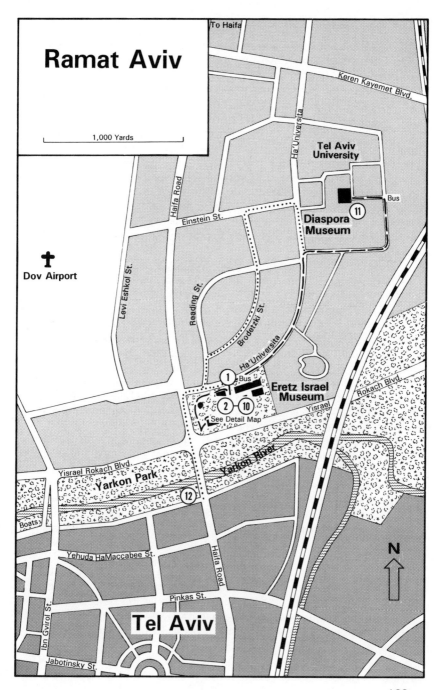

Ramat Aviv

1,000 Yards

To Haifa

Keren Kayemet Blvd.

Ha'Universita

Tel Aviv University

Haifa Road

Einstein St.

Diaspora Museum

Bus

(11)

† Dov Airport

Levi Eshkol St.

Reading St.

Brodetzki St.

Ha'Universita

(1) Bus

(2) (10)

See Detail Map

Eretz Israel Museum

Yisrael

Rokach Blvd.

Yisrael Rokach Blvd.

Yarkon Park

Yarkon River

Boats

(12)

Yehuda HaMaccabee St.

Haifa Road

Pinkas St.

N

↑

Ibn Gvirol St.

Tel Aviv

Jabotinsky St.

onstrated by a small selection of road vehicles and railway equipment. This little detour is worthwhile if you have an interest in the subject, otherwise head directly for the **Ethnography and Folklore Pavilion** (9). Traditional costumes and Jewish ethnic objects, both religious and secular, are on display here along with the interior of a 17th-century Italian synagogue with a magnificent Holy Ark.

For many visitors, the highlight of the entire Eretz Israel complex is not an exhibit in the normal sense, but an actual working archaeological dig on a low hill right in the center of the site. The ***Tel Qasile Excavations** (10) have unearthed a Philistine settlement dating from the 12th century B.C. at the bottom of a dozen layers of subsequent developments. You can see it all from raised walkways, then visit an authentically reconstructed dwelling of the Iron Age. The adjacent **Tel Qasile Pavilion** houses artifacts from the digs, and can provide you with an explanatory guide to the site.

The Eretz Israel Museum complex, phone (03) 641-5244, is open on Sundays through Thursdays from 9 a.m. to 2 p.m.; on Tuesdays also from 4–7 p.m.; and on Saturdays from 10 a.m. to 2 p.m. Leave it now and head for the other big attraction of Ramat Aviv.

From here it's a 20-minute walk or a brief ride on the number 25 or 27 bus to the Tel Aviv University campus and the ***Museum of the Jewish Diaspora** (*Beth Hatefutsoth*) (11). Enter through the gate on Prof. Yosef Klausner St. A "must-see" for visitors to Israel, the museum uses the most innovative means possible to present the age-old story of the dispersion and survival of the Jews in exile during the 2,500 years before the State of Israel was created. The emphasis here is on reconstructing a way of life rather than preserving artifacts and treasures from the past. Mini-theaters present short video shows on different aspects of Jewish life, computers answer questions and search out roots, and a host of visual aids bring history to life before your eyes. Among the highlights are the exquisite scale models of synagogues from around the world during different historical periods. If you know nothing at all about Jewish life, this is the place to learn; if you already know something, you'll learn even more. The museum, phone (03) 642-5161, is open on Sundays through Thursdays, from 10 a.m. to 5 p.m., and remains open until 7 p.m. on Wednesdays. It is closed on Fridays and Saturdays.

You can return to central Tel Aviv by taking a bus from the campus gate. Along the way, you might want to get off at **Yarkon Park** (12), a place to relax along the banks of Yarkon River. Admittedly, this is not the most beautiful river in the world, but you can rent a rowboat for some exercise, or visit the tropical gardens. After that, it's a quick ride back to the center of things.

Rishon LeZion

(Rishon LeTzion, Rishon LeZyyon)

"First to Zion" is the meaning of Rishon LeZion; an apt name for this early Zionist settlement founded in 1882. The town quickly became famous for its winery, the first in Israel since ancient times, and later for its outstanding museum of local history. Much of a century-old past still survives along the route of the "Pioneers' Way," while the cafés along the pedestrianized main street and a charming municipal park combine to make your visit here a thoroughly enjoyable—if not overly exciting—experience.

Rishon LeZion began as a *moshav*, or cooperative village, founded by Polish and Russian Zionists in the late 19th century. Within five years its agricultural base was failing, and the community turned to a wealthy Jewish philanthropist from France, Baron Edmond de Rothschild, for salvation. Wishing to help the Zionist cause, the baron sent agronomists to see what could be done. Their suggestion was to grow vineyards instead of grain. From this start evolved the wine industry that put Rishon LeZion on the map and that remains its major attraction. The town had other "firsts" as well, including the first synagogue erected in Israel since Biblical days, the first school to teach in the Hebrew language, the country's first orchestra, and the first performance of Israel's national anthem.

The suggested tour includes a delightful small museum of local life, a stroll through the old town, and a visit to the Carmel winery where you can sample the products. This daytrip can easily be combined in the same day with one to Rehovot, described in the next chapter. Buses number 200 and 201 leave from Rishon LeZion's bus terminal for the 10-minute ride to Rehovot.

GETTING THERE:

Buses depart Tel Aviv frequently for the quick trip to Rishon LeZion. The number 19 local bus leaves from Shalom Aleichem St., opposite the tourist office, and makes stops along Ben Yehuda St. and Allenby Road. The more comfortable Egged number 200 and 201 buses leave from the Central Bus Station.

By car, Rishon LeZion is about 8 miles southeast of central **Tel Aviv.** Take Route 1 or Route 44, then turn south on Route 412. From **Jerusalem,** it's 38 miles to the northwest. Take Route 1 almost to Tel Aviv, then Route 412 south.

PRACTICALITIES:

Both attractions are closed on Saturdays, and the winery is also closed on Fridays. Public transportation comes to a halt from Friday afternoon until Saturday evening. The local **Tourist Information Office**, phone (03) 968-2435, is in the town museum. Rishon LeZion has a **population** of about 110,000.

FOOD AND DRINK:

You'll find several attractive **outdoor cafés** along the pedestrian mall (Rothschild St.) between Herzl St. and the Village Well. For a lighter meal, try one of the **felafel stands** on Herzl St. between the mall and the bus station. At the bus station, the **Egged Restaurant** offers above-average cafeteria fare at low prices. If you'd rather bring a picnic lunch, head for the municipal park.

SUGGESTED TOUR:

If you came by bus number 200 or 201, you'll arrive at Rishon LeZion's **Bus Terminal** (1), which is also where you can get a ride to Rehovot. Bus number 19 goes directly to the **bus stop** (2) on Herzl St., two blocks farther south.

As soon as you arrive in town, head straight for the winery to make reservations for a tour later in the day *unless you have already made arrangements by phone.* The **Carmel Wine Cellars** (3), phone (03) 964-2021, are open on Sundays through Thursdays from 9 a.m. to 4 p.m. Pass through the gate on HaCarmel St. and go to the tour office in the first building to the right.

Having arranged for a wine tour, you're now free to explore the town. Stroll across the street and into the lovely **Municipal Park** (4), which began early in the town's history as an agricultural experiment by Rothschild's gardeners to see what grew best. Date palms obviously did well, as so many of them grace the paths. Toward the northern end there is a mini-zoo where farm animals delight the children.

Turn right on the broad, pedestrians-only Rothschild Street and follow it to the **Rishon LeZion History Museum** (5) on Founders' Square (*Kikar Hameyasdim*). Located in several small, century-old houses, the museum traces the story of the town's founding in the earliest days of Zionism, of the initial hardships and disasters that followed, and of the generous help received from Baron Rothschild. A highlight is the reconstructed street lined with craftsmen's workshops. The admission includes

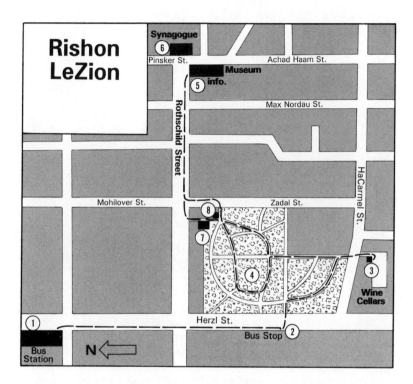

an indoor sound-and-light show at the Village Well, just a few blocks down the street. Visits may be made on Sundays, Tuesdays, Wednesdays, and Thursdays from 9 a.m. to 2 p.m.; on Mondays from 9 a.m. to 2 p.m. and 4–8 p.m.; and on Fridays from 9 a.m. to 1 p.m. For current information call (03) 968-2435.

The **Great Synagogue** (6), across the street, is nearly as old as the town. Interestingly, when it was built in 1885 it was officially listed as a "warehouse," as the Turkish authorities who then ruled Palestine would not allow a Jewish house of worship.

Head back down Rothschild Street to the **Village Well** (7), where water was at last discovered at a depth of 155 feet after all previous attempts in the area had failed. Prior to that, water was carried on the backs of animals from a source several miles away. An indoor **sound-and-light show** is given here in connection with your visit to the museum, where you can ask about current schedules for the English showing. Just beyond the well is the **Water Tower** (8), a landmark stone structure also financed by the good baron.

Looking up the pedestrian mall

Now return through the park to the **Carmel Wine Cellars** (3) for your tour. Built around 1890 to process the first vintage, these original buildings of Baron Rothschild's winery are today used primarily for wine storage as most of the actual production is done in modern facilities located elsewhere. Your tour includes an audio-visual show, a visit to the cellars and other historic structures, and a chance to sample the various types of wine produced. Those varietals bearing the *Rothschild* label, made from the Cabernet Sauvignon, Chardonnay, Sauvignon Blanc, or Emerald Riesling grapes are superb, while the others make a good, honest accompaniment to everyday meals.

Rehovot

A visit to the Weizmann Institute of Science at Rehovot reveals an entirely different face of Israel. You won't find anything of the past here, or of the arid land either. Instead, you'll explore some 250 acres of a lush, green oasis dedicated to the cutting edge of science and technology. Some of the nation's finest modern architecture is located here, along with several of its most beautiful gardens.

Israel's first president, Chaim Weizmann, settled in Rehovot in 1920 and in 1937 built the magnificent home where he lived until his death in 1952. Today this house, visited during his lifetime by so many world leaders, is open to the public and is an attraction not to be missed. Besides being a leader in the Zionist movement, Dr. Weizmann was a world-renowned scientist whose research during World War I proved invaluable to the British war effort and helped win some international support for the Jewish cause. In 1934 he founded the Sieff Research Institute here, which later became the Weizmann Institute. Today it has some 1,800 researchers and graduate students along with many visiting scientists from around the globe, all concerned with such topics as cancer, immunology, biotechnology, the neurosciences, heart disease, agriculture, physics, solar energy, and the environment.

Rehovot itself began in 1890 as a *moshav*, a cooperative farming village founded by Polish Jews. Although its main activity is still the cultivation of citrus fruits, the town also has large pharmaceutical and glass industries. After visiting the institute, you might want to stroll downtown past the fruit and produce market and take the bus back from there. This trip can easily be combined in the same day with the previous one to Rishon LeZion as there is good bus service between the towns.

GETTING THERE:

Buses number 200 or 201 leave Tel Aviv's Central Bus Station frequently for the 40-minute ride to Rehovot, stopping at Rishon LeZion en route. Get off at the Weizmann Institute of Science (on the left, sign in English), just before Rehovot's town center.

By car, Rehovot is about 14 miles southeast of central **Tel Aviv**. Take Route 1 or Route 44, then turn south on Route 412. From **Jerusalem**, it's 38 miles to the northwest. Take Route 1 to Lod, then head south on Route 40 and north through Rehovot on Route 412.

The Solar Tower

PRACTICALITIES:

Avoid making this trip on a Friday, Saturday, or major Jewish holiday, when the main sights are closed. For further information call the Visitors' Section of the Weizmann Institute at (08) 48-32-30 or 48-33-28. Rehovot has a **population** of about 70,000.

FOOD AND DRINK:

The town has several inexpensive restaurants and *felafel* stands, mostly along Herzl St. below the bus station. Recommended are:

Estate Restaurant (near the Weizmann home) A cafeteria with decent food in nice surroundings. X: Fri., Sat. $

Eternity (192 Herzl St., a few blocks south of the institute) Strictly vegetarian dishes with interesting meat substitutes. X: Fri. eve., Sat. $

SUGGESTED TOUR:

If you've come by bus, get off at the **stop** (1) opposite the main entrance of the **Weizmann Institute of Science**. Walk through this to the first large structure on the left, the **Stone Administration Building** (2), where you can get an information brochure and ask about guided tours at the Visitors' Section in room 307. A free documentary film on the institute's activities is shown in the nearby **Wix Auditorium** (3) on Sundays

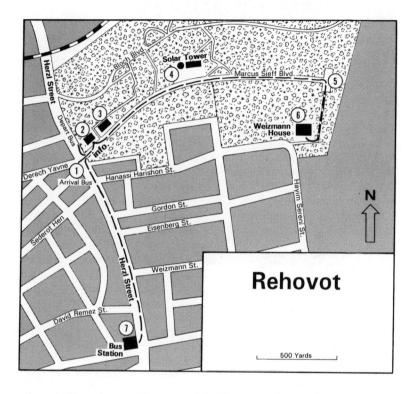

Rehovot

500 Yards

through Thursdays at 11 a.m. and 2:45 p.m., and on Fridays at 11 a.m. only.

Continue down Marcus Sieff Blvd. to the **Solar Tower** (4), a fantastic piece of architecture that's actually part of a nuclear particle accelerator. You can climb to the top of it, on Sundays through Fridays from 8 a.m. to 3:30 p.m., for a bird's-eye view of the campus.

The road leads straight ahead to the **Weizmann Memorial Plaza** (5) with its Holocaust Victims' Memorial sculpture. Turn right to the graves of Dr. Weizmann and his wife. Beyond this is the striking ***Weizmann House** (6), designed by the renowned architect Erich Mendelsohn, who had fled Nazi Germany for a career in Palestine and later the U.S.A. The house was built in 1937 on a lovely site chosen for its view of the Judean hills towards Jerusalem. Dr. Weizmann's presidential limousine, a Lincoln presented by Henry Ford II, may be seen outside. Don't miss taking a tour through the interior, given on Sundays through Thursdays from 10 a.m. to 3:30 p.m. For further information call (08) 48-33-28.

On the Weizmann Institute campus

Return to Herzl St., perhaps exploring other parts of the campus along the way. From here you can walk south for nearly a mile to the center of Rehovot, where there's a colorful produce market, several restaurants, and a **bus station** (7) from which you can get a ride back to Tel Aviv. The same bus can also be boarded at a stop just north of the main entrance to the Weizmann Institute.

Ashkelon

(Ashqelon, Askalon, Askelon)

There's an awful lot to see in Ashkelon; easily enough to keep you busy all day. Squatting next to the Mediterranean, this is among the oldest inhabited towns on Earth, and has plenty of ancient ruins to prove it. But that's not all. Within its widespread boundaries is a traditional Arab town, a prosperous modern community of today's Israel, a commercial center, a complete national park, and a leading seaside resort. The tour outlined here takes you to the best of the widely scattered sites and allows enough time to thoroughly enjoy both star attractions—the Old Town and the excavated site of Biblical Ashkelon.

Egyptian texts from around the 18th century B.C. mention Ashkelon as a Canaanite trading town, one of several along the coastal road linking Egypt with Syria. In the 12th century B.C. it was captured by the Philistines and became the most important of their five principalities. There are several Biblical references from this era, the most notable being David's lament over the death of King Saul—"Tell it not in Gath, publish it not in the streets of Askelon; lest the daughters of the Philistines rejoice; lest the daughters of the uncircumcised triumph" (2 Samuel 1:20). Changing hands several more times, Ashkelon flourished under Roman rule from the 1st century B.C. until the fall of the empire. According to tradition, Herod the Great was born here in 73 B.C. and later added considerably to the town's magnificence. During the 7th century A.D. Ashkelon fell to the Arabs, and then briefly to the Crusaders of the 12th century. The ancient town was finally destroyed forever by the Mamluks in 1270, although the Arab village of Migdal eventually developed on a site a little bit to the east.

GETTING THERE:

Buses (numbers 300 and 311) leave **Tel Aviv's** Central Bus Station frequently for the one-hour ride to Ashkelon, with returns until mid-evening. From **Jerusalem's** Central Bus Station there are hourly departures (bus number 437) for the 90-minute trip, with returns until early evening. Naturally, there is no service from mid-afternoon on Fridays until Saturday evenings, nor on some major Jewish holidays.

By car, Ashkelon is 39 miles southwest of **Tel Aviv** via Route 4. From **Jerusalem**, take Route 1 west, then Route 3 southwest, for a total distance of 45 miles. Use the car for getting to the sites; parking is usually easy.

GETTING AROUND:

Unless you have a car, you'll have to rely on local buses to reach the various sites, which are spread over a large area. Relevant bus stops are indicated on the map, and route numbers in the text. As in all Israeli towns, you pay the driver, who will also make change.

PRACTICALITIES:

Avoid visiting Ashkelon on Fridays, Saturdays, or on major Jewish holidays, when much of the town shuts down and transportation is difficult. Good weather is essential for this completely outdoor daytrip. The local **Government Tourist Information Office**, phone (051) 324-12, is in the Commercial Center of the Afridar district. Ashkelon has a **population** of about 62,000.

FOOD AND DRINK:

Some restaurant choices are:

Afridar Café (Zephaniah Sq., near the tourist office) Light meals and desserts in a pleasant setting. X: Fri., Sat. $

Nitzahon (30 Herzl St. in the Old Town, at Tzahal St.) Old-World Romanian cuisine for over 30 years, a local favorite. X: Fri. $

In addition, you'll find excellent *felafel* and other Middle Eastern street foods vended along the pedestrian shopping street in the Old Town of Migdal. There is a pub-restaurant as well as an outdoor café in the national park, and that old reliable standby, the Egged cafeteria at the bus terminal.

SUGGESTED TOUR:

From Ashkelon's **Central Bus Station** (1) on Ben-Gurion Blvd. you can either walk a little over a mile *or* take local bus number 4 or 5 to the Commercial Center (*Merkaz Afridar*) at the north end of HaNassi St. in Afridar. There you'll find the town's best source of current information and advice, the **Government Tourist Information Office** (2). Just across the square is the **Antiquities Courtyard** (3) where two magnificent Roman sarcophagi of the 3rd century A.D. are displayed under an open shelter. They were discovered nearby during digging operations in 1972. **Afridar** is an unusually pleasant neighborhood that serves as a model for some people's vision of Israel's future. It was founded in 1952 as an idealistic planned community by Jewish immigrants from South Africa, and retains much of that rather genteel atmosphere.

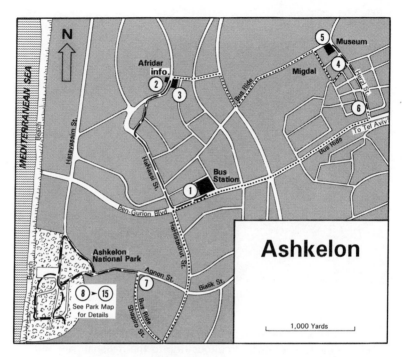

From the southeast corner of the same square you can take bus number 4, 5, or 7 to an entirely different kind of place, the old Arab town of **Migdal**. Then called *Majdal*, it was established in the early 19th century by Arab laborers brought here by the ruling Turks to work on the ultimately unsuccessful excavations led by Lady Stanhope, an English aristocrat who thought she knew where the treasures lay. In the war of 1948, most of the Arab residents were driven south to the nearby Gaza Strip, and the Old Town taken over by the victorious Israelis.

Get off the bus at the **stop** (4) near the upper end of Herzl St., the main shopping thoroughfare, and stroll north to the **Ashkelon Museum** (5), located in an old Arab caravanserai (*khan*) next to a mosque. The exhibits and audio-visual presentations here focus on the town's history from the Roman era until modern times. They may be seen on Sundays through Thursdays from 9 a.m. to 1 p.m. and 4–6 p.m., on Fridays from 9 a.m. to 1 p.m., and on Saturdays and holidays from 10 a.m. to 1 p.m.

Retrace your steps on Herzl St. and continue straight ahead to where it becomes a pedestrian shopping mall (*midrehov*). A colorful outdoor market is held here on Mondays, Wednesdays, and Thursdays; and there are always outdoor cafés, restaurants, *felafel* stands, and all manner of small shops to hold your interest.

The statue of Isis and Horus in the Roman Forum

At the bottom of Herzl St. (6), near the post office, you can board bus number 3 or 9 for a rather circuitous ride to the national park and its archaeological excavations. Get off at the **bus stop** (7) on Shapiro St. and walk west on Agnon St., which becomes a footpath, and into the park. *If you're coming by car, you'll have to use the north entrance, reached via Ben-Gurion Blvd.*

Enter the ***Ashkelon National Park** via the **Jaffa Gate** (8), where you can pick up a more detailed map and explanation of the site. The area of the ancient city enclosed by the great walls is about 600 *dunams* (150 acres) in size and opens directly to the sea along its western edge. Head south until you come to an intersection with an outdoor café. Just southwest of this is the site of the ***Roman Forum** (9), where various antiquities have been collected and are on display. At its southern end is a sunken area filled with interesting finds including a statue of the goddess Isis and her child-god Horus.

Continue down the road to the restored **Amphitheater** (10), which may have once been a well and behind which are remnants of the Crusader walls. Beyond the second parking lot is a cliff looking straight down on the **Crusader Harbor** (11) and a modern bathing site.

The path going past some current excavations brings you to the **Marine Stores** (12); digs below this have revealed remnants from the Persian period of 500 B.C. The trail leads down to the main parking lot,

where there's a restaurant and other facilities. The **Turkish Well** (13) near here has been partially restored; there's another one in even better shape behind the café. Follow the map to the ruined **Byzantine Church** (14) of about A.D. 400, which has four Roman columns and a frescoed apse. Those on foot can exit the park via the nearby **Jerusalem Gate** (15) and head directly back to the bus stop (7) on Shapiro St., where you can get a ride back to the Central Bus Station. The National Park, phone (051) 364-44, is open daily from 8 a.m. to 5 p.m., closing at 4 p.m. on Fridays.

Beersheba

(Be'ersheva, Be'er Sheva)

A trip to Beersheba is a must for anyone with a real interest in Biblical archaeology or the Bedouin way of life, although others may find it to be a day largely wasted on the edge of a wilderness. Truth to tell, this modern boom town in the desert resembles nothing so much as a prosperous suburb in the American southwest. Yet, the traditional Thursday morning Bedouin market is still a scene out of an Arabian movie, the Old Town still has the air of a turn-of-the-century Turkish village, and the magnificent digs at Tel Beer'Sheba, four miles to the northeast, reveal a civilization going back to the 12th century B.C. Exploring Beersheba is not easy, but with a little effort it can be a highly rewarding experience.

An ancient oasis in the desert and still something of a frontier town, Beersheba dates from the story of Abraham in the Book of Genesis, and in fact was inhabited by the first sheepherders as far back as 4000 B.C. Its name means "The Well of the Oath," referring to the patriarch Abraham's treaty with the king of the Philistines; "Thus they made a covenant at Beersheba: then Abimelech rose up, and Phichol the chief captain of his host, and they returned into the land of the Philistines" (Genesis 21:32).

Abraham's well remained an important source of water in the arid land, and it was here that his grandson Jacob received the vision to lead the Israelites into Egypt (Genesis 46:1-7). After the Exodus, Beersheba was given to the tribe of Simeon and became the southern boundary of the land of Israel, extending ". . . from Dan even to Beersheba . . ." (Judges 20:1, etc.). It never grew, however, to be anything more than a collection of wells where the nomad Bedouins watered their flocks.

Then, in 1900, the ruling Ottoman Empire built an administrative center here, soon linked by rail to the Sinai by the Germans. It was in Beersheba, during World War I, that Lawrence of Arabia was imprisoned and probably tortured by the Turks; shortly thereafter the town was liberated by Britain's General Allenby. Later falling into Egyptian hands, Beersheba was captured by Israel in October, 1948. Since then, it has grown from a dusty village of some 2,000 souls into today's urban sprawl, the fourth-largest city in the land.

The Negev Museum in the Old Town

Besides being a destination for daytrips from Tel Aviv or Jerusalem, Beersheba makes a fine stopover for travelers en route to Eilat, or a base for exploring the Negev desert.

GETTING THERE:

Buses (route 370) leave **Tel Aviv's** Central Bus Station frequently for the 80-minute ride to Beersheba, with returns until early evening. From **Jersusalem's** Central Bus Station, there are frequent departures (bus numbers 443, 445, and 446) for the one-hour ride, with return service until early evening. If you're on the way to **Eilat**, you can get there by bus numbers 393 or 394, a 3-hour ride departing hourly.

Cars are especially useful on this trip as they're an easy way to get to the digs. Beersheba lies some 70 miles south of **Tel Aviv** via routes 4, 41, and 40. From **Jerusalem**, it's 52 miles to the southwest going by way of Hebron on Route 60. This road, however, might be dangerous (depending on the current political situation) as it passes through the Occupied Territories of the West Bank. Cars with yellow Israeli license plates are often stoned. Play it safe and drive west on Route 1, southwest on 3, and south on 40 for a total distance of about 70 miles. **Eilat** lies about 150 miles to the south via routes 40 and 90.

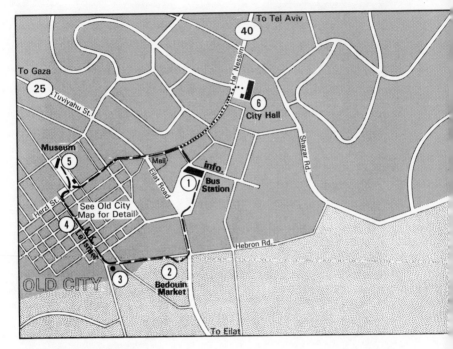

PRACTICALITIES:

An early start is necessary to really enjoy this trip. The weekly **Bedouin Market** is held on Thursdays from 6 a.m. to noon, with the most authentic action being in the earlier hours. The museums close early on Fridays and Saturdays, and public transportation comes to a halt from Friday afternoons until Saturday evenings. If you are visiting during the summer, or even spring or fall, be prepared for the desert. Wear a hat and sunglasses, use sun-block lotion, and drink plenty of liquids. The local **Government Tourist Information Office**, phone (057) 236-001, is on Nordau St. opposite the bus terminal. Beersheba has a population of nearly 130,000.

FOOD AND DRINK:

Some recommended restaurants are:

Papa Michel (95 Histadrut St., in the Old Town) Middle Eastern cuisine with a French touch. $$

Jade Palace (79 Histadrut St., corner of Yair St., in the Old Town) Good Chinese food in an attractive setting. $$

Bulgarian Restaurant (on K.K. L'Israel shopping street in the Old Town) Eastern European specialties. $

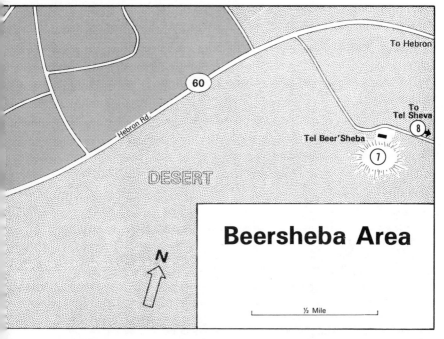

Beersheba Area

N

½ Mile

In addition, the Qanyon indoor shopping mall near the bus station has a lower-level food court with everything from burgers to Middle Eastern dishes. Alternatively, you could have a cheap and delicious lunch at one of the *felafel* and *shwarma* stands along the K.K. L'Israel shopping street in the Old Town, especially at the outdoor café at the corner of HeHalutz St.

SUGGESTED TOUR:

Follow the map from Beersheba's **Central Bus Station** (1) to the nearby ***Bedouin Market** (2), where the nomadic Bedouins come in from the desert to trade on Thursday mornings from 6 a.m. to noon. All manner of goods and foods are sold here, including what might be some good buys in Arab handicrafts such as beaten copperware, handwoven rugs, and embroidered bags. Should the urge strike, you can even purchase goats, sheep, and other livestock, but it's your problem getting them home. Be prepared to haggle over prices, beginning with less than you think the item is worth, and increasing slowly. Even if you don't come on a Thursday morning, you can still catch some of the flavor at the adjacent **Municipal Market** located under the arched rooftops. This *shuk*, or flea market, is open on all normal business days.

Continue down the road to **Abraham's Well** (3), a restored ancient well believed by some to be the very one dug by the patriarch himself. Although it's now surrounded by a tourist restaurant, you can go around the rear and enter the courtyard for a look. The historical marker sign dates it from at least the 12th century B.C., which may be correct, but most archaeologists now think that a similar well at Tel Beer'Sheba (visited later) is the actual one described in the Bible. In any case, this well is not very impressive in its present setting.

You are now entering the **Old City**, established in 1900 by the Turkish authorities as an administrative center for the Negev region. Before then, Beersheba was nothing but a watering spot for the nomadic Bedouins; all the rest of today's city dates from after the founding of the State of Israel in 1948. Stroll up the main shopping street, **Keren Kayemet Le'Israel** (4), usually referred to simply as "K.K.L.," passing numerous shops, restaurants, and cafés along the way. Some of the side streets around here are also worth exploring.

At the top, across Herzl St., is the **Allenby Garden**. First planted by the Turks in the early 1900s, it was later dedicated to General Sir Edmund Allenby, who liberated Beersheba and defeated the Ottoman forces throughout Palestine during World War I. Cross Ha'Atzma'ut St. to the **Negev Museum** (5), located in a former Turkish mosque built in 1906 and aligned to face Mecca. A visit here is recommended before making the trek out to Tel Beer'Sheba (7), as the displays here will help you to understand the digs at the actual site. Artifacts unearthed at the *tel* and exhibited here range in age from about 4000 B.C. to around A.D. 700, and include a reproduction of the great four-horned altar of the 9th century B.C. that suggests a non-conformist cult among the Israelites of the time. The original of this is in the Israel Museum in Jerusalem. Another treasure is the 6th-century Byzantine church mosaic with that archaeological rarity, an actual date (August 4, A.D. 576) inscribed in Greek letters. The museum, phone (057) 391-05, is open on Sundays, Mondays, Wednesdays, and Thursdays from 8 a.m. to 2 p.m., on Tuesdays and Fridays from 8 a.m. to 12:30 p.m., and on Saturdays from 10 a.m. to 1 p.m.

Facing the museum entrance is the **Governor's Residence** of 1906, which served as the city hall until recently. It now houses a small museum of contemporary art, with the same hours and admission as the Negev Museum.

Now follow the map out of the Old City, pass the Qanyon indoor shopping mall, and return to the Central Bus Station (1). Ask at the information counter there about service on bus route 55 to Tel Beer'Sheba, also called Tel Sheva. If you have a wait for the next bus, you might want to make a little side trip to the nearby **City Hall** (6), a handsome modern structure with a concrete tower that resembles a fist raised in determination.

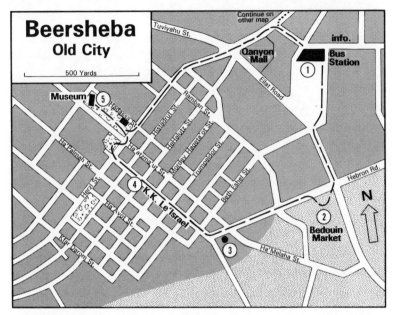

Unless you have a car, the only way to get to the archaeological digs at Tel Beer'Sheba is to take either a taxi or the none-too-frequent bus number 55. Make sure that the driver understands that you want the site, not the Bedouin village of the same name that's a half-mile farther down the road.

*Tel Beer'Sheba (7), four miles northeast of the modern city, is the site of the original town dating from the 12th century B.C. A small fort existed here in the time of King Saul (1023–1004 B.C.), over which a town was built by King David (1004–965 B.C.). Soon after that it was destroyed by fire, possibly resulting from an Egyptian invasion in 925 B.C. Although it rose again from the ashes and prospered, the town was totally devastated in the late 8th century B.C. by Sennacherib, King of Assyria, after which the survivors moved to where modern Beersheba now stands. The mound was used as a fortress by the Persians in the 4th century B.C., and again by the Romans during the 2nd and 3rd centuries A.D. Enter the excavations and explore the partially-restored ruins, including the 10th-century-B.C. **gate**, the 12th-century-B.C. **well** that might have been dug by Abraham, a group of **houses** of various ages, and the **Roman fort** of the 2nd century A.D. There is also the **"Man in the Desert" Museum of Bedouin Life**, a cafeteria, and a restaurant. The museum is open on Sundays through Thursdays from 10 a.m. to 5 p.m., and on Fridays and

Inside the Museum of Bedouin Life

Saturdays from 10 a.m. to 1 p.m.; while the entire complex is open daily from 9 a.m. to 5 p.m.

Before returning to modern Beersheba, you could take a 10-minute walk farther along the road to **Tel Sheva** (8), a contemporary village designed by an Arab architect and financed by the Israeli government in an attempt to lure the nomadic Bedouin into settling down. This was only partially successful, as you'll note by the surrounding tents and goat herds that are preferred by more traditional Bedouin. To get back to the Central Bus Station in Beersheba, you can board bus number 55 either at the bus stops in the village or outside the excavation.

Section III

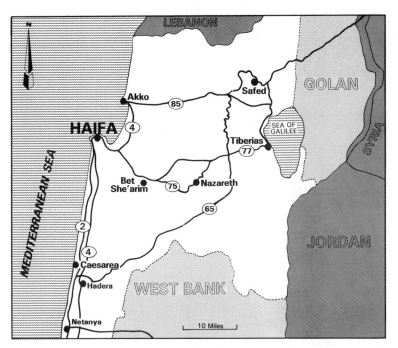

DAYTRIPS IN
NORTHERN ISRAEL
• from Haifa

Although it is perfectly possible to make daytrips into northern Israel from Jerusalem or Tel Aviv, especially by car, you'll find it much more comfortable to use Haifa as your base. Often overlooked by tourists, Israel's gorgeous port city is within easy striking distance of several of the country's most exciting destinations. It is the transportation hub of the entire north, and offers a superb selection of hotels, restaurants, and other guest facilities in all price ranges. Staying here for a few days will spare you hours of travel time, cost a bit less, and introduce you to a side of Israel that not every traveler sees.

*Haifa

(Hefa)

The City on the Hill

Tumbling down a mountainside and spilling into a beautiful bay, Haifa enjoys one of the Mediterranean's most spectacular settings. Yet, Israel's third-largest and most secular city is a treat that all too many travelers miss, or spend too little time exploring. Besides being a great base for daytrips to all of northern Israel, Haifa has plenty of attractions of its own, including the Baha'i Shrine, Elijah's Cave, the Carmelite Monastery, several good museums, and a superb zoo. But mostly it's the place itself, and the no-nonsense people who live and work there, that makes a stay so rewarding.

Although the site has been occupied since prehistoric times, Haifa itself is not mentioned in the Bible. Mount Carmel, on whose northern slope most of the city is built, is sacred to Jews, Christians, Moslems, and Druze alike as the place where the prophet Elijah triumphed over the priests of Ba'al during the 9th century B.C. Sacked by the Crusaders in the 12th century A.D., Haifa remained an insignificant village until the 19th century, when the coming of steamships made its large, deep harbor vital to the shipping trade. After rail links to Egypt and Damascus were established in the early 20th century, the city's economy really took off and has not stopped growing ever since. Haifa today is a bustling, blue-collar industrial city with two major universities and a strong base in the sciences and high-tech businesses; a place where Jews and Arabs manage to co-exist in peace; and surely one of the most enjoyable towns to visit in all of Israel.

As it ascends the mountainside from harbor to peak, the city is essentially divided into three tiers, or levels. At the bottom is the colorful port area, the oldest part of town. Above this is the Hadar HaCarmel district, usually just called "Hadar," a densely-populated middle-class community of busy shops, restaurants, and residences with a distinctly Eastern European air about it. The slopes now become quite steep as the roads twist their way up to Central Carmel, a prosperous area of contemporary life overlooking the whole scene. This is where most of the hotels are located, and where the walking tour starts. Fortunately, it's all downhill from here. The suggested route ends at Kikar Paris, where you can easily get a ride back up the hill, or continue on the next walking tour, whose description starts on page 154.

GETTING THERE:

Buses depart **Jerusalem's** Central Bus Station (routes 940, 966) frequently until early evening for the 2-hour ride to Haifa. From **Tel Aviv**, take bus number 900 or 901, a 75-minute ride that runs frequently until mid-evening from the Central Bus Station. There is no service from mid-afternoon on Fridays until Saturday evenings, nor on major Jewish holidays. It is best to purchase your ticket before boarding, and to wait in line at the posted departure platform, where the signs are in English on one side, Hebrew on the other.

Sherut Taxis operated by several different firms depart from various points in Jerusalem and Tel Aviv for Haifa. These shared vehicles, usually stretch Mercedes, have fixed fares that are roughly the same as buses, with higher fares on the Sabbath. Ask locally for current information.

Trains from Tel Aviv's Central Train Station run nearly hourly until early evening, with no service from early Friday afternoons until Sunday mornings. They arrive at Haifa's main station, behind its Central Bus Station. Trains are slower and cheaper than buses, offer good views, and have on-board snack bars.

By air, passengers arriving at Tel Aviv's Ben-Gurion Airport can travel by bus or sherut taxi straight to Haifa. Arkia Israeli Airlines flies directly from Haifa to Eilat, with special package deals available, and also to Jerusalem and Tel Aviv.

By car, Haifa is about 100 miles northwest of **Jerusalem** via Route 1 to Tel Aviv, then Route 2 north to Haifa. From **Tel Aviv**, it's about 60 miles north on Route 2. From **Eilat**, head north via Beersheba and Tel Aviv for about 280 miles.

GETTING AROUND:

You'll need to use public transportation to get back up the mountain to Central Carmel, as it's much too steep to walk. The options are:

Local buses operated by Egged which run from early morning until about midnight, with considerably reduced service from late Friday afternoon until Saturday evening and on major Jewish holidays. Signs at the bus stops have route numbers and destinations in both English and Hebrew. Tell the driver where you're going and he will sell you the correct ticket, which you keep until leaving the bus.

Carmelit Subway, the only one in Israel, is an underground funicular that links Kikar Paris (the end of this walk) with Central Carmel, with intermediate stops in Hadar. It does not run on the Sabbath. Built in 1959, it has been closed for renovations and should reopen sometime in 1993.

Taxis, usually called "Specials," can be hailed in the street or summoned by phone. Expect to pay extra on the Sabbath.

PRACTICALITIES:

This walk can be taken on any day, noting that a few of the minor sights may be closed on Fridays and/or Saturdays. Public transportation is limited from late Friday afternoons until Saturday evenings and on major Jewish holidays. The **Government Tourist Information Office**, phone (04) 66-65-21, is at 20 Herzl St. in Hadar, midway along the walk. There is also a **Municipal Information Office,** phone (04) 38-36-83, at 106 HaNassi Ave. in Central Carmel near the start of the walk, and another, phone (04) 66-30-56, at 23 HaNevi'im St., near Herzl St., in Hadar. Haifa has a **population** of about 250,000.

FOOD AND DRINK:

Some choice places to eat along or near the route of this walking tour are:

La Trattoria (119 HaNassi Ave. in Central Carmel) French and Italian cuisine, indoors or out. $$ and $$$

Abu Yousef (2 Kikar Paris, corner of Yafo St.) A well-known Arab restaurant with Middle Eastern dishes. $$

Prego (23 Nordau St., on the pedestrian mall in Hadar) An Italian pizzeria, café, and restaurant. $ and $$

Nargila (125 HaNassi Ave. in Central Carmel) Exciting Yemenite food, very popular with the young crowd. Both sidewalk tables and indoor dining room. Sign is in Hebrew only, but there's an English menu. $

Ha Tzimchonit (30 Herzl St., near the tourist office in Hadar) A traditional Jewish dairy restaurant with vegetarian and fish dishes. X: Fri. eve., Sat. $

Kapulsky (11 Nordau St., on the pedestrian mall in Hadar) Light meals at a European-style café, with outdoor tables. $

What some people regard as Israel's best *felafel* stands are spread around the corner of HaNevi'im and HeHalutz streets in the Hadar district, 3 blocks northwest of the tourist office.

SUGGESTED TOUR:

Begin your walk at the intersection of HaNassi Ave. and HaLevanon St. in Central Carmel, just a stone's throw from the major hotels and easily reached by bus or subway. HaNassi Ave. is a broad, elegant boulevard lined with parks, shops, outdoor cafés, and high-rise hotels. On the west

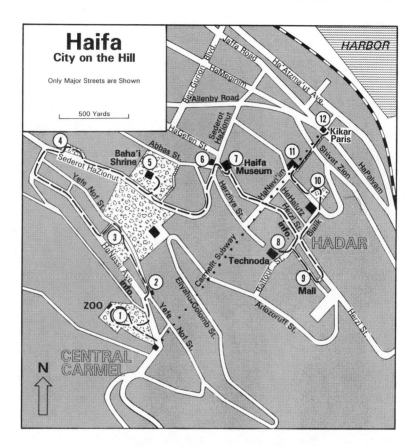

side of the intersection is **Gan Ha'em Park** (1), whose delightful ***Zoo** features animals native to Israel. Although it's not a large zoo, the layout is exceptionally attractive as it combines nature walks with lush botanical gardens and magnificent views down the far side of the mountain and across the Mediterranean. There's also an outdoor café and a small natural history museum. The zoo, phone (04) 37-70-19, is open on Sundays through Thursdays from 8 a.m. to 4 p.m. (6 p.m. in summer), on Fridays from 8 a.m. to 1 p.m., and on Saturdays from 9 a.m. to 4 p.m. (6 p.m. in summer). At its far end is the **Stekelis Museum of Prehistory**, where daily life along the slopes of the Carmel Range during the Stone Age is re-created in dramatic dioramas. Visits to the museum, phone (04) 37-18-33, may be made on Sundays through Thursdays from 8 a.m. to 2 p.m., and on Saturdays from 10 a.m. to 2 p.m. The museum is accessible only through the zoo. Allow at least an hour to visit both.

In the Sculpture Garden

Now follow HaNassi Ave. past the Municipal Information Office and turn right to the charming **Mané-Katz Museum** (2). This was the last home of the French-Jewish artist Mané-Katz, who was born in the Ukraine in 1894 and died in Tel Aviv in 1962. A follower of the Expressionist school, his work is often reminiscent of Marc Chagall's. Besides the paintings, the exhibits include the artist's collection of Judaica, Oriental rugs, and antiques. The whitewashed stucco home and studio, clinging to the side of Mount Carmel with a stunning view of the bay, is open on Sundays through Thursdays from 10 a.m. to 1 p.m. and 4–6 p.m., and on Fridays and Saturdays from 10 a.m. to 1 p.m. Winter hours are somewhat different; phone (04) 38-34-82 for current schedules.

Continue on Yefé Nof St. to the **Louis Promenade** (3), an elevated garden walk alongside the street, for the best possible *view of Haifa—whose bay is nearly a thousand feet below you. Off in the distance you can easily see the ancient port of Akko (Acre), described later in this book; and on a clear day even the border with Lebanon, some 20 miles to the north. Just behind the promenade is the **Tikotin Museum of Japanese Art**, which is closed at the time of writing but which may reopen in the near future.

Return to HaNassi Ave. and follow it downhill, turning sharply right onto Sederot HaZionut (Zionism Blvd.). Until 1975 this, like many main thoroughfares in Israel, was called United Nations Blvd. On November

The Baha'i Shrine and Gardens

10th of that year the U.N. General Assembly passed a motion equating Zionism with racism; immediately thereafter the street names were changed!

On the left is the entrance to the **Gan HaPesalim** (4), a lovely **sculpture garden** overlooking the city. Featuring 18 modern bronze statues by Ursula Malbin, it makes a great spot to relax before pressing on. Exit from the lower level onto the same street.

Continue downhill and turn left into Haifa's most famous attraction, the ***Baha'i Shrine and Gardens** (5). This is the center of the Baha'i faith, an independent religion that claims some four million adherents worldwide. Founded in the mid-19th century, it teaches that truth is progressive, never final; that God educates humans through a series of prophets which in the past has included Moses, Zoroaster, Buddha, Christ, Mohammed, and Baha'u'llah, the founder of the faith. Others will follow. The religion derives from the prophecies of Mirza Ali Mohammed of Shiraz, a Shi'ite Moslem from Persia who declared himself to be the *Báb*, or Gateway to God, in 1844. For this heresy he was executed in Tabriz, Iran, in 1850. One of his followers, Mirza Hussein Ali, took the title *Baha'u'llah* (Glory of God) as the long-awaited Messiah, and started the faith in 1863. He was promptly exiled to Constantinople and later to Akko, just north of Haifa, where he died in 1892 and where his shrine stands today.

The *Baha'i Shrine here in Haifa contains the remains of the Báb, which were smuggled out of Iran in 1909. Completed in 1953, the present superstructure over the grave combines European and Moorish architectural styles, and caps it all off with a golden dome that can be seen for miles around. The surrounding *Persian Gardens are an oasis of manicured tranquillity, a place of almost unworldly beauty that simply must be seen by every visitor to Haifa. Visits to the garden may be made daily from 8 a.m. to 5 p.m.; to the shrine daily from 9 a.m. to noon. There is no admission charge, and contributions are accepted only from members of the faith. You are requested to dress modestly, to remove your shoes before entering the shrine, and to refrain from smoking, eating, or photographing the interior. It should be noted that the many splendid ornamental decorations throughout the premises have no special religious significance, so don't try to figure out what they mean. For further information, call (04) 52-17-61.

Just across the street and a bit higher on the hillside stand the administrative buildings of the Baha'i faith, including the striking white marble, colonnaded Universal House of Justice. It faces the Shrine of the Baha'u'llah in Bahji, just north of Akko, across the bay. A committee of nine, elected every five years by secret ballot among the members of the National Spiritual Assemblies of the Baha'is throughout the world, meets here to coordinate all Baha'i activities. These buildings are not open to the public.

Stay on Sederot HaZionut (Zionism Blvd.) as it curves steeply downhill to the Artists' House (6), a gallery with changing exhibitions of contemporary Israeli art. Admission is free, and the house is open on Sundays through Thursdays from 9 a.m. to 1 p.m. and 4–7 p.m., and on Saturdays from 10 a.m. to 1 p.m.

Cross the street to the Haifa Museum (7), which combines the Museum of Ancient Art, the Museum of Modern Art, and the Museum of Music and Ethnology under one roof. The most interesting displays here are those of archaeological finds from Israel and the Mediterranean world, especially the mosaic floors from the digs at Tel Shikmona on the western side of Haifa. Musical instruments mentioned in the Bible, costumes from the Diaspora, and regional household utensils are among the sort of things you'll find in the changing exhibitions, along with art from the late 18th century to the present. The museum, phone (04) 52-32-55, is open on Sundays through Thursdays and Saturdays from 10 a.m. to 1 p.m., and on Tuesdays, Thursdays, and Saturdays also from 5–8 p.m.

Continue on Shabbetai Levy St. and into the heart of the Hadar district. The Government Tourist Information Office at 20 Herzl St. is open to assist you on Sundays through Thursdays from 8:30 a.m. to 5 p.m., and on Fridays from 8:30 a.m. to 2 p.m., but never on the Sabbath.

From here, you can make a little side trip by going uphill on Balfour St. for two blocks to the **National Museum of Science and Technology** (8), also known as the **Technoda**. This was the original home and campus of the Technion, Israel's foremost academy of technology, but most of the school has since moved to a new campus at Technion City, on the southeastern slopes of Mount Carmel. Children—and gadget-minded adults as well—will drool over the displays here, which are mostly interactive and allow you to have lots of hands-on fun while learning all about physics, mechanics, chemistry, mathematics, and related subjects. The instructions are in English as well as Hebrew. On the other hand, the museum is usually overrun with noisy kids and has all the charm of a run-down video arcade. If you're interested, it's open on Mondays, Wednesdays, and Thursdays from 9 a.m. to 5 p.m.; on Tuesdays from 9 a.m. to 7 p.m.; on Fridays from 9 a.m. to 1 p.m.; and on Saturdays from 10 a.m. to 2 p.m. Strangely, it's closed on Sundays. The phone number is (04) 67-13-72.

The nearby **Nordau Mall** (9) is a *midrehov*, or pedestrian shopping street lined with boutiques, outdoor cafés, restaurants, and art galleries. It's a wonderful place to sit down and just watch the street theater going on all around you.

Follow the map along Herzl and Bialik streets to City Hall and the **Gan HaZikaron** (10) Memorial Park across from it. From here you'll get superb close-up views of the port and lower town. Continue on to **Kikar Boneh** (11), a square fronting the modern HaNevi'im Tower Shopping Mall. Steps lead sharply downhill into the Old City, centered around **Kikar Paris** (12). This is the main square of the lower town, and the bottom terminus of the Carmelit Subway (temporarily closed for renovations), which returns you to the very beginning of this walk in minutes. Alternatively, you can get there via bus routes 3, 3a, 5, 22, or 092. The new office building to the right houses the local ticket office of El Al Israel Airlines. Kikar Paris is also the starting point for the other walking tour of Haifa, whose description begins on page 154.

Haifa
(Hefa)
Along the Bay

Although Haifa's most famous attractions are up on the hill, some of its more unusual sights lie scattered along the waterfront. This walk begins where the previous one left off, at Kikar Paris in the Old City. Until the late 19th century, maritime trade favored the ancient port of Akko (Acre) across the bay, but the development of steamships required a larger and deeper harbor. This was provided at Haifa by the construction of a jetty in 1898 and expanded shortly thereafter by rail lines to Damascus and then on to Egypt. The modern deep-water port was opened in 1931; following independence in 1948 this became Israel's sole shipping link to the outside world. Vast industrial development took place on the flat plains to the east of the port.

The walk described here is mercifully level all the way, except for a possible side trip to the Carmelite Monastery. Frequent buses operate along the entire route, so if you get tired you can always get a ride back. In addition to the historic port and some colorful old neighborhoods, the tour features two first-rate museums as well as religious sites associated with the prophet Elijah.

GETTING THERE:
Take a bus, taxi, or the Carmelit Subway to Kikar Paris in the Old City near the port, where the previous tour ended.

GETTING AROUND:
See this entry for the previous trip on page 147.

PRACTICALITIES:
Several of the sights close at 1 p.m. on Fridays and are closed all day on Saturdays. Return transportation will be difficult on the Sabbath or on major Jewish holidays. If you plan to visit the Railway Museum, note that it is closed on Mondays, Wednesdays, Fridays, and Saturdays. The Dagon Silo Museum tour is at 10:30 a.m. daily except Saturdays, unless other arrangements are made in advance. There is a **Tourist Information Office** in the Central Bus Station in addition to the ones listed on page 148.

FOOD AND DRINK:

Some good restaurants in this part of Haifa are:

Shmulik and Dany (7 HaBankim St. at Yafo Rd., 4 blocks northwest of Kikar Paris) Real kosher cooking. X: Sat. $$

Allenby (43 Allenby Rd., near HaZionut St. in the Arab quarter) A simple place for superb Middle Eastern cuisine. $$

Pagoda (1 Bat Gallim Ave., 5 blocks northwest of the bus station) Szechuan and Cantonese cuisine. $$

Misadag (29 Margolin St., 5 blocks northwest of the bus station) A famous seafood restaurant overlooking the sea. $$

In addition, there are some wonderful *felafel* and *shwarma* stands with indoor dining along Yafo (Jaffa) Rd., just west of the bus station. The Egged Cafeteria in the bus station offers decent food at low prices.

SUGGESTED TOUR:

Begin your walk at **Kikar Paris** (1), a square named in honor of the French firm that built the **Carmelit Subway** in 1959. By the time you read this, Haifa's unusual underground funicular should be back in operation after a lengthy renovation. It climbs over 900 feet during the 7-minute ride from here up to Central Carmel, making five stops along the way.

If you are really nutty about trains, you should follow the map east past the El Al ticket office and Kikar Feisal to the East Railway Station, site of the **Railway Museum** (2). Those not afflicted with railfan fever would do better to head directly to the next attraction instead, and save a lot of walking. This is definitely not one of the world's major rail museums, but the fact that Israel has even a little one is rather amazing. At one time you could travel by train from here to Beirut, Cairo, Amman, or Damascus. Today you are limited to a few closer destinations such as Nahariya, Akko, Tel Aviv, and (awkwardly) Jerusalem. The building complex dates from Ottoman times, as the Turkish plaque near the entrance attests. Inside, you'll find several diesel locomotives, freight cars, an 1893 Egyptian coach, and a magnificent 1922 British private car used by the Palestine Railway to transport the governor and other dignitaries in style. The latter may be boarded. There is also a collection of artifacts, photos, timetables, and tickets dating from as far back as the 1880s. The museum has rather limited hours, being open on Sundays, Tuesdays, and Thursdays from 9 a.m. to noon only. For further information phone (04) 56-42-93. From here, you can avoid the long walk back by taking bus number 17, 42, or 193 to the next destination at Kikar Khayar.

However you get there, the lively commercial area along Ha'Atzma'ut Ave. near Kikar Khayar is lined with interesting buildings from an earlier era. This was once the waterfront, so the structures on the south side often predate the construction of the port, while those on the north are

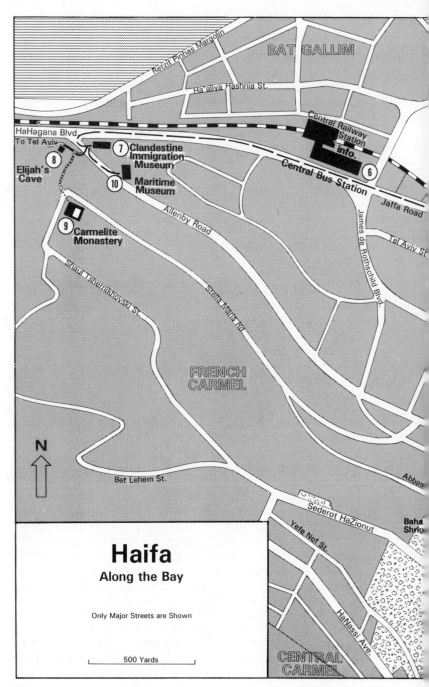

BAT GALLIM

Retzit Pinhas Margolin

Ha'aliya Hashnia St.

Central Railway Station

info.

HaHagana Blvd
To Tel Aviv

⑧ Elijah's Cave

⑦ Clandestine Immigration Museum

Central Bus Station ⑥

⑩ Maritime Museum

Jaffa Road

⑨ Carmelite Monastery

Allenby Road

James de Rothschild Blvd

Tel Aviv St

Shaul Tshernikhovski St.

Stella Maris Rd

FRENCH CARMEL

N

Bet Lehem St.

Abbas

Sederot HaZionut

Baha Shrin

Yefe Nof St.

Haifa
Along the Bay

Only Major Streets are Shown

500 Yards

HaNassi Ave.

CENTRAL CARMEL

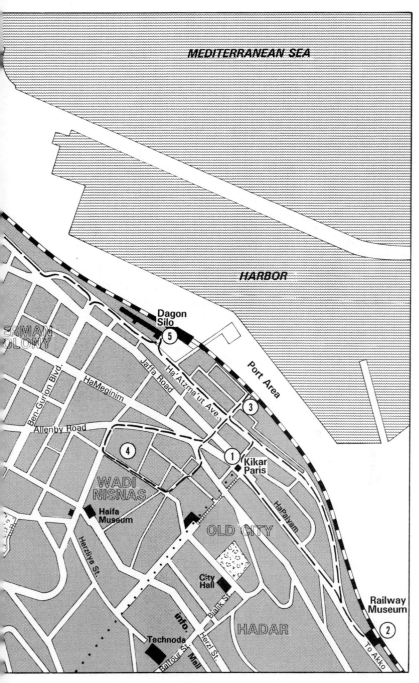

MEDITERRANEAN SEA

HARBOR

Dagon
Silo

Port Area

GERMAN
COLONY

Ben-Gurion Blvd.

HaMeginim

Jaffa Road

Ha'Atzma'ut Ave.

Allenby Road

Kikar
Paris

WADI
NISNAS

Haifa
Museum

Herzilya St.

HaPalyam

OLD CITY

City
Hall

Blank St.

info.

Technoda

Balfour St. Mall

Herzl St.

HADAR

Railway
Museum

To Akko

157

on landfill that resulted from the dredging. While not very elegant, these streets teem with an intense vitality as merchants hawk their wares. Turn right to **Sha'ar Palmer** (Palmer Gate) (3), the main passenger entrance to the port area. Around you are bars and other entertainment spots catering to sailors, including the U.S. Sixth Fleet when they're in port. You may be able to get into the dock area itself by showing your passport at the gate; this of course depends on the current security situation.

From here, you can make an interesting **side trip** by going slightly uphill into **Wadi Nisnas** (4), a colorful old Arab neighborhood whose sights, sounds, and smells will remind you that this is the Middle East, not Europe. There are some wonderful little restaurants around here that specialize in the foods of Lebanon, Egypt, Syria, and other Arab lands. Unlike some other parts of Israel, Arabs and Jews get along quite fine in Haifa.

Other than the Baha'i Shrine, Haifa's most prominent landmark is undoubtedly the **Dagon Silo** (5), a huge concrete edifice that stores most of Israel's grain. Now, you might not think of a silo as being a tourist attraction or a piece of great architecture, but this one is both. Vaguely resembling a modern version of a Crusader fortress, it houses a fascinating little **museum** on the history of grain cultivation, handling, storage, and distribution from the Neolithic era to the present. There is also a collection of archaeological artifacts including some stale grains of wheat that are about 4,000 years old, Egyptian art depicting grain cultivation, and beer containers from the Early Iron Age. Visits are by free guided tours only, which are held on Sundays through Fridays at 10:30 a.m. Appointments for other times may be made by phoning (04) 66-42-21. Enter through the small administration building facing Plumer Square.

Just beyond the silo, Ben-Gurion Blvd. heads straight up through the old **German Colony**, a neighborhood of attractive houses built by Christian German Templars in the late 19th century. The group survived until World War II, when they were forcibly removed. Many of them are buried in the small graveyard on Yafo Rd., next to the British Military Cemetery from World War I, between the row of enticing *felafel* stands and the bus station.

Take a look up Ben-Gurion Blvd. for a good view of the Baha'i Shrine (see page 151), then continue on Yafo (Jaffa) Rd. to the **Central Bus Station** (6). This amazingly well-designed terminal has a tourist information office on its lower level, numerous shops, and inexpensive snack bars. You can get a bus from here to anywhere in Haifa, or to just about anywhere in Israel. Long-distance departures are from the lower level, arrivals are on the upper level, and all local buses use the middle level. The Central Railway Station, just behind the bus terminal, can be reached via a tunnel next to bus platform 34 on the lower level.

Follow HaHagana Blvd. west to the ***Clandestine Immigration and**

The Dagon Silo

Naval Museum (7), which in the most compelling terms chronicles the smuggling of Jewish refugees into Palestine from 1934 until the establishment of the State of Israel in 1948. The museum is built around an actual ship, the *Af-al-pi-chen*, in whose cramped hold some 434 survivors of the Holocaust crossed the Mediterranean and where an audio-visual show now relates their ordeal. You can climb all over this boat, then visit the rest of the museum, which is mostly devoted to the Israeli Navy and includes a collection of naval guns on the outdoor terraces. A visit here is a moving experience that can be made on Sundays through Thursdays from 8:30 a.m. to 3 p.m., and on Fridays from 8:30 a.m. to 1 p.m. On Sundays and Tuesdays it remains open until 4 p.m. For further information phone (04) 53-62-49.

A flight of steps just across Allenby Rd. leads up to **Elijah's Cave** (8), a holy place for Jews, Christians, Muslims, and Druze alike. Tradition holds that this is where the prophet Elijah rested before (or after?) his encounter with the false priests of Ba'al (I Kings 18: 17–46) in the 9th century B.C. Many Christians also believe that the Holy Family stayed here on their return from Egypt. Visits may be made on Sundays through Thursdays from 8 a.m. to 5 p.m., and on Fridays from 8 a.m. to 1 p.m.; entry is free.

If you have lots of energy left, an interest in the story of Elijah, and don't mind climbing a rough trail, you can make a short-but-steep **side trip** up, up, up to the **Carmelite Monastery** (9). Built in 1836 over another cave in which the prophet Elijah is thought to have lived, the present monastery replaces predecessors dating from Crusader times on, each destroyed by Moslems. One of these was used by Napoleon during his unsuccessful 1799 campaign at Akko as a hospital for wounded soldiers, who were brutally massacred by the Turks after his retreat. Step into the chapel to view paintings and stained-glass windows depicting Elijah in his chariot of fire, King David and his harp, the Holy Family, and other Biblical figures. There is also a small statue of the Virgin Mary as Our Lady of Mount Carmel, with a porcelain head made in Genoa in 1820 and a cedar body from a century later. Some ruins from the previous structures are displayed in the adjacent museum. The monastery, phone (04) 52-34-60, is open daily from 6 a.m. to 1:30 p.m. and 3–6 p.m. Admission is free, but dress modestly—no shorts or bare shoulders.

Continuing up Allenby Rd., you'll soon come to the **National Maritime Museum** (10), an unusually good collection of seafaring artifacts. Over 5,000 years of maritime history, mostly in the eastern Mediterranean, is celebrated through rich archaeological finds, boat models, charts, maps, and navigational instruments from the earliest times to the present. Among its treasures is a bronze ram from an ancient warship found off a nearby coast. If you love the sea, you'll enjoy this museum, which is open on Sundays through Thursdays from 10 a.m. to 4 p.m., and on Saturdays from 10 a.m. to 1 p.m. Buses back to the town center leave from across the street.

*Akko

(Acco, Acre)

Directly across the bay from Haifa lies the ancient port of Akko, historically known as Acre and today one of Israel's most delightful attractions. Its existence is documented in Egyptian texts going back as far as the 19th century B.C. Among the earliest seaports of the Mediterranean world, Akko's protected harbor remained commercially viable until modern times, when ships of larger draft began using the deeper waters of Haifa as their anchorage.

Throughout its long history, Akko has been conquered and reconquered by many diverse peoples including the Canaanites, Egyptians, Phoenicians, Israelites, Persians, Greeks, Syrians, and Romans. Its greatest era was during the 12th and 13th centuries A.D. when, under the name St.-Jean-d'Acre, it at first became the main port for the Crusaders and later the capital of their Latin Kingdom. At the height of its prosperity it was visited by the likes of St. Francis of Assisi, Marco Polo, the Holy Roman Emperor Frederick II, and the French King Louis IX (St. Louis); as well as by innumerable traders and merchants. Then, in 1291, the revenging Mamluks of Egypt attacked and Akko was utterly destroyed in a bloody siege as its population fled to Cyprus.

For the next 450 years the port lay in a state of virtual ruin, until a Bedouin leader had it rebuilt as part of his independent fiefdom. From 1775 until 1804 it was ruled for the Ottoman Empire by a fascinating Albanian adventurer named Ahmed Pasha, better known as el-Jazzar ("The Butcher") for his unconventional methods of dealing with people he didn't like. With help from the British fleet, Ahmed handily defeated Napoleon in his invasion of 1799, safely securing the port for Turkey, in whose hands it remained until the British took over in 1918. During the Mandate period Akko's Citadel was used as a British prison for captured members of the Jewish underground, several of whom were hanged there. The port fell to Israeli forces almost immediately after the State of Israel was created in 1948.

Akko is really two cities; one modern, the other ancient. The new part of town, where the bus and train stations are located, is prosperous, clean, Jewish, and unfortunately dull. What you want to see is the colorful Old City, still inhabited by Arabs and surrounded by fortifications and the sea. This is the perfect place for a walking tour as it's almost impossible to drive through the narrow, twisted alleyways. You'll undoubtedly get lost, but that's part of the fun. While a few corners of the town do cater to tourists, for the most part this is a great place to experience a genuine Middle Eastern atmosphere.

GETTING THERE:

Buses (routes 271 or 272) leave Haifa's Central Bus Station frequently for the half-hour ride to Akko (Acre), with reduced service on the Sabbath.

Trains leave Haifa's Central Train Station (behind the bus station, use the tunnel next to bus platform 34) every hour or so for the 45-minute run to Akko. There is no service from early Friday afternoons until Sunday mornings. Trains are cheaper and more comfortable than buses.

By car, Akko is 15 miles northeast of Haifa via Route 4. There is a large parking lot on Weizmann St., just inside the walls of the Old City.

PRACTICALITIES:

Most of Akko's sights are open daily, but note that some close early on Fridays. You'll need to follow the twists and turns of the map carefully as very few streets in the Old City have names. The **Municipal Tourist Information Office**, phone (04) 91-02-51, is on El-Jazzar St. opposite the mosque. If it's closed, ask at the adjacent entrance to the Subterranean Crusader City. Akko has a **population** of about 40,000.

FOOD AND DRINK:

Some recommended dining spots in the Old City are:

Abu Christo (at the south end of the fishermen's harbor) Seafood and grilled meats overlooking the harbor. Everyone eats here. $$

Ouda Brothers (Khan-el-Faranj, near the City Market) A popular Middle-Eastern restaurant with grilled meats, seafood, and salads. $$

Monte Carlo (Salah-a-Din St., just east of El-Jazzar Mosque) A favorite for Middle-Eastern and Continental cuisine. $$

In addition, there are several inexpensive *felafel* and *shwarma* stands near the El-Jazzar Mosque, some with outdoor tables. In the modern city, you'll find plenty of snack shops and pizza parlors along Weizmann and Ben-Ammi streets. Finally, there's always the reliable Egged Cafeteria at the bus station.

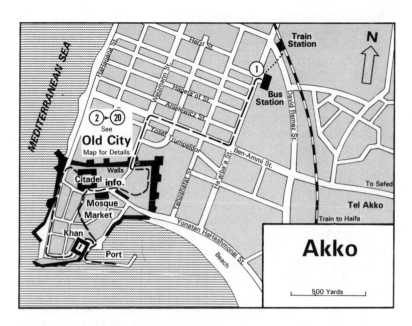

SUGGESTED TOUR:

Whether you've come by bus or train, you'll probably want to take a **local bus** from Platform 16 of the **Akko Bus Station** (1) to the outer walls of the Old City along Weizmann St. Otherwise, it's a boring one-mile trek. Those coming by car can park at a lot just inside the walls.

Once inside the outer walls, turn left and climb the steps up to the **Land Wall Promenade** (2) atop Ahmed el-Jazzar's sturdy 18th-century fortifications. From here you'll enjoy superb **views** of Haifa Bay and, a mile to the east, of the original site of the ancient town at Tel Akko, also known as Napoleon's Hill as this is where that warrior almost met his Waterloo in 1799. The **Burj-el-Kummander** fortress in the northeast corner is built on the foundations of the medieval tower on which King Richard I ("Lionheart") ordered the Duke of Austria's banner to be lowered in 1191, setting off a chain of events that included Richard's imprisonment at Dürnstein on the Danube and his nasty brother John's premature grab at the throne of England, thwarted in legend by the intervention of one Robin Hood. As you can see, there's a lot of history in these stones.

Descend the massive staircase leading into a park and follow the map past the 18th-century **Souk el-Abyad** (3), an old Turkish covered market that's still active today. At its far end is the impressive ***El-Jazzar Mosque** (4), built in 1781 on what were probably the ruins of a Crusader cathedral.

This is surely one of the finest mosques in Israel, as its benefactor had a lot of sins to atone for. Ahmed Pasha el-Jazzar, affectionately known as "The Butcher," was an 18th-century Ottoman governor who apparently enjoyed strangling his wives, mutilating disobedient servants, and having enemies buried alive. He also gave Akko its very best architecture.

Step into the spacious **courtyard**, which is lined on three sides with ancient columns taken from the ruins of Caesarea (see page 194) and Tyre. The small domed structure near the minaret contains the **tombs** of el-Jazzar and his adopted son, Suleiman Pasha, who succeeded him. As the entire complex sits on top of the ruined Crusader city, there are interesting things to see underground on a tour of the cisterns. Before entering the mosque itself, the faithful stop at the lovely octagonal **fountain** for a ritual washing of the feet. You may enter at any time that prayers are not going on, and should remove your shoes if you're going beyond the vestibule. The simple-but-elegant **interior** is beautifully carpeted with Persian rugs and decorated with inlaid designs and Arabic texts. The *Mihrab*, or prayer niche, faces south towards Mecca. Upstairs, in the women's gallery, is a green cage containing a hair from the beard of the prophet Muhammad, shown to the public only on the 27th day of Ramadan. The El-Jazzar Mosque is open daily from 8:30 a.m. to 5 p.m. except during prayers, and a small admission is charged. Modest dress is required. Self-appointed guides will probably offer to show you around for a few shekels; if you accept, be sure to settle on the price first to avoid a scene later.

After the great Crusader city of St.-Jean-d'Acre was destroyed by the Mamluks in 1231, its magnificent Gothic structures were buried in rubble to prevent their ever being used again. The street level rose to as high as 25 feet above the previous level, and new buildings were eventually erected on top of the old; whose existence was in time largely forgotten. Then, in the 1950s, excavations began to unearth the past.

Enter the spooky ***Subterranean Crusader City** (5) through the gate of a 19th-century Turkish building, directly across from the mosque and to the left of the tourist information office. Above you and to the north looms Ahmed el-Jazzar's massive 18th-century Citadel, which you'll be visiting later on this walk. For the moment, however, the tour explores what lies below parts of both the castle and the Old City. Excavations to date have uncovered only a small portion of the Crusader City, as further digs might cause the Arab town above it to collapse. Still, there's a lot to see here.

In the **first room** (6) beyond the entrance hall you'll notice a mixture of architectural styles; Crusader Gothic at the bottom and Turkish at the top. There are traces of a **wine press** here, used secretly by thirsty Turks, whose Moslem faith forbids alcoholic beverages! Adjacent to this is a **courtyard** (7) from which you can see the mighty Citadel towering some

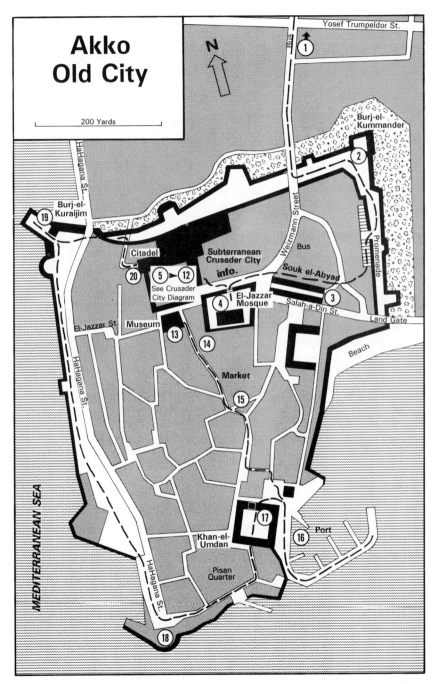

Akko
Old City

200 Yards

MEDITERRANEAN SEA

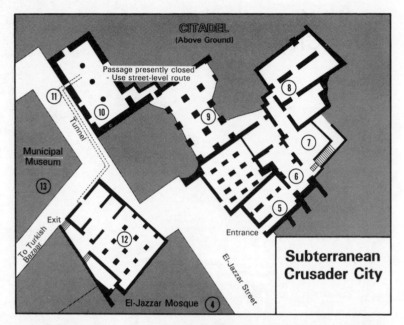

CITADEL
(Above Ground)

Passage presently closed - Use street-level route

⑪ ⑩

Tunnel

⑧

⑨

Municipal Museum

⑬

Exit

To Turkish Bazaar

⑫

Entrance

El-Jazzar Street

⑦

⑥

⑤

Subterranean Crusader City

El-Jazzar Mosque ④

120 feet above you. A monumental **Turkish gate**, from which (according to legend) their prisoners were once hanged, leads into the wonderfully-preserved 12th-century ***Knights' Halls** (8). Although only three of these have been opened, there are actually seven—corresponding to the nations represented by the Knights Hospitallers: England, France, Auvergne, Provence, Germany, Italy, and Spain. The first hall contains modern sculpture on a Crusader theme, while another is used for occasional chamber music concerts. Between them is a hall whose ceiling bears a patch of modern concrete, the result of a failed jailbreak in 1947. Captured members of the Jewish underground were being held by the British in the Citadel above; when their secret tunnel led only to this then-rubble-filled chamber they returned to their cells and plotted another escape that did succeed.

Continue into the **Grand Maneir** (9), a huge, partially-excavated chamber that was probably used as an administrative center. From here, a narrow passage leads down to the so-called ***Crypt** (10), which was actually a large dining room, or refectory, for the Knights of St. John. Marco Polo, who stopped by on his way to China in 1271, was almost certainly one of the guests honored here. Construction on the room began in the Romanesque style, but evolved into the earliest form of Gothic after a visit by Louis VII of France in 1148, attested to by the *fleur-de-lis* pattern engraved on some of the stones.

A staircase next to the last column in the crypt takes you down into a claustrophobic **tunnel** (11) that may have once been a pre-Crusader sewer. It goes under a street and then up a flight of steps into what was most likely the medieval knights' hospital, now known as **Al-Bosta** (12), or The Post. From here you leave the world of the Crusaders and exit into a narrow street. The Crusader City complex, phone (04) 91-38-34, is open on Saturdays through Thursdays from 8:30 a.m. to 4:45 p.m., and on Fridays from 8:30 a.m. to 1:45 p.m. Its ticket also admits you to the next attraction.

Step across the street to the **Municipal Museum** (13), located in Ahmed el-Jazzar's very own Turkish bathhouse (*hammam*) of 1780. This temple of cleanliness continued to operate until 1947, after which it was converted into a museum. The whole rich history of Akko is on display here, mostly in the form of artifacts from local digs. There are also displays relating to local folklore and Islamic culture. The museum is open at the same time as the Crusader City, and the same ticket applies.

Now follow the map through the **Turkish Bazaar** (14) and thread your way into the **City Market** (15), or *souk*. Although more than a few tourists find their way here, the trading is almost entirely among Arabs and the atmosphere completely genuine. You'll surely get lost in the maze of tiny passageways, but the water is always nearby, and that brings you to the ***Fishing Port** (16). This colorful spot is all that's left of the ancient harbor,

The Fishing Port

In the Khan el-Umdan

once the only protected port along the Palestinian coast. In those days, the breakwater extended all the way to the Tower of the Flies, still partially visible in the bay, while another one reached out from what is now the eastern beach. During the 12th century as many as 80 seagoing ships could safely anchor in the calm waters of the harbor. Today, the modern marina is used only by small fishing craft and pleasure boats, some of which offer rides around the harbor. If you take one of these short excursions, be sure to settle on a fair price first, lest you be fleeced.

Near the small mosque by the harbor stands the most magnificent of Akko's many *khans*, or caravanserais; a kind of Middle Eastern inn that once accommodated camel caravans. Overlooked by its Ottoman clock tower of 1906, the **Khan el-Umdan** (17) was built in 1785 on the site of the Crusaders' Dominican monastery by none other than Ahmed el-Jazzar. Its courtyard is surrounded by a two-storied structure with columns looted from Caesarea. Animals were housed on the ground floor while people slept upstairs. They may do that again, as there are plans afoot to turn the old *khan* into a tourist hotel. In the meantime, it is often possible to climb the clock tower for a fabulous close-up view of the harbor. Ask at the tourist office about this.

Continue south into the Pisan quarter, a venerable neighborhood where traces of Crusader structures are still visible. What remains of one of their early churches now serves as a foundation for St. John's Church, built in 1737 near the **Lighthouse** (18) and the youth hostel. Just beyond this is a great breach in the seawall, caused by an earthquake in 1837.

Amble north along the walls, which can be climbed in places for nice panoramic views, despite the signs reading: "Walking on the walls is dangeres end forbidden end it is on your own responsibility." The **Burj el-Kuraijim** (19) is a Turkish bastion that guards the northwest corner of the Old City from sea attacks. For some reason it is often called the "English Fort," perhaps because it is built on Crusader foundations.

Now carefully follow the map into the ***Citadel** (20), which sits on top of the Subterranean Crusader City. Another imposing 18th-century structure erected by Ahmed el-Jazzar, this is where the ruler lived and kept both his loot and his prisoners, including the founder of the Baha'i faith, Baha'u'llah (see page 151). From 1918 until 1948 the fortress served as the main British prison in Palestine, a place where captured members of the Jewish underground were incarcerated and sometimes executed. Their story is told in the dramatic **Museum of Heroism** that occupies much of the fortified complex, with an emphasis on the mass escape of 1947. Be sure to enter the horrifying **Gallows Chamber** that claimed the lives of eight Jewish political prisoners hanged by the British between 1938 and 1947. The noose is still in place; the trapdoor open. Visits to the museum, phone (04) 91-39-00, may be made on Sundays through Thursdays from 9 a.m. to 5 p.m., on Fridays from 9 a.m. to noon, and on Saturdays from 9:30 a.m. to 5 p.m.

From here you can either follow the northern wall back into the New City, or walk along El-Jazzar St. to the area of the El-Jazzar Mosque, where you'll find a local bus stop near the parking lot.

Bet She'arim

(Beth Shearim, Beit Shearim)

Amateur archaeologists and students of Jewish history will surely appreciate this short excursion into the long-buried past, although others may not find it to be all that stimulating. Practically forgotten for over 1,500 years, Bet She'arim was once the spiritual center of the Jewish world. In A.D. 352 it was destroyed by the Romans and not rediscovered until the late 19th century. Excavations from 1936 to 1940 and 1953 to 1957 have so far revealed the remains of an impressive town, and a major necropolis consisting of a fantastic series of catacombs.

After the failure of the First Revolt in A.D. 70, this northwest corner of the Jezreel Valley fell under Roman control. The recognized leader of the Jewish people during the 2nd century A.D. was Rabbi Judah HaNassi, who moved his Sanhedrin, or Supreme Rabbinical Council, here when the emperor Marcus Aurelius presumably offered him the land. It was also at Bet She'arim that HaNassi compiled the Mishnah, the first written record of the Oral Law that forms much of the Talmud. In A.D. 220 he was buried here in his family tomb.

For centuries, Jews preferred to be interred on Jerusalem's Mount of Olives, where the Messiah was expected to appear. When this became impossible after the Jews were expelled from the city, many of them followed the revered Rabbi HaNassi's lead and chose Bet She'arim as an alternative place of burial. This created a vast necropolis, a veritable city of the dead populated by Jews from all over the Holy Land and far beyond, and supported a thriving industry of stonecutters and sculptors. Then, in A.D. 352, it all came to an end as the Romans burned the town, which was eventually covered by earth and forgotten.

A visit to Bet She'arim makes a good half-day trip that can easily be combined with one to nearby Nazareth (see page 174) if you get off to an early enough start. Both places are on the same bus route. Unless you have a car, however, there will be a few miles of walking involved.

Entrance to a catacomb

GETTING THERE:

Buses leave Haifa's Central Bus Station frequently for the half-hour ride to Kiryat Tiv'on (Qiryat Tiv'on). Take bus number 75, 301, or 338. Get off at the second stop in the village, and follow signs to Bet She'arim on foot over local roads, about a mile or so to the south. There is no bus service from Friday afternoons until Saturday evenings, or on major Jewish holidays.

By car, Bet She'arim is 12 miles southeast of Haifa. Take Route 75 (in the direction of Nazareth) as far as Kiryat Tiv'on (Qiryat Tiv'on), then follow signs over local roads to the right.

PRACTICALITIES:

The site is open on Sundays through Thursdays from 8 a.m. to 6 p.m., on Fridays from 8 a.m. to 1 p.m., and on Saturdays from 8 a.m. to 4 p.m. Phone (04) 83-16-43 for current information.

FOOD AND DRINK:

You won't really need lunch on this short trip, but if you do get hungry there is a café by the parking lot that opens during the tourist season. This is also a nice place for a picnic. In addition, there are a few simple restaurants not far from the bus stop in Kiryat Tiv'on.

SUGGESTED TOUR:

From the **bus stop** (1) at Kiryat Tiv'on it's a walk of a bit over a mile following signs to the Bet She'arim National Park site and the necropolis. Shortly before entering the park, you'll come to excavated remnants of the ancient town itself, destroyed by the Romans in A.D. 352. On your left is the ruined **Synagogue** (2) that probably dates from the 2nd century A.D., and was at that time among the largest in the land. Archaeologists date the destruction of Bet She'arim on the basis of some 1,200 4th-century coins, none of which were minted later than A.D. 351, found in the two-story building between the synagogue and the road.

Continue on to the nearby ruins of a 4th-century **Olive Press** (3), where oil was extracted by crushing baskets of olives onto a circular grooved stone, from which it flowed into a basin cut in the rock floor. From here you can climb slightly uphill to the late-2nd-century **Basilica** (4), whose name is used in the Roman sense of the word, meaning a place of public assembly rather than a church. Two rows of columns divide the simple rectangle, with a raised platform opening onto a court at the far end.

Follow the road around a bend to the right and enter the **Bet She'arim National Park**, paying a small admission at the **kiosk** (5). This is where most of the necropolis is situated. So far, some 31 catacombs have been discovered; eerie caves dug into the soft limestone of the hills and filled with now-empty stone sarcophagi. **Catacombs 12 and 13** (6) catered to different degrees of wealth and social class, the first being spacious and elegant while in the second the bodies were almost crammed in.

Catacomb 14 (7), with its unfinished entrance, is probably the family tomb of Rabbi Judah HaNassi himself, although the inscriptions refer only to his sons Simeon and Gamliel. One of the earliest burial places was **Catacomb 20** (8), a rambling, disorganized series of spooky tunnels and chambers lined with sarcophagi. There is a small **museum** here with explanatory notes in English and an ancient relief of a *menora* that almost looks contemporary.

Close to the catacombs is a parking lot, **snack bar** (9), and rest rooms. On the way back to the bus, you might want to visit the **Statue of Alexander Zaid** (10), who guarded this site for many years and served as a mediator between Arabs and Jews until being killed in the riots of 1938.

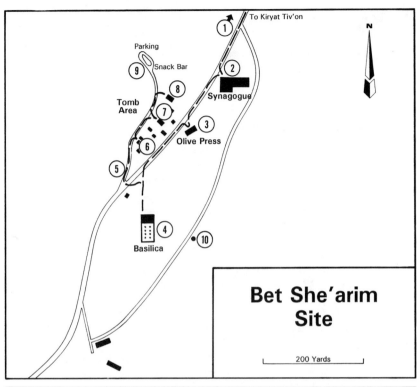

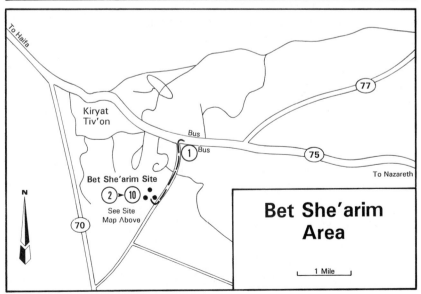

Nazareth

(Nazerat, Natzeret, Natsrat, En-Nasra)

At first sight, you might agree with the question posed in the Gospel of St. John (1:46): "Can anything good come out of Nazareth?" This undistinguished, somewhat dingy town isn't even mentioned in the Old Testament, but Christians around the world revere it as the hometown of Jesus Christ and a center of their faith. As to physical appearances, the overall dullness evaporates instantly when you step into the magnificent Basilica of the Annunciation, which may well be the largest and most beautiful church in the entire Middle East. Well worth the trip in itself, this structure comes as a revelation after seeing Israel's other Christian churches. Close to it are several more places of immense spiritual and historic significance, as well as a real Arab *souk* that isn't geared to tourists.

Whether Mary and Joseph lived in Nazareth before Jesus was born is open to question, as the Bible might seem to contradict itself on this matter. Luke 2:4–5 says yes; Matthew 2 could imply that they were from Bethlehem. In any case, the most credible evidence clearly states that Jesus himself was raised in Nazareth and spent most of his short life there.

Although the town was only an obscure village before Christian times, archaeological digs show that it was certainly inhabited as far back as the 2nd millennium B.C. There seems to have been a Judeo-Christian community there during the 2nd and 3rd centuries A.D., but this most likely died out and the town was destroyed in 614 by the Persians. From then on not much happened until the time of the Crusaders, who made it the capital of Galilee in 1099, only to eventually be driven out by the Mamluks. In 1620 the Franciscans were allowed to purchase the ruined church, and Christians have lived there ever since despite occasional persecutions.

There are really two Nazareths. The lower Old Town, which you will visit, is almost entirely populated by Arabs, nearly half of whom are Christians; while the modern upper town of Nazerat-Illit is Jewish.

Since Nazareth lies along the same road and bus route as the previous trip to Bet She'arim, you might want to combine the two on the same day. Be sure to get off to an early start if you do this.

The Basilica of the Annunciation

GETTING THERE:

Buses leave Haifa's Central Bus Station about once an hour for the one-hour ride to Nazareth, where they stop along the main street rather than at a station. Take bus numbers 341 or 431. There is no service from Friday afternoon until Saturday evening.

By car, Nazareth is 22 miles southeast of Haifa via Route 75.

PRACTICALITIES:

In Nazareth, the Sabbath is celebrated on Sundays, not Saturdays, so the most important religious sites are closed on Sunday mornings. They also close every day between noon and 2 p.m. Be sure to dress modestly, meaning no shorts or bare shoulders. Women should think twice about traveling alone here; even nuns get harassed. As very few of the streets have names, you'll have to navigate with extra care. The **Government Tourist Information Office**, phone (06) 57-05-55, is on Casa Nova St., just down from the Basilica. The Old City of Nazareth has a **population** of about 40,000.

FOOD AND DRINK:

You'll pass numerous *felafel* stands between the bus stop and the Basilica, along with an assortment of rather undistinguished restaurants offering mostly Middle Eastern fare. The best choices are:

Astoria Restaurant (Northeast corner of Casa Nova and Paul VI streets) Basic Middle Eastern cuisine in an unpretentious setting. $

Israel Restaurant (Casa Nova St. near Paul VI St.) A favorite for inexpensive Middle Eastern dishes. $

SUGGESTED TOUR:

Leave the **bus stop** (1) on Paul VI St. and follow the map up Casa Nova St. past the tourist office to the ***Basilica of the Annunciation** (2). Built on the traditional site of the Virgin Mary's house, where many believe the archangel Gabriel appeared to announce the forthcoming birth of Jesus (Luke 1:26–35), the present structure is the fifth in a series of churches that have stood on this same spot since the 3rd century A.D. It was completed in 1969 in a modern version of the Italian Renaissance style and is simply the most splendid Christian church in the Middle East.

Mosaic panels depicting the Annunciation decorate walls of the courtyard to the right, while the basilica's west façade has reliefs of Biblical figures. Enter through the great **bronze doors**, sculpted with events in the life of Jesus, and step into the **Lower Church**. Remnants of the earlier 12th-century Crusader church are visible along the north wall and in the three apses at the east end. Under the octagonal dome is a large opening in the floor, where you can look down into the ***Grotto of the Annunciation**, the presumed site of Mary's house and of the 3rd- and 4th-century churches, parts of which remain. A staircase near the north wall descends into this crypt, taking you past "Mary's Kitchen," the Chapel of St. Joseph, and to the Altar of the Annunciation with its inscription "*Verbum caro hic factum est*" ("And the Word was made flesh"; John 1:14). To the left of this is Gabriel's Column, where according to tradition the angel stood; and Mary's Column, where she received the message.

Stairs at the western end of the lower church lead to the **Upper Church**, which is used for services, and which contains a remarkable ***collection of wall murals** with images of Mary, donated by Christian groups from all over the world. Spend some times examining them, and then take another look down at the Grotto through an octagonal opening in the floor under the dome.

Exit the basilica via a door along the north side of the upper church. This takes you into a courtyard where you can look down into **excavations of ancient Nazareth** that date from the time of Christ. The Basilica is open daily from 8:30–11:45 a.m. and 2–5 p.m., closing at 6 p.m. in

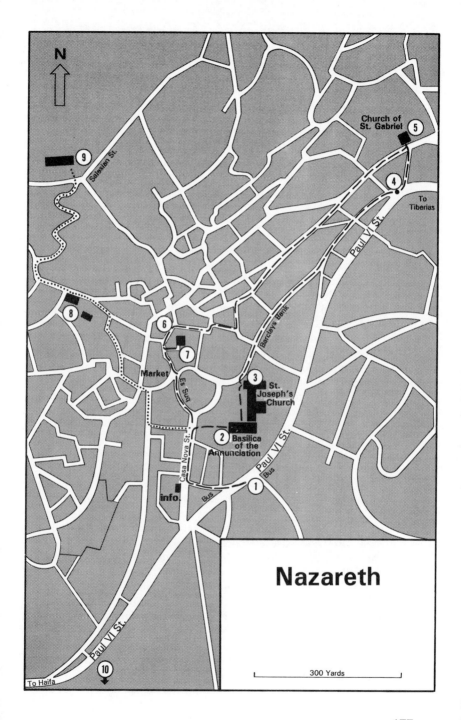

N

Church of
St. Gabriel ⑤

⑨ Salesian St.

④

To
Tiberias

Paul VI St.

Barcleys Bank

⑧

⑥

⑦

③ St.
Joseph's
Church

Market

Es Suq

② Basilica
of the
Annunciation

Casa Nova St.

Bus

① Bus

Paul VI St.

info.

Paul VI St.

Nazareth

To Haifa ⑩

300 Yards

summer, and closed on Sunday mornings except for those attending mass. Admission is free, courtesy of the Franciscans. Modest dress is required.

Continue across the courtyard, passing the Franciscan monastery on the right. This takes you to **St. Joseph's Church** (3), built in 1914 atop remnants of a 13th-century Crusader church. It stands on what many believe to be the site of Joseph's carpentry shop, although there is no valid evidence of this and some digs seem to indicate that a synagogue occupied this spot at the time. In any case, the church is well worth a visit for its fascinating ***Crypt** where you can view an underground cave, cistern, and storage pits that must have been there when Jesus was alive, and may in fact date from the Stone Age. St. Joseph's Church is open daily from 8:30–11:45 a.m. and 2–5 p.m., closing at 6 p.m. in summer.

Now follow the map to the so-called **Mary's Well** (4), a modern outlet for the town's ancient source of water. What you see today is actually a simple fountain where people without running water can fill their buckets. Just a short distance uphill from this is the actual spring that dates from Biblical times, located inside the 17th-century Greek Orthodox **Church of St. Gabriel** (5). As is so often the case throughout the Holy Land, there is disagreement as to where certain events supposedly took place. The Greek Orthodox faith believes, on the basis of apocryphal gospel, that the Annunciation happened by this spring while Mary was drawing water. Christian churches have stood here since as far back as the 4th century A.D. Step inside to see the spring itself, located downstairs in the rear of the church, and to admire the intricate Byzantine decorations. The church is open daily from 8:30–11:30 a.m. and 2–5 p.m., closing at 6 p.m. in summer.

Return to the center of town via another local street and begin wandering down through the labyrinth of narrow passageways in the noisy, crowded **Arab Market** (6), or *souk*. You will surely get lost. To find your way out, just keep heading downhill, following the drainage ditch past countless open shops that sell just about every imaginable item—and even some that you can't imagine. The market is closed from about 1:30–4 p.m. daily, on Wednesday afternoons, and all day on Sundays.

In the center of this bustling bazaar stands the **Greek Catholic Synagogue-Church** (7), reached via a doorway with a sign in French only. Tradition holds that this old Christian church is built on the site of the synagogue that Jesus attended, and where he later taught (Luke 4:16–30). Whether this is true or not, the church is certainly an interesting structure dating from Crusader times. No longer used for services, it is usually open for visitors; ask around the market for the caretaker if it's not.

You have now completed the circle and returned to the Basilica (1). For those with time and energy to spare, Nazareth offers several more churches of interest to tourists. These include the **Mensa Christi Church**

In the Greek Catholic Synagogue-Church

(8), a Franciscan chapel built in 1861 on the site where, according to tradition, Jesus dined with his disciples after the Resurrection. The large limestone block inside was the table. Considerably farther up the steep hill is the **Salesian Basilica of Jesus the Adolescent** (9), a beautiful French church erected in 1918 in the medieval style. For many, the ***views** from here justify the exhausting climb.

Those with cars may want to visit the **Chapel of Our Lady of the Fright** (*Notre Dame de l'Effroi*) (10, off the map), a Franciscan convent on the site where Mary is supposed to have witnessed the good citizens of Nazareth attempting to throw Jesus over the edge of a precipice (Luke 4:29–30). It is at the end of a lane leading south from Paul VI St. opposite the HaGalil Hotel. Those planning to visit any of these out-of-the-way places would do well to check with the tourist office first to see if they're open.

Tiberias

(Teverya, Tveriya)

Piety, history, and frivolous play go hand-in-hand at Tiberias, the sun-splashed, fun-filled capital of the Galilee. A hedonistic resort town ever since the Roman era, Tiberias is nestled along the shores of the Sea of Galilee, or Yam Kinneret, or Lake of Tiberias—as Israel's largest fresh-water lake is variously known.

Whatever you care to call it, the Sea of Galilee is situated some 683 feet below sea level, making it the second-lowest place on Earth. Large only by local standards, it measures about 14 miles long by seven miles wide, although hazy skies often make it appear larger. The lake is actually a basin in the Jordan River, and serves as Israel's major source of fresh water, supplying about a third of its consumption.

It was along these shores that Jesus began his ministry and performed his miracles (John 6:1, 23; 21:1), although he avoided Tiberias itself, which was at the time considered "unclean" for Jews. Less than two centuries later, Tiberias became the intellectual center of Judaism and is now regarded as one of the faith's four holy cities; the others being Jerusalem, Hebron, and Safed.

Tiberias was founded around A.D. 18 by Herod Antipas, the son of Herod the Great and the governor of Galilee; and named in honor of the ruling Roman emperor Tiberius. Built on the site of an ancient cemetery, it was considered unfit for Jewish habitation and consequently settled only by heathens. For Romans, who dearly loved to bathe, its 17 hot mineral springs made it the perfect health spa and recreational center. As the focus of Jewish life moved north from Jerusalem, the town was ritually purified and became the center of Jewish scholarship, acquiring its Hebrew name of Teverya, meaning the navel of the world. It was here that the *Mishnah* and the Talmud were completed, and the Hebrew alphabet perfected.

Christianity got a foothold as early as the 6th century, but soon the area was conquered by Arabs, and later destroyed by earthquake. The Crusaders rebuilt the town a bit farther north, and in 1187 lost it to

Saladin's Islamic forces. Changing hands several more times, Tiberias was again ruined by earthquake in 1837 and eventually redeveloped as the Jewish city that it is today.

The walk described here combines a little bit of history with a lot of pleasure, including the opportunity for a cruise on the lake, a visit to the hot springs, and plenty of chances to soak up the sun at waterside cafés.

GETTING THERE:

Buses depart Haifa's Central Bus Station frequently for the 90-minute ride to Tiberias. Use bus numbers 430 or 431. There is no service from Friday afternoons until Saturday evenings.

By car, Tiberias is 43 miles east of Haifa via routes 75 and 77.

PRACTICALITIES:

Tiberias is at its best during spring and fall, but can be uncomfortably hot and humid in summer. The Lehmann Museum and a few other sites are closed on Friday afternoons and all day on Saturdays and major Jewish holidays. The **Government Tourist Information Office**, phone (06) 72-09-92, is on the upper level of the pedestrian shopping mall, next to the Bezek Telephone Center. Tiberias has a **population** of about 30,000.

FOOD AND DRINK:

As a resort town, Tiberias abounds in tourist-oriented restaurants, most of which serve up mediocre-but-acceptable food at slightly inflated prices. Nearly all of the renowned "St. Peter's Fish" offered on most menus does not actually come from the lake, but from commercial breeding ponds nearby. Some choice establishments are:

> **Guy Restaurant** (HaGalil St., 2 blocks southwest of the pedestrian mall) Middle Eastern cuisine with a Moroccan touch, both indoor and outdoor tables. Kosher. X: Fri. eve., Sat. until sunset. $$

> **The Pinery** (Donna Gracia St., near the Crusader Castle) Chinese and Thai cuisine in an authentic setting. Kosher. X: Fri. eve., Sat. $$

> **Caramba** (on the waterfront promenade, near St. Peter's Church) A pleasant vegetarian and fish restaurant with creative dishes. Non-kosher. $$

> **Kapulsky** (on the pedestrian mall) Light meals at an Old-World café with outdoor tables. $

For the best *felafel*, head for HaYarden St. between the bus station and HaBannim St. Fast-food addicts will find burgers along the pedestrian mall, and pizza by the waterfront. The best value for a filling meal at a low price is the Egged Cafeteria in the bus station.

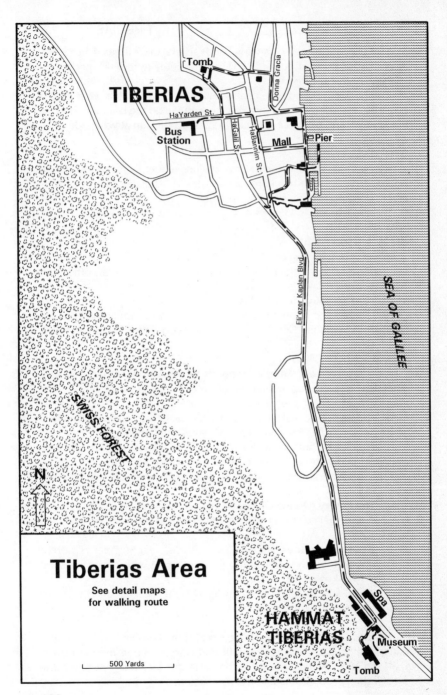

Tomb

TIBERIAS

HaYarden St.

Donna Gracia

Bus
Station

HaGalil St.

HaBanim St.

Mall

Pier

Eli'ezer Kaplan Blvd

SEA OF GALILEE

SWISS FOREST

N

Tiberias Area

See detail maps
for walking route

500 Yards

Spa

HAMMAT
TIBERIAS

Museum

Tomb

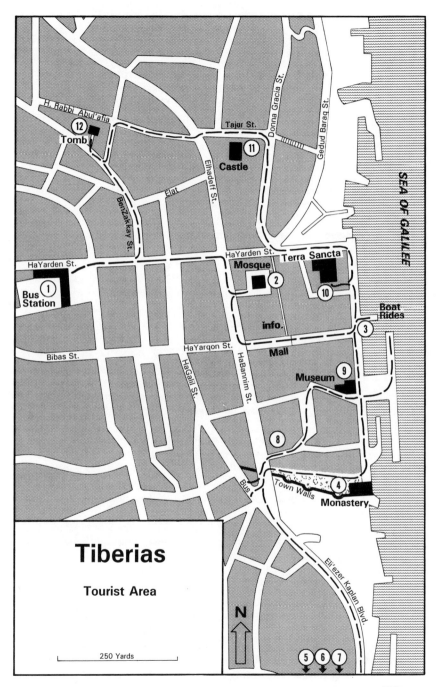

Tiberias

Tourist Area

250 Yards

N

SEA OF GALILEE

H. Rabbi Abul'afia
12 Tomb
Tajar St.
Donna Gracia St.
Gedud Baraq St.
11 Castle
BenZak'kay St.
Elhadeff St.
Elat
HaYarden St.
1 Bus Station
HaYarden St.
Mosque
2
Terra Sancta
10
Boat Rides
3
info.
Mall
HaYarqon St.
HaGalil St.
HaBannim St.
Bibas St.
Museum
9
8
Bus
Town Walls
4 Monastery
Eli'ezer Kaplan Blvd
5 6 7

SUGGESTED TOUR:

Leave the **Central Bus Station** (1) and follow HaYarden St. past a row of tempting *felafel* stands. A right turn on the main thoroughfare, HaBannim St., brings you to the **Great Mosque of El Omri** (2) in a courtyard surrounded by shops. Built in 1743 and no longer used as a place of worship, it is one of the few old buildings still standing in Tiberias. According to tradition, its construction cost in the 18th century was partially paid by the Jewish community as thanks to the local Bedouin sheik for allowing them to live there.

Continue around the corner to the outdoor **Pedestrian Shopping Mall**, or *midrehov* as it's called in Hebrew. The western part of this is lined with shops, outdoor cafés, and restaurants. On the second level, next to the Bezek Telephone Center, is the tourist information office, where you can get current schedules for cruises on the Sea of Galilee. The mall now opens into a wide expanse sloping gently down to the water's edge.

Along the lakeside promenade is a **pier** (3) from which *boat rides operated by the Kinneret Sailing Company depart. These usually go to **En Gev** on the east side of the lake, a somewhat commercialized *kibbutz* with many tourist facilities, a fish restaurant, and a show. The ride takes about 45 minutes each way.

Follow the promenade south until you can go no farther and are up against the walls of the **Greek Orthodox Monastery**, built in 1862 on the foundations of an earlier Christian monastery established in the 3rd or 4th century A.D. Turn right and stroll along the **Crusader Town Walls** (4) that were rebuilt in the 18th century and severely damaged by the earthquake of 1837.

From here you can either walk or take a bus south along the shore road, Eli'ezer Kaplan Boulevard, to the original **Hammat Tiberias** hot springs area. The total distance is less than a mile and a half—a lovely 25-minute stroll, level all the way. If you'd rather ride, you can board bus number 2 or 5 at HaGalil St. Archaeological digs along the way are revealing traces of Roman Tiberias.

Located immediately south of this, the ancient settlement of Hammat was known even in Old Testament times for its therapeutic hot springs. To the Jews, these healing waters were the work of God; the Romans found more hedonistic uses for them. According to legend, the springs began running hot when King Solomon, in need of a bath, sent demons deep into the earth to heat the water. To insure an everlasting warmth, he then made them deaf so they could never hear news of his death and perhaps stop stoking the flames. In truth, however, the hellishly hot (140°F!), sulfur-smelling water has probably been bubbling up for the last 10,000 years; providing relief for even Stone Age man.

The **Young Tiberias Hot Springs Spa Complex** (5), built in 1978 next to the lake, offers massages and relaxing "treatments" to the general public

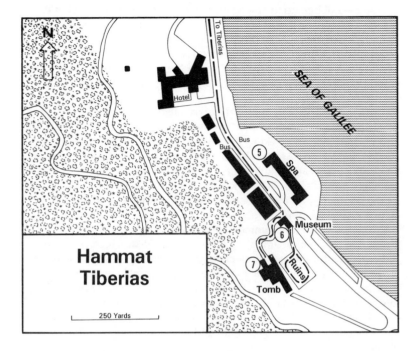

Hammat
Tiberias

250 Yards

at reasonable prices, and has a good fish restaurant. It is open on Saturdays through Thursdays from about 8 a.m. to 8 p.m. (or later), and on Fridays from 8 a.m. to 3 p.m.; phone (06) 79-19-67 for further information. The older spa across the street was built by the Turks in the 19th century and now caters to those with various skin problems.

Apart from its world-famous spa facilities, the major attraction of Hammat is surely the **Lehmann Museum** (6) and its adjacent ruins from antiquity, both forming the Hammat National Park. Enter through the museum, housed in an 18th-century Turkish bathhouse. The history and geology of the hot springs at Hammat are the focus of the displays here, along with artifacts dating from as far back as the 1st century A.D. Just behind the museum are the ruins of six ancient synagogues built atop one another between the 1st and 8th centuries A.D. Don't miss seeing the magnificent *mosaic floor from the 4th-century synagogue, the motifs of which pose questions as yet unanswered. During its heyday, Hammat and Tiberias were the center of Jewish theology; yet here are actual graven images, not only of the pagan Greek sun god Helios but also of a very naked Aquarius and other symbols of the Zodiac. Ponder this, then go look at (and smell!) the ancient hot-spring source itself. The museum and digs are open on Sundays through Thursdays from 8 a.m. to 5 p.m., and on Fridays from 8 a.m. to 2 p.m.

On the hill behind the museum stands the **Tomb of Rabbi Meir Ba'al HaNes** (7), one of the holiest places in the world for Jews. This 2nd-century rabbi helped to compile the *Mishnah* and is perhaps most revered for rescuing his sister-in-law from Roman captivity. Two 19th-century synagogues, one Sephardic and the other Ashkenazi, flank the tomb, which is open daily from 8 a.m. to 5 p.m. Modest dress is required.

Return on foot or by bus to Tiberias, alighting at the intersection of HaGalil and HaBannim streets, opposite the Crusader Town Walls (4). Just northeast of this, next to the River Jordan Hotel, recent excavations are forming the new **Archaeological Park** (8). Although it's not yet open to the public, you can look down at the digs and see the sights that have been uncovered so far. These include a great Crusader church, a section of the northern wall of Arab or even Byzantine Tiberias, and a synagogue with a marvelous mosaic floor.

Continue on to the **Municipal Museum** (9) opposite the marina. It is housed in the former Jami al Bahr Mosque of 1880, which served Arab fishermen with a special entrance for those arriving by boat. The water's edge has since moved a bit to the east. Temporarily closed for renovations, the museum is expected to reopen in the near future with its displays of archaeological artifacts, maps, and prints of old Tiberias.

Directly across from this is the main pier, with a host of tourist amenities. Stroll out to its northern end for a superb **view** of the modern resort.

Now follow the lakeside promenade north to **St. Peter's Church** (10), commonly known as *Terra Sancta*. Set back in a courtyard, this Franciscan church was first built by the Crusaders around 1100 A.D., and altered many times since. During its long and colorful history it has also been used as a mosque and later as a Turkish caravanserai. Its nave is shaped like a boat to honor St. Peter, who was a fisherman. In the tiny courtyard beyond this is a statue of the saint, copied from the one in St. Peter's Basilica in Rome, and a monument built by Polish soldiers stationed here during World War II that is dedicated to Our Lady of Czestochowa. The church is open daily from 8–11:45 a.m. and 2–5:30 p.m.

While along the water's edge, you might want to take advantage of this last opportunity to enjoy one of the lakeside outdoor cafés before pressing inland.

Head west on HaYarden St. and turn right onto Donna Gracia, a street named for the 16th-century Spanish lady who used her powerful position to bring about a brief period of Jewish enlightenment in Turkish-ruled Tiberias. To the left are parts of the so-called **Crusader Castle** (11), a fortress that was probably built in the 18th century using stones from the Crusader period. It now houses art galleries and a restaurant.

On the way back to the bus station, go just a few steps out of your way

View of Tiberias from the pier

to visit the **Tomb of Maimonides** (12), a 12th-century Jewish philosopher whose full name was Rabbi Moses ben Maimon, and who is often known by his acronym, Rambam. Born in Spain in 1135, he moved to Cairo and became physician to Saladin, the sultan of Egypt. At that time he was also the spiritual leader of the Jews in Egypt, an astronomer, a scientist, and an all-around intellectual giant whose writings on a wide variety of subjects are still highly regarded. Maimonides' most noted works were his simplification of Talmudic teachings and his *Guide to the Perplexed*, which explains Jewish beliefs. His remains were brought to the holy city of Tiberias after he died in Cairo in 1204. A lane lined with black pillars leads to the actual tomb, a white half-cylinder. From here it's a short stroll back to the bus station.

ADDITIONAL SIGHTS:

If you're spending more than a day in Tiberias, you might want to explore the New Testament sites around the Sea of Galilee. Doing this by car or even (for the energetic!) by rented bicycle is relatively simple, but using public transportation presents problems as most of the places are served infrequently if at all. Several guided tours are organized by various firms; ask at the tourist office for current information, or make inquiries at the Egged Tours office in the bus station.

*Safed
(Zefat, Tzfat, Safad)

Combine a holy city renowned for its strange mysticism with a thriving artists' colony, stick it on top of a high mountain, and you've got Safed, surely one of the most atmospheric places in Israel. And, at 3,000 feet elevation, the closest to Heaven. The serene beauty of this magical town in the upper Galilee is overwhelming, and well worth the trip.

Although the site of Safed was inhabited as far back as 2000 B.C., it is not mentioned in the Bible. A fortress may have been constructed here in the 1st century A.D. by Flavius Josephus, the Jewish governor of Galilee, who later sided with the Romans and became a notoriously unreliable historian. During Talmudic times, its mountaintop location was used for one of a chain of signal fires that announced the sighting of a new moon in Jerusalem, and thus the start of each new month.

The Crusaders built a mighty citadel atop the hill and made the town an important administrative center, losing it several times to the Arabs before it was finally abandoned to the Mamluks in 1266. By the 16th century, Safed had become a Jewish center under Ottoman rule, and attracted Jews from North Africa and Europe, especially those fleeing the Spanish Inquisition. What brought them to this remote mountain was its long association with the Kabbalah, a text of Jewish mysticism that developed here in the 2nd century A.D. With this, Safed entered its golden age as a place of spiritual learning and became one of Judaism's four holy cities; the others being Jerusalem, Tiberias, and Hebron.

Earthquakes, famine, disease, and Arab riots decimated the Jewish population during the 19th and early 20th centuries, reducing it to around 1,500 elderly persons who hung on out of religious devotion. Then, in 1948, fierce fighting drove the Arabs out and Safed was once again Jewish; the former Arab quarter now being populated by Israeli artists. Its temperate climate, magnificent views, and immensely picturesque Old City attract a great number of tourists and vacationers, for whom excellent facilities have developed.

GETTING THERE:

Buses depart Haifa's Central Bus Station frequently for the nearly-two-hour ride to Safed, with returns until mid-evening. Use bus numbers 361 or 362. There is no service from Friday afternoons until Saturday evenings.

By car, Safed (Zefat) is 45 miles northeast of Haifa. Take Route 4 north to Akko, then Route 85 east and routes 866 and 89 into Safed. Park as close to the bus station as possible, and don't even consider driving in the Old City.

PRACTICALITIES:

Avoid going to *Tzfat* on *Shabbat*; that is, Safed on the Sabbath, when nearly everything is closed. So lovely the rest of the year, this town can be dreary and dead in winter. Safed is a hilly town with some moderately steep climbs, so wear comfortable walking shoes. Modest dress is required to visit the synagogues, and men will need a head covering. The **Government Tourist Information Office**, phone (06) 93-06-33, is in the Municipality Building on Yerushalayim (Jerusalem) St. Safed has a **population** of about 17,500.

FOOD AND DRINK:

Out of the many restaurants in Safed, some good choices are:

HaMifgash (75 Jerusalem St., on the pedestrian mall) Middle Eastern and International dishes with a good wine selection. Kosher. X: Sat. $$

HaKikar (on Kikar HaMeginim in the old Jewish quarter) Decorated with local art, this Middle-Eastern restaurant features vegetarian and fish dishes. X: Fri. eve., Sat. lunch. $$

Big Mo's Dairy Experience (between Beit Yosef and Tarpat streets, near the steps) American-style pizza, bagels, blintzes, soyburgers, fish, and pastries. Kosher. X: Fri. eve., Sat. lunch. $

The best *felafel* can be found along the pedestrian mall, especially at **Universal Felafel**, 54 Jerusalem St., near the top of the steps. **Palermo Pizza**, near this, is also a good bet for a quick, cheap meal.

SUGGESTED TOUR:

Leave the **Central Bus Station** (1) and follow the map up Yerushalayim (Jerusalem) St. to the tourist office in the **Municipality Building** (2). To the left of this is the famous **Davidka Monument**, actually a primitive mortar used in the 1948 War of Independence. Although horrendously ineffective and more likely to maim the people who used it than the enemy, it made so much noise that the Arabs fled in sheer terror. On the traffic island across the street stands the former **British Police Station** from the Mandate era.

Climb the Ma'alot Moshe path and enter the heavily-wooded **Gan HaMetsuda* (3), a lovely park on the site of the ancient **Citadel**. Little remains of the 12th-century Crusader fortress, and even less of the presumed fortifications of Josephus, but recent digs have unearthed pottery fragments from the time of Abraham—and that was circa 1800 B.C.! Further excavations are planned, so you might be able to see one in progress. The *view from here is stunning, extending to the Golan Heights and across the Sea of Galilee. It's easy to see why this hill was chosen as a site for one of the bonfires that heralded each new moon in ancient times.

Follow the road along the top of the hill to the **Israel Bible Museum** (4), which is actually an art gallery primarily devoted to modern Biblical paintings and sculptures by Phillip Ratner. The house itself, dating from the late 19th century, was once the home of a Turkish administrator. Ratner, who immigrated to Israel from the U.S.A. in 1984 and lives in Safed, is well known for his stunning interpretations of Biblical figures. The museum, phone (06) 97-34-72, is open from March through September, Sundays through Thursdays from 10 a.m. to 6 p.m. and Saturdays from 10 a.m. to 2 p.m.; in October and November on Saturdays through Thursdays from 10 a.m. to 2 p.m.; and in December and February on Sundays through Thursdays from 10 a.m. to 2 p.m. It is always closed on Fridays and during January, and admission is free.

Return to the tourist office either the way you came or via the slightly longer route shown on the map. Whichever way, continue on Jerusalem St. to where it becomes a **pedestrian mall**. Amble on down between the shops and cafés until you get almost to the bottom of the hill. Steps on the left lead to a small park around the **Cave of Shem and Ever** (5), where according to legend both a son and great-grandson of Noah studied the Torah. Moslems believe that it was here that Jacob was told of the death of his son by a messenger, who was buried on the spot. If it's closed, you can ask the caretaker at the nearby synagogue to open the door. He'll expect a donation.

Continue downhill into the colorful *Artists' Colony, which until 1948 was the Arab part of town. Little has changed since then, although the tiny stone dwellings along the meandering passageways are now studios, where dozens of leading Israeli artists create, exhibit, and sell their works. The **Printing Museum** (6) commemorates the fact the Safed was the first town in what is now Israel to get a printing press, with its first Hebrew book being published in 1578. Exhibits here include models of historic printing equipment, a press, rare books, maps, posters, and the like. Admission is free, and the doors are open on Sundays through Thursdays from 10 a.m. to noon and 4–6 p.m., and on Fridays from 10 a.m. to noon. Phone (06) 92-09-47 for further information.

Wind your way along the lanes, passing a delightful little square called **Kikar Hama'ayan Haradum** (7), and stroll over to the **Permanent Artists' Exhibition** (8) housed in an old mosque easily identified by its minaret. This general exhibition of works by Safed artists, past and present, is open daily from 9 a.m. to 6 p.m., and on the Sabbath and holidays from 10 a.m. to 2 p.m. Phone (06) 92-00-87.

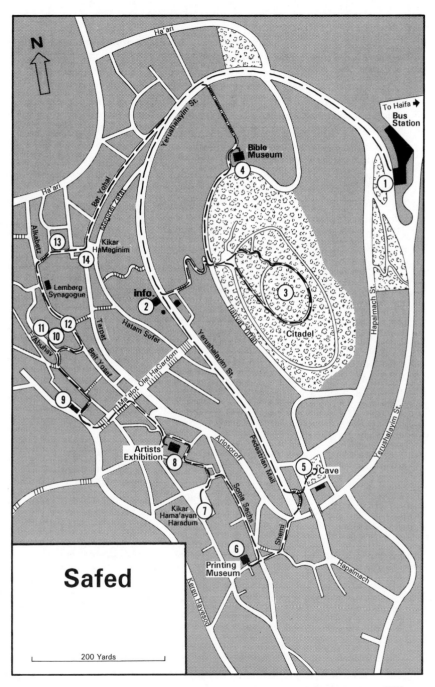

You'll soon come to the steep **Ma'alot Olei HaGardom,** a wide stairway built by the British to separate the Jewish and Arab quarters after a particularly bad riot. A gun position and searchlight on the roof of a building at the top served to keep the two sides apart. If you're bounding with energy, you might want to walk down to the next attraction—but remember that what goes down must come up.

The **Beit Hameiri Museum** (9), at the bottom of the hill, is housed in a restored 16th-century building that was once a center for Kabbalistic study. Its displays focus on Jewish life in Safed, especially in the late 19th and early 20th centuries, and include furnishings, clothing, tools, holy objects, and other artifacts. Visits may be made on Sundays through Thursdays from 9 a.m. to 2 p.m., and on Fridays from 9 a.m. to 1 p.m. Phone (06) 97-13-07 for further information.

Climbing back up the hill brings you into the center of the ***Old Jewish Quarter**, a highly atmospheric neighborhood with many **historic synagogues** recalling Safed's role as a holy city. Now, you surely won't want to visit them all, but those described below are among the more interesting. For the most part, they're open all day and require that you be modestly dressed. Cardboard *yarmulkas* (head coverings) are provided for males who didn't bring their own. You are expected to make a small donation to any synagogue that you visit. Signs throughout the area remind you to "Remember the Sabbath Day to Keep it Holy! On the Sabbath it is Forbidden to Smoke or to Carry Cameras."

The **Alshekh Synagogue** (10) was one of the few buildings in Safed not destroyed during the earthquake of 1837. It is named for Rabbi Moses Alshekh, a leading Kabbalist of the 16th century, and has a lovely domed ceiling. Note that many of the houses in this area are painted blue, a color symbolizing both Heaven and the reign of God.

A few steps farther along the same lane is the **Abuhav Synagogue** (11), an impressive structure honoring the great 15th-century Spanish sage, Rabbi Issac Abuhav. Its design is based on the Kabbalah, with four central pillars representing earth, water, air, and fire. The ten windows in its dome symbolize the Commandments, while the pictures in it depict the 12 tribes of Israel. A wooden ark on the right near the entrance houses the sacred Torah scroll written by Rabbi Abuhav, which is used only on Yom Kippur, Shavuot, and Rosh HaShana. It is said that only the wall containing this ark survived the devastating earthquake of 1837; the rest of the synagogue was destroyed.

Wind your way uphill to the ***Caro Synagogue** (12) on Beit Yosef St. Although rebuilt after the 1837 earthquake, this is the place where the 16th-century chief rabbi of Safed, Yosef Caro, produced his great works and teachings on living the perfect Jewish life. Tradition holds that an angel appeared to Rabbi Caro in the vault under this very floor. The ark contains three notable Torah scrolls which you can see, one of which is about 500 years old.

Kikar Hama'ayan Haradum in the Artists' Colony

Continue down the alleyway past the ruined Hassidic **Lemberg Synagogue**, now only partially restored. The route takes you up steps to the ***Ha'Ari Ashkenazi Synagogue** (13), one of several dedicated to the "Ari," a leading 16th-century figure in Jewish mysticism. There are some wonderfully intricate 19th-century carvings here, including an olive-wood ark. The hole in the pulpit, stuffed with written prayers, is the result of a 1948 Arab attack in which the entire congregation miraculously escaped harm. Be careful about sitting in Elijah's Chair in the small room at the rear of the synagogue—according to legend, any Jewish couple who does so will be blessed with a baby boy within the year. Guaranteed.

Heading back to Yerushalayim St., you will first pass the main square of the Old Jewish Quarter, **Kikar HaMeginim** (14). Once known as Kohlenplatz because charcoal for heating was sold here, it was the center of Jewish resistance during the 1948 War of Independence. From here, the route on the map takes you back to the bus station.

*Caesarea

Both the Romans and the Crusaders found the site at Caesarea irresistible, and so do today's travelers as they poke about in what may well be Israel's most intriguing archaeological digs. That it's also a delightful resort right on the Mediterranean only adds to the pleasure of a visit.

These shores were first settled around the 4th century B.C. by Phoenicians from Sidon, who used them as an anchorage for traders sailing to and from Egypt. At that time the site was known as "Strato's Tower" after its prominent landmark. Changing hands several times over the centuries, it was given to King Herod the Great of Judea by the Romans in 30 B.C. With his usual megalomaniacal zeal, Herod set out in 22 B.C. to build the most grandiose city imaginable. He succeeded, perhaps beyond his wildest dreams, and the result was named Caesarea in honor of his patron, the emperor Augustus Caesar.

When Judea became a proper Roman province around A.D. 6 this magnificent port was made its capital, which it remained for over six centuries. Pontius Pilate lived here from A.D. 26 to 36, and St. Paul was held captive in Herod's praetorium from A.D. 58 to 60 before being sent to Rome (Acts 23). The first conversion of a Gentile to Christianity occurred in Caesarea about A.D. 35 when St. Peter baptized the Roman centurion Cornelius (Acts 10; 11:1–18).

Clashes between local Jews and Gentiles led to a revolt in A.D. 66 that ultimately resulted in the destruction of Jerusalem, ending its role as the Jewish capital for the next 19 centuries. All but 2,500 of the survivors were sent to Rome as slaves; those Jews who remained were fed to the wild beasts in Caesarea's amphitheater. Another carnage occurred after the Bar Kochba Rebellion of A.D. 132, when ten Jewish sages were tortured to death in the same arena to amuse the pagans.

Slowly, things improved and many Jews returned to Caesarea, which eventually became a center of scholarship for both Jews and the emerging Christian faith. Then, in A.D. 640, the city was captured by the Arabs and declined dramatically. It fell to the Crusaders in 1101; among the booty taken was a hexagonal bowl of green glass that some believe to be the Holy Grail used by Jesus at the Last Supper, which is today on display in the Cathedral of San Lorenzo in Genoa. After changing hands several times, Caesarea was taken by King Louis IX (St. Louis) of France in 1251.

Louis enclosed a small part of the vast ancient city, including the harbor, with strong fortifications—and within those walls erected the splendid Crusader City that you see today.

The final end to Caesarea's glory came in 1265, when the Mamluks under Sultan Baybars utterly devastated the place as its inhabitants fled into the night. For the next 600 years it lay mostly buried beneath the sand, used only as a convenient quarry for builders up and down the coast.

Life returned to Caesarea in 1878 as a group of Moslem refugees from Bosnia were settled there by the Turks, and the small mosque that still stands next to the harbor got built. This village was abandoned during the 1948 War of Independence. Organized excavations began shortly after that, yielding the sights you'll see today. Much remains to be dug up yet, so future archaeologists have their work cut out for them.

Taking this daytrip yourself by public transportation is awkward, but well worth the extra effort if you don't have a car. Most commercial guided tours to Caesarea offer only a brief, hurried visit and miss the lesser-known sights along with the atmosphere of the place.

GETTING THERE:

Buses depart the central bus stations of both **Haifa** and **Tel Aviv** fairly frequently for the one-hour ride to **Hadera**, a large town midway between the two cities. Get off at Hadera's Central Bus Station and go directly to the information window, where you can get the current schedule of buses to Caesarea. These are on bus route number 76 and run roughly every two hours. The departure platform is well marked in English. If you have a long wait, you might want to visit Hadera's interesting Khan Historical Museum in an old caravanserai on Hagiborim St. next to the central synagogue. There is also a good Egged cafeteria at the bus station. When you board the bus, make sure the driver knows that you don't want the modern resort of Caesarea, which you come to first, but the ruins (ha'ateekot). Ride past the Crusader City and get off at the next stop, the Roman Theater. You will be returning from the bus stop opposite the Crusader City; check out the return buses on the printed schedule you got back in Hadera. As this is in Hebrew only, ask someone to mark the relevant times. There is no bus service from Friday afternoons until Saturday evenings, nor on major Jewish holidays.

All of this can be simplified by taking a **taxi** from the bus station in Hadera. The distance is no more than six miles, but be sure to arrange for a ride back.

NOTE: Some guidebooks tell you to change buses along the highway instead of in Hadera. While this route is no doubt shorter, it is also very risky and might leave you stranded in the middle of nowhere, facing a long walk in the hot sun. Go by way of Hadera and be safe.

By car, Caesarea is 24 miles south of **Haifa** or 36 miles north of **Tel Aviv** via *either* Route 2 or the slower Route 4. In either case, keep an eye out for the Caesarea exit and follow local signs to the Roman Theater and Crusader City sites.

PRACTICALITIES:

This trip is entirely out of doors, so good weather is essential. Be prepared for the hot summer sun with both a hat and sun-block lotion. The sites are open on Sundays through Thursdays from 8 a.m. to 4 p.m., and on Fridays from 8 a.m. to noon. In effect, this means that you should avoid coming on a Friday, Saturday, or major religious holiday. One ticket covers both enclosed sites. For **further information**, contact the Haifa or Tel Aviv tourist offices, or phone (06) 36-13-58.

FOOD AND DRINK:

Restaurants within the Crusader City site are:

> **Citadel Restaurant** (by the harbor) In a magnificent setting over- looking the harbor and sea. Specializes in fish. $$
>
> **Chez Charly** (near the harbor) Middle Eastern and fish dishes. $$

In addition, there is a **café** with outdoor tables just across from the Crusader City entrance, and another similar one at the Roman Theater entrance; as well as a few cafés by the harbor. If you have a wait at Hadera, you can get a cheap-but-decent meal at the Egged cafeteria in the bus station.

SUGGESTED TOUR:

Begin at the **bus stop** (1) in front of the Roman Theater. In its heyday as the capital of Roman Palestine, Caesarea extended from here to well north of the Crusader City and east past the Hippodrome; and had an estimated population of about 100,00 during late Roman times. The 1st-century Jewish-Roman historian Flavius Josephus marveled over the sheer size of the harbor facilities, the highly advanced system of sewers, the large dwellings and magnificent palaces, and the full range of tem- ples, theaters, and other public structures. Although Josephus was noto- rious for exaggerations, digs to date seem to confirm the accuracy of his description. The two areas excavated so far together form the **Caesarea National Park**, with a single admission ticket for both sites.

Enter the southern section of the park, where you'll find the ***Roman Theater** (2). Just inside the gate, to the left, is a small garden of archae- ological artifacts including an enormous stone foot and a replica of the famous **plaque** unearthed here a few decades ago. Its inscription is the only material proof that Pontius Pilate ever existed or ruled this area.

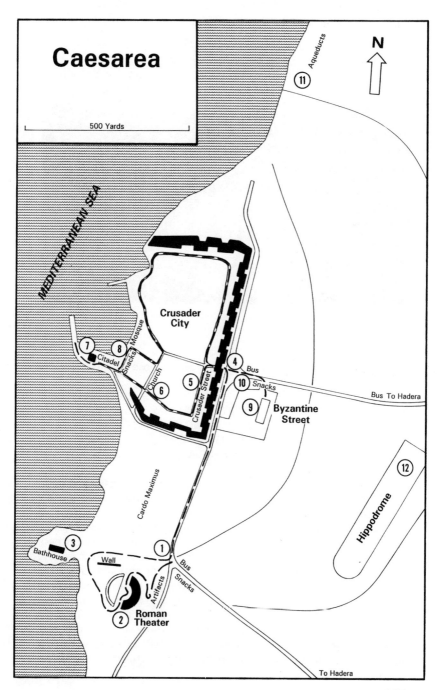

Caesarea

500 Yards

MEDITERRANEAN SEA

N

Crusader City

Citadel

Snacks Mosque

Church

Crusader Street

Bus

Snacks

Byzantine Street

Bus To Hadera

Hippodrome

Cardo Maximus

Bathhouse

Wall

Artifacts

Bus

Snacks

Roman Theater

To Hadera

Aqueducts

The Roman Theater

Although the letters are partially worn away (those in **bold face** are visible), it seems to read:

DIS AUGUSTIS **TIBERIEUM**
PONTIUS **PILATUS**
PRAE**FECTUS JUDA**EAE
FECIT DE DICAVIT

Translated, that means "Pontius Pilate, Prefect of Judea, made and dedicated the Tiberieum to the Divine Augustus." The original stone is safely displayed in the Israel Museum in Jerusalem.

The theater, not to be confused with the amphitheater where thousands of Jews were slaughtered and which has not yet been unearthed, was built by Herod and modified over the years. Now highly (some would say overly) restored, it is often used for outdoor concerts and other stage presentations. Most of the time, however, you can climb all over it and explore the stage area, perhaps testing out the acoustics. A semicircular platform behind this dates from the 3rd century A.D. and once formed a kind of arena. Many of the broken columns you see strewn about were quarried in Egypt over two millenia ago; the best of these were later appropriated by 18th-century Turks to build their architectural marvels at Akko (page 161).

Between the Theater and the sea stands a great stone wall erected in the 6th century A.D. as part of a fortification to protect the local ruler from his unhappy subjects. Down near the water's edge are scanty remnants of what appears to be a **Roman Bathhouse** (3), possibly from Herodian times.

Leave the theater site and stroll (or drive) along the paved road north to the part of Roman Caesarea that was enclosed and rebuilt by the Crusaders during the 12th and 13th centuries. Halfway between you and the sea, running parallel to the road, is the course of the Roman *Cardo Maximus*. Little has been excavated of this great street yet, but trial soundings indicate that it is about 20 feet wide, has a vaulted sewer under it, and roofed sidewalks on either side.

The mighty *****Crusader City**, surrounded on three sides by thick 13th-century defensive walls and a moat, faces the sea and opens onto the harbor. Although extensive in size, it occupies only about a third of Herod's original city, and about an eighth of Late Roman (Byzantine) Caesarea. At its height, the Crusader City supported a population of roughly 12,000.

Enter through the beautifully-restored *****East Gate** (4), the main land entrance to the town. Show your ticket, cross the moat, and pass into the L-shaped gatehouse, where invaders could easily be picked off by archers from above. Further defense was supplied by an iron portcullis gate and a solid wooden gate.

Turn left and amble over to the **Vaulted Crusader Street** (5), whose arches are in an early Gothic style. To the right of this, following the marked tourist route, is a Frankish Crusader house arranged around a central court. The unfinished **Crusader Church** (6) was unwittingly built atop storage vaults from Herod's time, on a platform that once supported a temple of Augustus and later a mosque. As construction progressed and the weight increased, the vaults below collapsed, bringing much of the church down with it but leaving the three apses more or less intact.

Out on the south jetty is the **Crusader Citadel** (7), which once defended the harbor and today houses a restaurant and tourist shops. Climb to the top for a good view and stroll out on the breakwater. Although the present harbor is not exactly small, in Roman times the Herodian breakwater sheltered a much larger port capable of handling a hundred war galleys at a time. Six colossal statues decorated the harbor entrance and the moles (jetties) were lined with great towers, with a wide promenade for those who disembarked. Alas, it was built over a geological fault line, and much of the breakwater sank beneath the waves, probably as early as the 1st century A.D. After that, ships preferred to use Akko as a port until repairs were made in the late 5th century. Jetties built since then have not extended out as far as the fault line, making the harbor safer.

The Vaulted Street of the Crusader City

Return to land and bear left past the 19th-century **Mosque** (8) built by the Turks for a group of Bosnian refugees. Their village was abandoned during the 1948 War of Independence; the buildings now house cafés, restaurants, and other tourist facilities.

At this point, more adventurous travelers should leave the marked trail and follow a rougher route north past the steep cliffs and the seacoast, then east and south along the 13th-century Crusader walls, climbing them occasionally for views. Few tourists ever venture into this secluded part of the ruins, so the atmosphere is much more romantically charged. The path is also somewhat overgrown with weeds, making the going just a little bit rough. If you'd rather not do this, take the shortcut on the map instead. Either way, you will wind up back at the East Gate (4).

Leave the Crusader City and walk across the street, past the café, to the **Byzantine Street Excavation** (9). Steps lead down to a mosaic pavement from the 6th century A.D. Two huge ***Roman statues** from the 2nd and 3rd centuries A.D. are the center of attraction here; both are enigmatically headless. Who were they, and why were they decapitated? The identity of the white marble figure remains a mystery, but the one in red porphyry probably represents the emperor Hadrian, who twice visited Caesarea around A.D. 130. It is quite possible that the heads were lost to religious zealots offended by graven images, or perhaps the fine bodies were simply recycled by later rulers who stuck on their own handsome,

The Harbor area and its Mosque

albeit temporary, noggins in place of those of their predecessors.

You can get a ride back to Hadera from the **bus stop** (10) next to the café on the corner here. However, if you have time and energy left, you might want to visit one or two of Caesarea's lesser sights, described below.

About a half-mile north of here, near the beach, stand two **Roman Aqueducts** (11) that once supplied the town with fresh water. The one closer to the sea was built by Herod, with additions made by Hadrian around A.D. 130. Marble plaques along the side facing the water are dedicated to the legions that were posted here. The other, low-level, aqueduct dates from the 4th or 5th century A.D. and ran about three miles north to an artificial lake.

Heading east on the main road, you will soon come to what little has been excavated of the **Roman Hippodrome** (12), a great racetrack for horses that was probably built by Hadrian in the early 2nd century A.D. By the 4th century, Caesarea was famous throughout the empire for its chariot races, and this track could accommodate some 20,000 fans at a time. A reconstructed archway marks the entrance to the site. Just beyond it is Israel's only 18-hole golf course, part of a modern luxury resort centered on the adjacent Dan Caesarea Hotel.

Index

Arts & Crafts, Christian Churches, Markets, Mosques, Museums, Roman Ruins, and Synagogues are listed individually under those category headings.

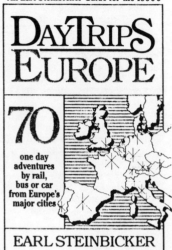

An Earl Steinbicker Guide for the 1990's

DAYTRIPS IN EUROPE

Created especially for travelers making the Grand Tour, *Daytrips in Europe* takes a fresh look at 70 of the most enjoyable destinations that can be explored on one-day excursions from London, Paris, Nice, Brussels, Luxembourg City, Amsterdam, Munich, Frankfurt, Vienna, Salzburg, Zürich, Geneva, Rome, Florence, Milan, Madrid, or Lisbon. Each trip description includes:

- A do-it-yourself walking tour
- A detailed town map
- Full travel directions by rail, bus, or car
- Time & weather considerations
- Price-keyed restaurant suggestions
- Photos and background information
- Concise descriptions of all worthwhile sights

92 Maps   97 Photos   432 Pages

DAYTRIPS FROM NEW YORK

100 one-day adventures by car from anywhere in the New York Metropolitan Area to the most enticing destinations in New York State, New Jersey, Pennsylvania, Connecticut, and Massachusetts. Includes descriptions of the sites, a bit of history, complete driving instructions, and practical information. 42 maps show you where the attractions are, and 42 photos help you preview them. 336 pages.

More

DAYTRIPS

TRAVEL GUIDES BY EARL STEINBICKER

DAYTRIPS/LONDON

Explores the metropolis on 7 one-day walking tours, then describes 23 daytrips to destinations throughout nearby southeastern England. 39 large maps, 58 photos, 240 pages.

DAYTRIPS IN BRITAIN

Takes a close look at 60 of the most exciting destinations for daytrips from London and Edinburgh. 65 maps, 107 photos, 353 pages.

DAYTRIPS IN FRANCE

Describes 45 one-day excursions—including 5 walking tours of Paris, 23 daytrips from the city, 5 in Provence, and 12 along the Riviera. 55 maps, 89 photos. 3rd edition, 336 pages.

DAYTRIPS IN GERMANY

55 of Germany's most enticing destinations can be savored on daytrips from Munich, Frankfurt, Hamburg, and Berlin. Walking tours of the big cities are included. 62 maps, 94 photos. 3rd edition, 336 pages.

DAYTRIPS IN ITALY

Features 40 one-day adventures in and around Rome, Florence, Milan, Venice, and Naples. 45 maps, 69 photos. 2nd edition, 288 pages.

DAYTRIPS IN HOLLAND, BELGIUM AND LUXEMBOURG

Many unusual places are covered on these 40 daytrips, along with all the favorites plus the 3 major cities. 45 maps, 69 photos, 288 pages.

• BY ROBERT D. WOOD •

DAYTRIPS TO ARCHAEOLOGICAL MEXICO

Describes 12 travel routes by car or bus to 100 Pre-Columbian archaeological sites all over Mexico, ranging from the world-famous to the virtually unknown. 23 maps, 6 photos. Revised edition, 176 pages.

"Daytrips" travel guides, written or edited by Earl Steinbicker, describe the easiest and most natural way to travel on your own. Each volume in the growing series contains a balanced selection of enjoyable one-day adventures. Some of these are to famous attractions, while others feature little-known discoveries. For every destination there are historical facts, anecdotes, and a suggested do-it-yourself tour, a local map, travel directions, time and weather considerations, food and lodging recommendations, and concise background material.

SOLD AT LEADING BOOKSTORES EVERYWHERE

Or, if you prefer, by mail direct from the publisher. Use the handy coupon below or just jot your choices on a separate piece of paper.

Hastings House
141 Halstead Avenue
Mamaroneck, NY 10543

Please send the following books:

_____copies	DAYTRIPS IN LONDON @ $12.95 (0-8038-9329-9)	_____
_____copies	DAYTRIPS IN BRITAIN @ $12.95 (0-8038-9301-9)	_____
_____copies	DAYTRIPS IN GERMANY @ $12.95 (0-8038-9327-2)	_____
_____copies	DAYTRIPS IN FRANCE @ $12.95 (0-8038-9344-2)	_____
_____copies	DAYTRIPS IN HOLLAND, BELGIUM AND LUXEMBOURG @ $12.95 (0-8038-9310-8)	_____
_____copies	DAYTRIPS IN ITALY @ $12.95 (0-8038-9343-4)	_____
_____copies	DAYTRIPS IN EUROPE @ $15.95 (0-8038-9330-2)	_____
_____copies	DAYTRIPS FROM NEW YORK @ $12.95 (0-8038-9332-9)	_____
_____copies	DAYTRIPS TO ARCHAEOLOGICAL MEXICO @ $12.95 (0-8038-9336-1)	_____
_____copies	DAYTRIPS IN ISRAEL @ $12.95 (0-8038-9342-6)	_____

New York residents add tax: _____

Shipping and handling @ $2.50 per book: _____

Total amount enclosed (check or money order): _____

Please ship to: _____

_____

_____